Rethinking Chinese Politics

Understanding Chinese politics has become more important than ever. Some argue that China's political system is "institutionalized" or that "win-all/lose-all" struggles are a thing of the past, but, Joseph Fewsmith argues, as in all Leninist systems, political power is difficult to pass on from one leader to the next. Indeed, each new leader must deploy whatever resources he has to gain control over critical positions and thus consolidate power. Fewsmith traces four decades of elite politics from Deng Xiaoping to Xi Jinping, showing how each leader has built power (or not). He shows how the structure of politics in China has set the stage for intense and sometimes violent intra-elite struggles, shaping a hierarchy in which one person tends to dominate, and, ironically, providing for periods of stability between intervals of contention.

JOSEPH FEWSMITH is Professor of International Relations and Political Science, Pardee School of Global Studies, Boston University.

D1565438

Rethinking Chinese Politics

JOSEPH FEWSMITH

Boston University

CAMBRIDGE
UNIVERSITY PRESS

University Printing House, Cambridge CB2 8BS, United Kingdom

One Liberty Plaza, 20th Floor, New York, NY 10006, USA

477 Williamstown Road, Port Melbourne, VIC 3207, Australia

314–321, 3rd Floor, Plot 3, Splendor Forum, Jasola District Centre, New Delhi – 110025, India

79 Anson Road, #06–04/06, Singapore 079906

Cambridge University Press is part of the University of Cambridge.

It furthers the University's mission by disseminating knowledge in the pursuit of education, learning, and research at the highest international levels of excellence.

www.cambridge.org
Information on this title: http://www.cambridge.org/9781108831253
DOI: 10.1017/9781108923859

First published 2021

A catalogue record for this publication is available from the British Library.

Library of Congress Cataloging-in-Publication Data
Names: Fewsmith, Joseph, 1949– author.
Title: Rethinking Chinese politics / Joseph Fewsmith.
Description: Cambridge, United Kingdom ; New York, NY : Boston University, Cambridge University Press, [2021] | Includes bibliographical references and index.
Identifiers: LCCN 2020058385 (print) | LCCN 2020058386 (ebook) | ISBN 9781108831253 (hardback) | ISBN 9781108926607 (paperback) | ISBN 9781108923859 (ebook)
Subjects: LCSH: China – Politics and government. | Political leadership – China. | Communism – China.
Classification: LCC JQ1510 .F486 2021 (print) | LCC JQ1510 (ebook) | DDC 324.251/075–dc23
LC record available at https://lccn.loc.gov/2020058385
LC ebook record available at https://lccn.loc.gov/2020058386

ISBN 978-1-108-83125-3 Hardback
ISBN 978-1-108-92660-7 Paperback

In memory of
Roderick MacFarquhar, Ezra F. Vogel, and
Rudolf G. Wagner
Friends, Mentors, and Sources of Inspiration

Contents

Tables

Figures

Acknowledgments

Although writing a book can be a solitary exercise, no one writes a book alone. One accumulates debts, often without even remembering when or where one picks up ideas. This is especially true in a book like this. I have been watching – and discussing – politics in China for four decades, and during that time I have had many, many conversations with scholars and officials throughout the world. As those familiar with the writings of the late Tang Tsou will readily tell, much of my approach is still informed by his insights into Chinese politics. Indeed, one of the main questions motivating this research was whether and to what degree Chinese politics had moved beyond the framework he articulated so well many years ago. Since moving to Boston some thirty years ago, the Fairbank Center for Chinese Studies at Harvard University has become my intellectual home. In thinking about Chinese politics, I was privileged to share ideas with the late Roderick MacFarquhar and Ezra Vogel many times. It is hard to believe they are not with us any more.

Over some four decades, I have discussed and argued about Chinese politics with Alice Miller, Cliff Edmunds, Li Cheng, Bob Suettinger, and many others. On many trips to China, I have benefited from many conversations with scholars and officials. In writing this book, I have had the critical input of Steven M. Goldstein, Charles Parton, Timothy Heath, and Barry Naughton, as well as the diligent reading of anonymous readers for Cambridge University Press. They have all forced me to clarify my thoughts and state my views more clearly.

In researching this book, I have had the support of the Smith Richardson Foundation, which provided me with the time to focus on the research. I have also had the research assistance of Shen Ao and Sun Xiao. In straightening out my sometimes tortured English and fractured footnotes, I have the privilege of once again thanking Nancy Hearst, the peerless librarian at the Fung Library at the Fairbank Center for Chinese Studies, Harvard University. Unfortunately, for the remaining errors and lack of clarity, I alone have to take responsibility.

Abbreviations

ACFTU	All-China Federation of Trade Unions
CAC	Central Advisory Commission
CASS	Chinese Academy of Social Sciences
CCP	Chinese Communist Party
CDIC	Central Discipline Inspection Commission
CMC	Central Military Commission
CPPCC	Chinese People's Political Consultative Congress
CPSU	Communist Party of the Soviet Union
CYL	Communist Youth League
DIC	discipline inspection commission
GMD	Guomindang
GPD	General Political Department
MOS	Ministry of Supervision
NDRC	National Development and Reform Commission
NGO	nongovernmental organization
NPC	National People's Congress
PAP	People's Action Party
PB	Politburo
PBSC	Politburo Standing Committee
PCA	Permanent Court of Arbitration
PLA	People's Liberation Army
PRC	People's Republic of China
PRI	Institutional Revolutionary Party
SOE	state-owned enterprise
TVEs	township and village enterprises
WTO	World Trade Organization

Introduction

On October 1, 2019, China's leader, Xi Jinping, presided over the most expansive military parade in the history of the PRC. Some 100,000 troops escorted "missiles, missiles, and more missiles" down the Avenue of Eternal Peace as China's most advanced aircraft flew above. Driving home the nationalistic message, Xi declared that "no force can shake the status of this great nation."[1]

In celebrating its seventieth anniversary, the PRC marked itself as one of the world's longest-lasting autocracies. The Soviet Union had lasted seventy-four years and the Institutional Revolutionary Party (PRI) in Mexico held uninterrupted power for seventy-one years. The Workers Party of Korea (WPK) has held power in North Korea since 1945, some seventy-six years and counting. Some monarchies have lasted even longer, such as the House of Saud in Saudi Arabia and the House of Khalifa in Bahrain, but authoritarian regimes generally do not last very long. The general explanation for those regimes (other than the monarchies) that beat the odds and survive for lengthy periods of time is that they develop party systems and institutions that define relations among the top elite. That is to say, they become institutionalized.

"Institutionalization," however, is a vexed word. Different people use it in different ways. Douglass North famously defines institutionalization as "the rules of the game" or, in more formal language, "the humanly devised constraints that shape human interaction." For North, all systems are institutionalized in the broad sense that all have "rules of the game," defined in formal or informal terms, or

---

[1] Andrew S. Erickson, "China's Massive Military Parade Shows Beijing Is Military Superpower," *National Interest*, October 1, 2019; and Emma Graham-Harrison and Verna Yu, "China Celebrates 70th Anniversary as Xi Warns 'No Force Can Shake Great Nation'," *The Guardian*, October 1, 2019, retrieved from www.theguardian.com/world/2019/oct/01/china-celebrates-70-years-military-parade-xi-jinping-hong-kong, accessed September 15, 2020.

both. What interests North is that some institutions are conducive to economic development and others are not.[2] This is a useful definition for his purposes. For others, however, what North calls "organizations" are seen as "institutions." This redefinition plays down the "rules of the game," which are abstract and often informal, in favor of the study of specific organizations.[3]

When analysts of China talk about institutionalization, they usually mean that the political system is typified by decision-making rules that define how leaders are promoted and chosen. In particular, an institutionalized system means one in which leadership can be passed from one leader to another without power struggles because there is a widely accepted decision-making rule. The implication of this is that there are constraints on power that mean that a leader cannot and does not need to "consolidate" power by cultivating a "faction" of supporters and removing members of a rival network. Institutionalization also means the development of an administrative system that more or less resembles a Weberian-style rational–legal bureaucracy; that is, one in which members of the bureaucracy are recruited and promoted on the basis of knowledge. This understanding does not mean that the system is frozen in place, immune to change, but it does mean that the use of raw power, including the building of personal factions, is not central to the political system.

Certainly Milan W. Svolik, the eminent political scientist at Yale University, was thinking in terms of decision-making rules and constraints on power when he wrote about Xi Jinping, then still heir apparent, "He will be expected to serve no more than two five-year terms and be accountable to a set of institutions within the Communist Party of China that carefully balance two major political coalitions as well as regional and organizational interests within the Chinese political system."[4] This was a reasonable prediction, based on what China specialists were writing, but it turned out to be sadly mistaken. Why was it mistaken? Because the Chinese system had not institutionalized

[2] Douglass C. North, *Institutions, Institutional Change and Economic Performance* (Cambridge: Cambridge University Press, 1990), p. 1.
[3] See, for instance, Paul Pierson, *Politics in Time: History, Institutions, and Social Analysis* (Princeton, NJ: Princeton University Press, 2004). See also James Mahoney and Kathleen Thelen, eds., *Explaining Institutional Change: Ambiguity, Change, and Power* (Cambridge: Cambridge University Press, 2010).
[4] Milan W. Svolik, *The Politics of Authoritarian Rule* (New York: Cambridge University Press, 2012), p. 85.

the way many observers thought it had. It is certainly true that the Chinese Communist Party (CCP) certainly has its own "rules of the game," hence it is meaningful to talk of norms and traditions, but those rules of the game have continued to stand in the way of institutionalization as defined above.

Since there are substantial numbers of intra-party rules and systems built up within the CCP over the years, one might well have thought that the CCP would have taken on more of the look of a Weberian-style bureaucracy. But it has not. On the contrary, we find that the personalization of power, factionalism, the arbitrary abuse of power, corruption, and the lack of discipline within the party continue to plague the party and stand in the way of institutionalization. Indeed, these problems stem both from the revolutionary past and from the inauguration of reform (see Chapter 4), and Xi Jinping's efforts to fight corruption and reshape the party are a response to such problems. Whether he is successful or not, it is clear that the party as a system is not developing clear decision-making rules and checks on power; on the contrary, the personalization of power is overwhelming whatever norms the party seemed to be developing, even though Xi Jinping emphasizes law and intra-party regulations. Susan Whiting has argued convincingly that the elaboration of a legal system can, in fact, legitimize authoritarian political systems.[5] The same appears to be true about the promulgation of regulations governing intra-party relations. Such laws and regulations turn out to be means by which the ruling elite can control and dominate society, not constrain their own exercise of power. The question for political scientists should not be explaining institutionalization but rather explaining its absence. The answer lies in certain pathologies of its one-party system. These pathologies will be explored in the course of this book.

Despite the lack of institutionalization, the idea that China has institutionalized is widespread throughout the field of political science and among those who study China. I suggest that the idea that the Chinese system has institutionalized derives from three separate literatures that have converged, however unintentionally, in recent years. Together, they have provided a framework for much of our understanding of contemporary China. However, these literatures are

---

[5] Susan H. Whiting, "Authoritarian 'Rule of Law' and Regime Legitimacy," *Comparative Political Studies*, Vol. 50, No. 14 (December 2017): 1907–1940.

misleading. Indeed, by focusing on "institutionalization," they miss some of the most important aspects of China's political system. It is necessary to rethink how that political system works.

One body of literature comes from the field of political science. This literature is directed at understanding authoritarian systems in general rather than China specifically, though some of the most important works do address China. Indeed, one of the problems with the general authoritarian literature is that there is no commonality to authoritarian systems. Authoritarian rule is a residual category; authoritarian countries are those that are not democratic.[6] Thus, it is necessary to break down the category "authoritarian"; the most common breakdown is monarchical, military, and one-party systems, though other taxonomies have been suggested.

The category "one-party system" seems most promising, not only because China is a one-party system but also because the literature concludes that one-party systems tend to be long-lived. But the category of one-party systems contains a wide variety of countries, and most of them do not look or act like China. Golkar in Indonesia, the United Malays National Organization (UMNO) in Malaysia, and the Falange in Franco's Spain are quite different from each other and also different from China. The People's Action Party (PAP) in Singapore at first glance seems to be a bit closer, but Singapore has a legal system that has nothing in common with that in China. Moreover, Singapore's bureaucracy really is Weberian, and the PAP has little of the mobilizing characteristics so apparent in the CCP. While the term "authoritarian" has become the term of the day, it really does not tell us very much about China. The term "Leninist" is less used these days, apparently because China does not seem as "totalitarian" as it used to be under Mao (though it seems to be moving back in that direction) and there is a lingering sense of the Cold War that clings to the term, yet "Leninism" remains the best term for describing the CCP. Leninist systems are, of course, authoritarian, but they function differently than the personalistic, patron–client dominated systems often described in the literature. Using the concept of Leninism can tell us a great deal about China's system, so there is no reason to discard what we know about Leninist systems just to conform to political-science currency.

[6] Ibid., p. 26.

Ken Jowitt, who wrote as well as anyone about Leninist systems, argues that the distinctive feature of such systems is the "charismatic impersonalism" of the cadre system. He emphasizes the structure of Leninism because he wants to distinguish between Leninism, on the one hand, and authoritarian systems, including Nazism, on the other. Thus, in his opinion, the *Führerprinzip* – a leadership principle – was the defining characteristic of Nazism, whereas the "correct line" – an organizational characteristic – is the defining characteristic of Leninism.[7]

Jowitt's concept of Leninism is also useful because he sees Leninism as passing through stages – transformation, consolidation, and inclusion – that make it a much more useful concept than the static notion of totalitarianism.[8] We will explore this thesis more below. In any event, Leninism refers to a system that extends hierarchically from the top of the system to the bottom. The most important principles holding the system together are that "the party controls the cadres" (*dangguan ganbu*) and a common ideology that is enforced on the basis of a "correct line."

One has to be careful in identifying the chief characteristics of Leninist systems because they, too, have a need for strong leadership. Indeed, as we will see in the pages below, leaders of the CCP have worked to consolidate their power, and the most successful leaders – Deng Xiaoping and Xi Jinping – have concentrated so much power that they appear to be more above the party than simply the highest leader in the party. There is also an inherent tension between the individual cadre and the organization to which he or she is supposed to be subordinate. The individual cadre in a leadership position, say a county party secretary, concentrates power by building a personal network which may act in a predatory fashion. Indeed, in the Chinese case, the natural tendency to form vertical factions has been heightened because in 1984 the CCP adopted the system of one level supervising the level below it (*xiaguan yiji*). Corruption has grown because of this organizational feature.[9] There are systems in place to try to stop such

---

[7] Ken Jowitt, "The Leninist Phenomenon," pp. 1–49, in *New World Disorder: The Leninist Extinction* (Berkeley: University of California Press, 1992).

[8] Ken Jowitt, "Inclusion and Mobilization in European Leninist Systems," *World Politics*, Vol. 28, No. 1 (1975): 69–96.

[9] Minxin Pei, *China's Crony Capitalism: The Dynamics of Regime Decay* (Cambridge, MA: Harvard University Press, 2016).

corruption, such as the discipline inspection commissions (DICs) at each level, but such systems have never been very effective for the simple reason that the head of the local DIC has traditionally been subordinate to the local party secretary. To the extent that local networks reinforce their own power, they sometimes ignore orders coming from the top. Xi Jinping has been trying to centralize the discipline inspection system, but we will have to wait to see how effective his efforts will be. It is clear, however, that there are tensions inherent in the organizational structure of Leninism.

One reason for emphasizing a Leninist structure is that it provides for a great deal of stability. Leninist systems are very effective in penetrating society and rewarding and sanctioning compliance and deviance respectively. One does not need to explain longevity by reference to institutionalization when reference to the Leninist system provides a more parsimonious explanation. Leninism, unlike the broader universe of authoritarian systems, transforms society and then rules through penetration of the basic social institutions. Although the lowest level of the party-state bureaucracy in China is the township (below the county), the party system extends into the villages. The cadre system can itself be a source of conflict, but its control of society and its control of cadres through its organizational hierarchy are, on balance, a source of stability.

The other reason to call attention to China's Leninist system is because the literature on authoritarian governments often treats the top leadership as a group of individuals, each of whom possesses political and often military assets and thus can bargain with the leader. The literature defines the central issue as the establishment of a set of "rules" that will define roles and divide spoils equitably, or otherwise will lead to the personalization of power or the ouster of the leader. As Geddes et al. write, when united militaries or disciplined parties lead to authoritarian seizures of power, "lieutenants are likely to be able to resist extreme concentration of power in the dictator's hands."[10]

However, this certainly does not apply to China under Mao or Deng, or apparently under Xi. The party is certainly more than a collection of leaders that a coup might bring to power. Each leader has a position in the system; that position and its importance can be challenged, but it

[10] Barbara Geddes, Joseph Wright, and Erica Frantz, *How Dictatorships Work* (Cambridge: Cambridge University Press, 2018), p. 79.

makes coups more difficult, though not impossible (as Khrushchev learned). The game in China, as we will see below, is always to concentrate power in the hands of the leader, and the lieutenants are there to support the leader, not to challenge him. A leader who cannot secure a majority of the top leadership will not survive. Leadership splits can happen, as when deep differences developed between Mao Zedong and Liu Shaoqi, but sooner or later the hierarchical order is restored.

This tendency to concentrate power in the hands of the leader means that opposition is handled differently from what is described in the literature on authoritarian rule. Leaders are often seen as "buying off" potential opposition by offering the opposition positions in legislatures or other organizations, but in China losers are rarely offered concessions.[11] Mao beat out Li Lisan, Zhang Wentian, Bo Gu, Wang Ming, and others in his quest for power. All were retained in the elite, but they were stripped of power. They were not bought off. Other threats, such as Liu Shaoqi, were dealt with more harshly. In the reform era, losers have been deposed, and, under Xi, many have been jailed. Concessions are few and far between.

Although one can never discount the possibility of a general secretary being deposed (Jiang Zemin faced a precarious environment when he first took the position of general secretary and there have been numerous rumors, none confirmed, of assassination attempts against Xi Jinping), one has to look at the checks and balances within the system that make such actions difficult. Just as the disparate composition of the Politburo (PB) and Politburo Standing Committee (PBSC) can make a new general secretary's life difficult, it also makes coordination among potential opponents problematic. Moreover, there is always a reason (perhaps several reasons) why the general secretary emerged as top dog in the first place. Unless that dynamic changes, it is tough to mount a challenge. Moreover, the monitoring of the movements and communications of top officials makes co-ordination both difficult and dangerous. Finally, there is the issue of legitimation – those who purge a leader need to put forward a persuasive reason, and the Chinese system, with its elaborated ideology, makes that complicated.

---

[11] Jennifer Gandhi and Adam Przeworski, "Authoritarian Institutions and the Survival of Autocrats," *Comparative Political Studies*, Vol. 40, No. 1 (November 2007): 1279–1301.

In any event, the literature on authoritarian governments concludes that institutional arrangements make for more stable regimes; in China, however, longevity has occurred through manipulation and violation of the rules, not through the creation of binding institutions.

The Cadre Management System

A second body of literature focuses on the cadre system in China. One of the first efforts to argue that the cadre system had institutionalized and that that institutionalization could control cadre behavior by providing important incentives is by Zhou Li'an. Zhou Li'an, an economist at Peking University, argues that the reason why China could sustain growth over the decades was its promotion system. Promotions were conducted as "tournaments" – cadres who did a better job than their rivals were promoted. Such competition over promotions incentivized cadres to build their local economies. The same lever allowed the central (or provincial) government with a means of controlling lower-level officials. This system, which propelled officials to work hard on behalf of their communities, discouraged predatory behavior because such behavior would hurt economic growth and those who engaged in predatory behavior would lose out in the competition for higher office.

In a co-authored article, Zhou and Hongbin Li note that the "strong pro-business role of Chinese local officials stands in stark contrast with the rent-seeking behavior (the 'grabbing hand') of local officials in other transitional and developing countries." Unlike Weingast and others who attribute this phenomenon to "market-preserving federalism," Zhou and Li believe that it is the result of the promotion incentives facing Chinese officials. As they conclude, "the Chinese central government tends to promote provincial leaders who perform well economically and terminate provincial leaders who perform poorly."[12]

Although impressive, there are many questions about Zhou's thesis. One is simply the question of how much impact a leader can have on

---

[12] Gabriella Montinola, Yingyi Qian, and Barry Weingast, "Federalism, Chinese Style: The Political Basis for Economic Success in China," *World Politics*, Vol. 48, No. 1 (October 1995): 50–81; Hongbin Li and Li-an Zhou, "Political Turnover and Economic Performance: The Incentive Role of Personnel Control in China," *Journal of Public Economics*, Vol. 80 (2005): 1743–1962, at 1760.

the economy of a place in the course of a single term. The economic development of a place is determined by so many factors, including its geographical location, transportation networks, capital stock, investment, and so forth. Leadership can certainly make a difference, but it is not clear how much of a difference it can make within a short period of time.

The more important question is the degree to which the incentive system, as measured through the cadre evaluation system, can control cadre behavior. Although much has been written about the cadre evaluation system, there remains much that is not known. For instance, application of the system seems to vary greatly from place to place. In some places, cadre evaluation seems to be taken seriously and discussed during party meetings. In other places, only the party secretary and the head of the Organization Department see the results, and they are only advisory. The "democratic evaluation" part is especially suspect. Cadres with a bad boss will certainly give him or her high marks – if their recommendation is accepted, they get rid of the bad boss and open up the position, into which one of his subordinates can move.[13]

Moreover, although the CCP has adopted a number of regulations regarding promotions, the formal regulations are simply impossible to follow. As Chien-wen Kou and Wen-hsuan Tsai point out, if cadres were promoted strictly according to the regulations, which means abiding by the rules that cadres serve their full five-year term in a given position and are promoted step by step, then not a single cadre could be promoted to the bureau-director (*ting*) level.[14] The regulations were designed in a way that there had to be exceptions – and there are. As Kou and Tsai note, one can rise up through the Communist Youth League (CYL), which allows faster promotions, and then transfer to a regular party position. (It should be noted that in 2016 when the Central Discipline Inspection Commission (CDIC) cracked down on the CYL its fast promotions were one of the

---

[13] Interviews with various local officials.
[14] Chien-wen Kou and Wen-hsuan Tsai, "'Sprinting with Small Steps' towards Promotion: Solutions for the Age Dilemma in the CCP Cadre Appointment System," *China Journal*, No. 71 (January 2014): 153–171. The regulations are "Zhonggong Zhongyang bangongting fayin 'Dangzheng lingdao ganbu kaohe gongzuo tiaoli'" (The Central CCP Office promulgates 'Regulations on the evaluation work of leading party and state cadres), retrieved from www .xinhuanet.com/politics/2019-04/21/c_1124395835.htm. Accessed October 10, 2020.

criticisms). Or one can accept a position in an external unit (*guazhi*), which allows the transferred cadre to return to his or her original unit at a higher level. Or a cadre can be the recipient of a "non-regulation promotion" that allows him/her to be promoted in fewer than the five years required by the regulations.[15] Altogether it is estimated that the majority of cadres serve only three years at a given post.[16]

Pang Baoqing and his colleagues push this argument further by suggesting that there is a political intention behind the design of the regulations. They argue that the regulations act as a regular track that is intended to halt the progress of most cadres below the bureau-director level, but other cadres are "fast-tracked" to be promoted to higher levels faster. Hopefully "merit" is one reason why some cadres are fast-tracked, but this design certainly allows other considerations to be factored in. Pang et al. argue that this two-track system creates a core of cadres that is loyal to the regime. But one has to argue that this loyalty is bought at the expense of the institutionalization that sup-posedly underlies the longevity of the regime.[17]

This is an important point with broader application to understand-ing China's political system. The implication of Pang Baoqing's argu-ment is that the elaboration of rules within the party does not imply institutionalization. After all, if the rules apply only to those not on the fast track, it suggests that others, those who are core to the functioning of the system, are not subject to such constraining rules. On the con-trary, promotions, particularly promotions to important, even critical, positions entail political support above and beyond the factors that guide the promotions of most cadres. We certainly see this in high-level promotions when some cadres are able to enjoy "helicopter promo-tions," meaning promotions of more than one rank.

The literature's focus on "institutionalization" and (generally) step-by-step promotions also sidesteps the actual functioning of the cadre system. Perhaps the most useful insight in this literature is Yang Xuedong's concept of a "high-pressure system" (*yalixing tizhi*). The notion of a high-pressure system is obviously related to the idea that the cadre system is a mobilization system. This mobilization system is

---

[15] Interviews with various local officials.
[16] Interview with expert on local politics.
[17] Pang Baoqing, Shu Keng, and Lingna Zhong, "Sprinting with Small Steps: China's Cadre Management and Authoritarian Resilience," *China Journal*, No. 80 (2018): 68–93.

rooted in the party's revolutionary history when cadres mobilized peasants or soldiers to accomplish specific tasks. That basic mobilization system has, with some modification, continued to the present.[18] To take an example from today's headlines, when Vice Premier Sun Chunlan visited Wuhan to implement emergency measures to control the deadly COVID-19, she ordered medical workers to form teams that would work twenty-four hours a day and go from house to house to check the temperatures of all residents.[19] Details were not provided, but clearly cadres from different offices had to have been mobilized to join these teams. This sort of mobilization effort is not something normal bureaucracies can do.

To take a more typical example, local officials in Weng'an, Guizhou, felt pressured by their superiors to achieve economic goals that would both enrich officials (at both levels) and show "political accomplishments" (*zhengji*) that would pad resumés and perhaps pave the way for promotions. In this case, officials pushed too hard and large-scale riots broke out.[20] This sort of pressure was the result not of local cadres trying to attain the goals set out on their "cadre evaluation forms," but rather trying to fulfill the "tasks" (*renwu*) set out by their superiors. Such tasks are the specific measures that superior officials really care about, and fulfilling one's tasks is more important than achieving the goals enumerated in the formal evaluation system.[21] The tasks put pressure on lower-level officials who have to find the resources (both personnel and material) to accomplish them if they want to move ahead.

It is this high-pressure, task-oriented system that makes the Chinese cadre system more personal than is normally associated

18 Yang Xuedong, "Yalixing tizhi: Yige gainian de jianmingshi" (High-Pressure System: A History Clarifying a Concept), *Shehui kexue*, No. 11 (2012): 4–12. See also Rong Jingben et al., *Cong yalixing tizhi xiang minzhu hezuo tizhi de zhuanbian: Xianxiang liangji shengzhi gaige* (Changing from a High-Pressure System to a System of Democratic Co-operation: Political System Reform at the County and Township Levels) (Beijing: Zhongyang bianyi chubanshe, 1998).

19 Amy Qin, Steven Lee Myers, and Elaine Yu, "China Tightens Wuhan Lockdown in 'Wartime' Battle with Coronavirus," *New York Times*, February 7, 2020, available at www.nytimes.com/2020/02/06/world/asia/coronavirus-china-wuhan-quarantine.html, accessed September 15, 2020.

20 Joseph Fewsmith, *The Logic and Limits of Political Reform in China* (New York: Cambridge University Press, 2013), Chapter 1.

21 Interview.

with the term "bureaucracy." It suggests why the term "cadre" is more suitable than the term "civil servant," even if cadres now take an exam and are called *gongwuyuan* ("civil servant"). It is a mobilizational system, not a Weberian bureaucracy based on rational–legal authority.

Of course, Weng'an was not the only place where cadres' interests clashed with those of the peasants. The number of "mass incidents" rose from 8,700 in 1993 to 180,000 in 2010.[22] Not only were there more incidents, but also the number of participants grew, as did the level of violence. And party publications placed the blame on cadres, not peasants. One should not blame these incidents on a "few bad apples"; they reflect structural problems in the cadre system.[23] Of course, the party could and did change policies, albeit slowly, to address these issues,[24] but dysfunctional aspects of the cadre system continued to manifest themselves in other ways, such as the vehicles for local finance and the growth of local debt.

It is no doubt too early to judge whether Xi's campaign against corruption and his efforts to make localities more responsive to Beijing's wishes will be successful, but it seems likely that informal politics will continue to play an important role in the cadre system for long into the future.

Elite Politics

Elite politics is less central to the study of Chinese politics than it used to be, perhaps following the trend in political science at large. Given the nature of the Chinese regime, however, elite politics remains critical. Like the general literature on authoritarian politics, this literature in recent years has focused on the relative stability of elite politics. It was widely assumed in the field that a factionalized political system that had manifested ideological bankruptcy and had

[22] Sun Liping, "Shehui zhixu shi dangxia de yanzhong tiaozhan" (Social Order Is a Serious Challenge at Present), *Jingji guanchabao*, February 25, 2011.
[23] Zhonggong zhongyang zuzhibu ketizu, ed., *Zhongguo diaocha baogao: Xin xingshixia renmin neibu maodun yanjiu, 2000–2001* (China Investigation Report: Research on Contradictions among the People under the New Situation, 2000–2001) (Beijing: Zhongyang bianyi chubanshe, 2001).
[24] Christopher Heurlin, *Responsive Authoritarianism in China: Land, Protests, and Policy Making* (New York: Cambridge University Press, 2016).

violently suppressed the democratic aspirations of its citizens could not last long. The context mattered as well. Following the Tiananmen massacre, socialism fell in Eastern Europe and the Soviet Union. Surely China would not be far behind. Andrew Nathan supplies the first and most persuasive explanation in his seminal article "Authoritarian Resilience." Nathan's answer resonates with the literature on authoritarian rule. He sees increasingly strong succession norms, growing meritocracy, weakening factionalism, greater professionalism, and the emergence of input institutions that provide feedback to the regime as leading to an institutionalization of the political system.[25]

Since Nathan, there have been a number of works that have pursued the institutionalization thesis. For instance, Bo Zhiyue has written about the institutionalization of elite management,[26] Suisheng Zhao on the emergence of a distinct China model,[27] and Melanie Manion on the role of people's congresses in providing feedback, among others.[28] In short, institutionalization has become the predominant explanation for the relative political stability China has experienced since Tiananmen.

Cheng Li has conducted the most detailed study of elite politics in recent years, focusing on the Xi Jinping era. He argues that China has developed intra-party democracy that "emphasizes deal-making and compromise between competing factions or coalitions." This collegial approach to decision making, Li argues, allows the leadership to practice "collective leadership." He focuses largely on the groups that formed around Jiang Zemin's "Shanghai Gang" on the one hand and Hu Jintao's reliance on the CYL on the other. Although such factionalization has proven fatal in the past, Li argues that each faction brings different backgrounds and skill sets to the table, and thus is able to

---

[25] Andrew J. Nathan, "Authoritarian Resilience," *Journal of Democracy*, Vol. 14, No. 1 (January 2003): 6–17.
[26] Bo Zhiyue, "The Institutionalization of Elite Management in China," pp. 70–100, in Barry Naughton and Dali Yang, eds., *Holding China Together: Diversity and National Integration in the Post-Deng Era* (New York: Cambridge University Press, 2004).
[27] Suisheng Zhao, "The China Model: Can It Replace the Western Model of Modernization?" *Journal of Contemporary China*, Vol. 19, No. 65 (2010): 419–436.
[28] Melanie Manion, *Information for Autocrats* (New York: Cambridge University Press, 2015).

compromise. Thus, although Li focuses on the relations among leaders ("factions"), ultimately his explanation lies in the notion of institutionalization.[29]

The same is true of Alice Miller, who comes out even more strongly in favor of institutionalization. As she writes, "Since the beginning of the Deng Xiaoping era, elite politics in China has undergone deliberate, incremental institutionalization. As institutionalized processes of leadership decisionmaking have taken hold, the dynamics of leadership competition have been changing, in favor of an increasingly consensus-building collective leadership."[30] Unfortunately, the data do not bear out the assertion, and the Xi Jinping era has turned decisively against these hoped-for trends. Indeed, this is understandable. Institutionalization would undermine the basis of Leninism, and such undermining has not occurred.

These various efforts to use institutionalization to explain Chinese politics seem misplaced. When applied to politics, institutionalization is first and foremost a concept that applies to the state. One thinks of the growth of government bureaucracies, mostly in the nineteenth century, as a product of war or revolution but always seeking a way to rationalize the state along rational–legal lines.[31] Effective state institutions recruit and develop expertise and are based on law. Formal institutions need to have "third-party enforcement,"[32] primarily courts, to limit the abuse of institutions and the ability of individuals to profit from their positions. When this does not happen, one ends up with weak states, often accompanied by patronage politics and/or organized crime.

It is important to keep in mind that in China the state bureaucracy is weak, a mere appendage to a powerful party organization. Some years

[29] Cheng Li, *Chinese Politics in the Xi Jinping Era: Reassessing Collective Leadership* (Washington, D.C.: The Brookings Institution, 2018).
[30] Alice L. Miller, "Institutionalization and the Changing Dynamics of Chinese Leadership Politics," pp. 61–79, in Cheng Li, ed., *China's Changing Political Landscape: Prospects for Democracy* (Washington, D.C., The Brookings Institution, 2008), p. 61.
[31] On bureaucratic formation, see Bernard S. Silberman, *Cages of Reason: The Rise of the Rational State in France, Japan, the United States, and Great Britain* (Chicago: The University of Chicago Press, 1993).
[32] On the importance of third-party enforcement, see Wolfgang Streek and Kathleen Thelen, "Introduction: Institutional Change in Advanced Political Economies," pp. 1–39, in Wolfgang Streek and Kathleen Thelen, eds., *Beyond Continuity: Institutional Change in Advanced Political Economies* (Oxford: Oxford University Press, 2005), pp. 10–11; North, *Institutions, Institutional Change and Economic Performance*, pp. 35 and 58.

ago, Hong Yung Lee hoped that the state bureaucracy would eventually reduce the role and arbitrariness of the party, and China would take its place as a modern administrative state.[33] But as Xu Xianglin points out, China's cadre force has never had an existence separate from the party and has always been used by the party to implement the party's vision.[34] Reform did not rationalize the state; it changed the party's goals. With Xi Jinping's declaration at the Nineteenth Party Congress that the "party leads in everything," the weakness of the state is even clearer than in the past.

Institutionalization and Balances

If institutionalization cannot be used to explain the relative political stability of China over the past four decades, what can? As suggested above, the Leninist system structures Chinese politics. It defines the hierarchy and it penetrates deeply into society. Propaganda defines the limits of acceptable speech, while intelligence and security forces maintain both compliance and societal order. Although Leninism stresses the party organization, it necessarily relies on cadres to carry out party policy. Leading cadres at various levels, unencumbered by effective legal constraints, are routinely invested with authority that greatly exceeds anything seen in a Weberian-style bureaucracy. This suggests that their power is more derived from who they are than from the offices they hold; office holding has surely become more important over the years, but one's power derives not just from the office one holds but also from the connections one has developed over the years.

This suggests that there are centrifugal forces in the Leninist bureaucracy that must be controlled lest individual authority overwhelm the party bureaucracy. One way to do this is through establishing formal and informal balances. At first glance, balances seem incompatible with Leninism. Leninist organizations are supposed to be highly disciplined, hierarchical structures. But in the real world, even hierarchical systems are bound to have different interests. These might grow out of an

---

[33] Hong Yung Lee, *From Revolutionary Cadres to Party Technocrats in Socialist China* (Berkeley, CA: University of California Press, 1991).

[34] Xu Xianglin, "Hou Mao shidai de jingying zhuanhuan he yifuxing jishu guanliao de xingqi" (The Turnover of Elites and the Rise of Dependent Technocrats in the Post-Mao Period), *Zhanlüe yu guanli*, No. 49 (December 2001): 65–76.

individual's contributions to the revolution, from organizational interests, from the growth of individual success in accumulating supporters, or from some combination of these. Forcing such diverse interests into a rigid frame, desirable as it might be from an organizational point of view, is often unrealistic. Informal arrangements are needed to supplement organizational structures; this was especially true in the Dengist period.

Sometimes balances can be incorporated into the system. For instance, county party secretaries are in a position in which they can potentially accumulate a great deal of personal power. They are constrained by at least two mechanisms. On the one hand, as at other levels of the system, a new party secretary comes into office with many of his or her colleagues already decided. Since terms in office are usually staggered, many of those on the party standing committee will be left over from the previous administration. But when they are transferred to other positions or when there is a party congress to decide on new leadership, the party secretary has the opportunity to promote cadres of his or her own choosing. The party secretary has a strong interest in choosing people that he or she believes will be supportive, but the party secretary only has the right to nominate such people. The superior official, in this example the municipal party secretary, has the right to veto these selections. So the party secretary must keep in mind the views of his or her superior when making personnel decisions. In other words, a balance must be struck. This system binds different levels of the system together in a way that is not readily apparent from the organizational chart.

Informal balances are also an important part of elite politics. There are at least two functions of such balances. On the one hand, balances allow a dominant leader (such as Deng Xiaoping) to build a coalition. Coming out of the Cultural Revolution, there was a wide variety of opinions within the party, with some hoping to re-establish the structures they were familiar with from before the Cultural Revolution, and others pushing for more radical reform. As a pragmatist, Deng was eager to avoid ideological battles, which he had seen deeply divide the party. Maintaining a balance between different interests could minimize ideological disputes and, for a while at least, political turmoil. This was most apparent in the economic sphere, as we will see in Chapter 1. Balances have also been used at different times for different purposes, such as balancing elders and younger, frontline, leaders. The problem with balances, of course, is that they shift over time, as leaders die or as views become polarized. Ultimately balances are unstable, and this adds to the uninstitutionalized nature of the system.

In addition to balances, norms are an important part of the system. Norms come closer to what many people have thought of as institutionalization. The CCP has held party congresses every five years since 1977, and this is a norm that might be considered institutionalized. The retirement system means that many cadres will have to retire at each party congress, but the idea that roughly half of the full members of the Central Committee will retire is more a norm than a rule. New members of the Central Committee are promoted either from the list of alternate members or directly from the wider body of officials. There are no known rules governing this process. We know that a committee of half a dozen senior officials will be appointed before each party congress to vet those being appointed to the Central Committee, but we do not know the criteria they use to approve or deny a promotion. In any event, the head of the party will have the most decisive voice. There is obviously room in this process for manipulation, and the degree to which personnel selection is biased has to be guided by norms – a sense that different interests in the party are appropriately "represented." But such norms are not rules, and they can be violated, as they have been in recent years.

One impact of these and other norms is that a new general secretary (party head) does not get to pick his colleagues. His (and so far the party head has always been a "he") colleagues could be left over from the previous term, or they could have just been promoted but reflect the preferences of other interests in the party. This arrangement sets up a sort of checks-and-balances situation. And such checks and balances have, by and large, supported stability. In a leader's second term, he has much greater control over personnel decisions (another norm) and the PB is likely to reflect the general secretary's preferences to a greater degree. So general secretaries tend to go from weak to strong over time, reflecting the relative dispersion of power in the first term and the relative concentration of power in the second term. We sometimes take this as reflecting "institutionalization," but it is useful to remember that in the reform era (since 1978) there have only been four party heads, and only two of them have followed this pattern. Xi Jinping seemingly has broken with the two-term norm.

Moreover, leaders often manipulate party organizations. For instance, in the Deng Xiaoping era, many policies were routed through the Secretariat to avoid the more conservative PB. Similarly, Xi Jinping has created new leadership small groups to enhance his power, and the CDIC has played an outsized role under the Xi administration that it had never played before. Leaders manipulate norms and organizations to strengthen their own positions, which would not be necessary if the system were institutionalized. Similarly, each leader, from Deng Xiaoping through Xi Jinping, has strengthened his position over time by recruiting allies. They put these allies into critical positions to enhance their own power. This book is largely about this process.

Balances and norms are informal mechanisms that can add stability to the system, but they are hardly institutionalized mechanisms that can pass power from one leader to the next or prevent struggles for power or the concentration of power.

Critical Positions

Not all positions are of equal importance; some are more important for the general secretary to keep and enhance his power. These posts are *critical positions*. The notion of critical positions can be clarified with a simple mind experiment. Imagine, if you will, being dropped into the general secretary's chair at the first PB meeting following a party congress. You would look around the room and see a lot of people, some friendly, others not so much. What do you have to do to secure power and keep it? As unrealistic as this scenario sounds, it is not unlike the situation facing Jiang Zemin when he was suddenly promoted to the top job in 1989.

As you contemplate your situation, you realize that some jobs are more important, in terms of keeping power, than others. Obviously, the single most important group for your survival is the PBSC – how many votes can you count on? The whole membership of the PB is also important. They only meet once a month (the PBSC meets once a week), but they run important ministries, provinces, and cities. And, with some exceptions, the membership of the next PBSC will come from the PB. You will also quickly realize that the position of the head of the General Office is critical. The General Office does everything from organizing the flow of paperwork to overseeing the Central Guard, roughly the Chinese equivalent of the American Secret Service. It was from this office that Wang

Dongxing directed the arrest of the Gang of Four. Next you might think of the Organization Department, which oversees the training and promotion of the *nomenklatura*, the centrally managed cadres (*zhongguan ganbu*). And then there is the Propaganda Department, your way of messaging the Chinese people as well as signaling to your colleagues. Other critical departments include the CDIC, the Ministry of State Security, and the Ministry of Public Security. Last but certainly not least, there is the CMC. There is no question that the military has become more professionalized over time, but general secretaries who can't control the CMC (such as Hu Jintao; see Chapter 3) do not fare as well.

The Secretariat is also a critical body because it is in charge of implementing PB and PBSC decisions and organizes major events. It also supervises the four departments directly under the Central Committee, namely the Organization Department, the Propaganda Department, the International Liaison Department, and the United Front Work Department.[35]

Together the members of these leading organs – the PBSC, the PB, the Secretariat, and the CMC – are referred to as party and state leaders. It is they who run the country. That is not to say that lower-level leaders – the Central Committee members from the PLA, the State Council, and provinces – are not important; on the contrary, we often see central leaders trying to build support among them, but they clearly rank below the national leadership, and it is often useful to distinguish these levels when discussing the elite.

I emphasize those in critical positions because it leads me to a different research strategy than most. Although the whole membership of the Central Committee is important, it makes sense to look first and foremost at who is occupying these critical positions. Doing a statistical analysis of the whole Central Committee, including alternate members, does not tell one very much. After all, only about 25 or 30 percent of the alternate members will be promoted at the next party congress, and they cannot vote until they become full members. By watching who is controlling these critical positions, one can get a rough gauge of the degree to which power is centralized. The normal pattern is for power to be less centralized in a general secretary's first term, and then become more centralized in his second term. We can see this

---

[35] Cheng Li, *Chinese Politics in the Xi Jinping Era*, p. 54.

because those moved into critical positions are usually close associates of the general secretary. Having friends in high places makes being general secretary more secure.

To lay out this mental map of the most critical positions in the system, however, is not to say that their relative importance stays the same over time. As suggested above, the party leadership has considerable leeway to realign the power of various organs, another reason why it is difficult to speak of institutionalization. For instance, in the late 1980s and early 1990s, Qiao Shi was a member of the PBSC and head of the Politics and Law Commission. He was succeeded as head of the Politics and Law Commission by Ren Jianxin, who was a member of the PB and Secretariat, but not the PBSC. His successor was Luo Gan, who moved up to the PBSC at the Sixteenth Party Congress. The importance of the Politics and Law Commission rose with his leadership and whether he had a position on the PB or its Standing Committee. Critical positions are always important, but their importance can vary over time, depending on who the leader is and whether he is able to emphasize or marginalize a particular bureaucracy. There is nothing mechanical about analyzing Chinese politics.

Looking at the rest of the Central Committee, there are usually about ten to fifteen people who head party organs – *People's Daily*, the Party History and Document Research Office, the All-China Women's Federation, and so forth. Then there are those who have leadership positions in the State Council. The State Council is the "state" side of the party-state system, though all ministers and commission heads of the State Council are party members. There are usually about sixty people on the Central Committee who lead State Council offices. The military is also well represented on the Central Committee. Uniformed military officers, including those on the CMC, make up about 20 percent of the Central Committee. Military representation on the Central Committee reached its peak at the Ninth Party Congress in 1969, when the Cultural Revolution was – prematurely – declared over. It dropped to 20 percent at the Twelfth Party Congress in 1982 and has remained at that level ever since. There are also about fifty-five people representing the provinces. Normally each province has two representatives, the party secretary and the governor. Some places, particularly Xinjiang and Tibet, often have three representatives, reflecting the difficulty of governing those two minority areas. Finally there are usually a small number, roughly ten people, who have retired from active service and taken up positions on the National People's Congress (NPC) and the Chinese People's Political Consultative Congress (CPPCC). These two bodies are more honorific than they are centers of power; they are ways of retiring people honorably. Following these critical positions allows the analyst to better understand the ebbs and flows of power.

This book is about power, how it is organized, accumulated, and sometimes thwarted. Leninism provides a framework, but that framework does not provide for accountability or effective constraints on power; it certainly does not provide a decision-making rule for passing power on to the next leader. It thus provides incentives for developing personal networks and setting up struggles for power. Informal balances can leaven politics, but such balances inevitably change, igniting a new round of struggle. As Tang Tsou noted many years ago, compromise is possible in Chinese politics but only as a tactical measure, a way to prepare for an inevitable decisive conflict.[36] Unfortunately, that still seems to be the case. The institutions that should make compromise possible have failed to develop.

Plan of the Book

Because the focus of this book is on the way in which Leninism shapes political action and stands in the way of institutionalization, there is necessarily a narrow focus on the leadership. As we will see, the Leninist party, at least in China, is not an inflexible structure that binds leaders, colleagues, and challengers in a rigid framework. On the contrary, as leaders pursue a concentration of power and seek to extend their influence beyond their formal terms, they use a variety of mechanisms, from different sorts of balances, through the manipulation of party organizations, to articulating new evolutions of Marxist ideology and purging opponents. Norms, particularly retirement norms, do influence politics, and leaders have sometimes appealed to institutionalization, but such appeals have not, during the last four decades, led to a political system or bureaucracy (party or state) that can reasonably be called institutionalized. And the reason lies squarely with the Leninist party.

[36] Tang Tsou, "The Tiananmen Tragedy: The State–Society Relationship, Choices, and Mechanisms in Historical Perspective," pp. 265–327, in Brantly Womack, ed., *Contemporary Chinese Politics in Historical Perspective* (Cambridge: Cambridge University Press, 1991), p. 319.

The main task of this book is to trace how different leaders during the reform period have gone about consolidating power. As will be seen, power is not something that can be passed easily from leader to leader; the best one leader can do for another is to position him well, assuming the predecessor really wants to pass on power. The successor must still do what is necessary to garner power in his own right or he will suffer as a weak leader. As one follows these trials and tribulations, one sees that power arrangements at the top of the Chinese system are constantly shifting, sometimes because of deaths, sometimes because of political maneuvering, and sometimes because of purges.

We start our investigation with Deng Xiaoping. Deng had very definite ideas on what had gone wrong during the Cultural Revolution and how power should be arranged. It is indeed tempting to call Deng an institutionalist, except that the CCP cannot be institutionalized without destroying what makes it a Leninist party – a hierarchal, mobilizational, task-oriented party that relies on cadres. Deng should get great credit for launching the economic reforms. It took great fortitude – and power – to move as far and as fast as he did away from the Maoist legacy. But Deng wanted to make Leninism work, not institutionalize it. Part of making the party work was not allowing his successor (Jiang Zemin) to name his successor. But Jiang Zemin undermined Deng's plans, and the power of Hu Jintao, by accumulating power. Tracing this process is the task of Chapters 1 and 2.

Chapter 3 looks at Hu Jintao's difficulties in managing as general secretary. Hu is generally regarded as a weak leader, but it is more accurate to say that he was never permitted to grasp the tools he needed. Those critical positions were always out of his reach.

When Ken Jowitt wrote about Leninism, he assumed that such parties would be consumed by corruption and/or factionalism once they reached the reform stage. Once the revolutionary mission and mobilization that had once kept them together was lost, the party would lose its discipline. That is exactly what happened to the CCP. The growing organizational corrosion and dysfunction are explored in Chapter 4.[37]

---

[37] Jowitt, *New World Disorder.*

It is only by understanding the pathologies of the Leninist system in China that we can understand Xi Jinping's rise to power and how he has gone about trying to revive Leninism in China. It is far from certain that Leninism can be revivified – one can look far and wide before finding someone who fully subscribes to Xi Jinping Thought on Socialism with Chinese Characteristics for a New Era – and the CCP will certainly again discover that passing power on to a successor will be difficult. How Xi has altered political arrangements in China and the implications of doing so are explored in Chapters 5 and 6.

1 | *The Dengist Structure of Power*

In the final months of his life, Mao Zedong worried about Deng Xiaoping. The Chairman knew that Deng was extremely competent, but he doubted that Deng could be trusted to uphold what Mao considered one of his greatest legacies: the Great Proletarian Cultural Revolution. When Tiananmen Square was occupied on Qingming (grave sweeping) festival in April 1976 by mourners coming to express their grief at the passing of Premier Zhou Enlai, the "Gang of Four" (Jiang Qing, Zhang Chunqiao, Wang Hongwen, and Yao Wenyuan) accused Deng of having orchestrated the demonstrations. Mao dismissed that charge, but was alarmed on April 7 when his nephew, Mao Yuanxin, told him that the crowds had "embraced the banner of Deng Xiaoping [and had] furiously pointed its spearhead at the great leader Chairman Mao." Angered, the chairman ordered that Deng Xiaoping be removed from all his positions. He also ordered that Hua Guofeng be named first vice chairman, a new title and clear indication that he would be successor.[1]

But Deng was too talented a person, with too much support among veteran leaders to be sidelined forever. During a party Work Conference in March 1977, Marshall Ye Jianying and veteran economic policy specialist Chen Yun appealed for Deng's return to work. Hua Guofeng yielded to the pressure, and in July, Deng reappeared in public. The following month, the CCP held its Eleventh Party Congress and Deng rejoined the party leadership as vice premier and a member of the PBSC. Thus started his quest to become "paramount" leader and to bring reform to China.[2]

---

[1] Frederick C. Teiwes and Warren Sun, *The End of the Maoist Era: Chinese Politics during the Twilight of the Cultural Revolution, 1972–1976* (Armonk, NY: M. E. Sharpe, 2007), p. 489.

[2] Yu Guangyuan, *Deng Xiaoping Shakes the World: An Eyewitness Account of China's Party Work Conference and Third Plenum (November–December 1978)*, ed. Ezra F. Vogel and Steven I. Levine (Norwalk, CT: EastBridge, 2004); Ezra F. Vogel, *Deng Xiaoping and the Transformation of China* (Cambridge, MA: Belknap Press of Harvard University Press, 2011), pp. 229–240.

China was in desperate need of reform. The Mao period had not been kind to the Chinese people. Not only had the Cultural Revolution sent thousands of intellectuals to the countryside to learn from the peasants at a time when the country needed their talents, but mass movements had separated families, brought about death and destruction, and brought the economy to the brink of collapse. Urban workers saw their annual wages fall on average from about 700 yuan in 1957 to 630 yuan in 1976, a decline of 10 percent.[3] The average per capita income of urban residents was 316 yuan, and that of rural residents was only 134 yuan. Over one-quarter of China's rural population had an annual per capita income of less than 50 yuan. Chen Yun bluntly warned that if the livelihood of the peasants did not improve, party secretaries would lead peasants into the cities to demand food.[4]

Figure 1.1 Chairman Hua Guofeng after being named Mao Zedong's successor (Bettmann via Getty Images)

---

[3] Andrew G. Walder, *China under Mao: A Revolution Derailed* (Cambridge, MA: Harvard University Press, 2015), p. 328.

[4] Joseph Fewsmith, *Dilemmas of Reform in China: Political Conflict and Economic Debate* (Armonk, NY: M. E. Sharpe, 1994).

During the Cultural Revolution, Deng was exiled to Nanchang, the capital of the central south province of Jiangxi, where he worked in a tractor factory located next to the army base where he lived. Walking back and forth every day to the tractor factory, Deng had plenty of time to think about what had gone wrong and what he would do differently if he ever were to have the chance. Some years later, he summed up his thoughts in one of the best-known passages in his works:

The errors we made in the past were ... more attributable to the problems in our organizational and working systems. If these systems are sound, they can place restraints on the actions of bad people; if they are unsound, they may hamper the efforts of good people or indeed, in certain cases, may push them in the wrong direction ... Stalin gravely damaged socialist legality, doing things which Comrade Mao Zedong once said would have been impossible in Western countries like Britain, France, and the United States.[5]

Unfortunately, Deng did not devote any time to discussing what precisely had caused the Chinese political system to push Mao to commit the errors he made later in life, but Deng did lay out with some specificity what he thought would provide for a stable and effective system.

Perhaps the most important problem the system faced was the "overconcentration of power." The overconcentration of power, Deng said, "means the inappropriate and indiscriminate concentration of all powers in the name of strengthening centralized party leadership." The problem was that the overconcentration of power often "turns into leadership by individuals" – which, in turn, meant that most cadres had no decision-making power at all. In China, many senior leaders held multiple posts simultaneously. Limiting that practice would spread responsibility, would allow those with greater expertise to focus on their area of knowledge, and would bring more leaders into the decision-making process.[6] Overconcentration of power meant that "democracy" was being impaired. As Deng put it, "Without democracy, there can be no socialism and no socialist modernization."[7] By "democracy," Deng certainly did

---

[5] Deng Xiaoping, "On the Reform of the System of Party and State Leadership," in *Selected Works of Deng Xiaoping (1975–1982)* (Beijing: Foreign Languages Press, 1983), p. 316.

[6] Ibid., pp. 303, 309.

[7] Perhaps surprisingly, this sentence appears in Deng's speech "Uphold the Four Cardinal Principles," but the fact that it does shows how Deng thought "democracy" in terms of consulting the relevant experts could be combined with discipline. See *Selected Works of Deng Xiaoping (1975–1982)*, p. 176.

not mean public participation but rather he meant that those officials who should be involved in a decision be adequately consulted and their opinions should be brought to bear on decisions.

Overconcentration of power, Deng also said, was connected to the problem of bureaucratism.[8] Because lower-level officials felt they had no decision-making power, they inevitably referred decisions up the chain of command, and nothing was done until a senior leader could get around to making a decision. And since senior leaders were tasked with making decisions across a wide range of issues, the limitations of their knowledge would inevitably lead to the commission of errors.

Overconcentration of power was also related to "feudalism." This was not only a problem of party culture but also a problem of Chinese culture in general. "Feudalism" meant deference to higher-ranking and more senior cadres on the one hand and to arrogance and ordering people around on the other. Deng made the point that although ranks differed, as party members they were all equal.[9]

These concerns were all related to cadre policy. Like Chen Yun, Deng was acutely aware that party leaders were too old; they would have to think of the overall interest of the party and retire in favor of younger leaders. Thinking of the forthcoming Twelfth Party Congress (which was held in September 1982), Deng said that he hoped that the party would name fifty people below the age of fifty to the Central Committee (they missed; see below).[10] Deng's interest in promoting younger leaders was not only because he saw younger leaders as having better training and greater willingness to reform, but also, like leaders everywhere, he had a desire to see his policies continued when he was no longer around. After all, he was acutely aware of Wang Hongwen's threat that within ten years he and other Cultural Revolution leaders would be back.[11]

---

[8] Deng Xiaoping, "On the Reform of the System of Party and State Leadership," p. 309.

[9] Ibid., p. 311.

[10] Deng Xiaoping, "Adhere to the Party Line and Improve Methods of Work," in *Selected Works of Deng Xiaoping (1975–1982)*, p. 266.

[11] Quoted in Teiwes and Sun, *The End of the Maoist Era*, p. 311. In Deng's 1983 speech at the Second Plenary Session of the Twelfth Central Committee, Deng, in reference to the "three types of people," said that there were those among them who bragged that in ten or twenty years they would be back. See Deng Xiaoping, "Dang zai zuzhi zhanxian he sixiang zhanxianshang de poqie renwu" (The Party's Urgent Tasks on the Organizational and Ideological Fronts), in

Cadre policy was not only a matter of age but also of selection. Cadres would have to be carefully vetted for both their political integrity and their professional competence. Political integrity was always a slippery concept because it was so easily interpreted differently by different people. In general, it did indeed mean loyalty, but hopefully loyalty to the party, not only loyalty to an individual. Deng railed on several occasions against the factionalism of Lin Biao and Jiang Qing; newly promoted cadres would have to be those who would not engage in factionalism (something that would prove to be difficult even for Deng).[12]

In addition to reforming the structure of power, Deng also wanted to limit the scope of the party. Deng was always conscious of the need to find the right person for the job, and that often involved technical expertise. This respect for expertise led him to call for the separation of party and government. The government, specifically the State Council system, possessed expertise that many party leaders did not have. Although these leaders were themselves party members, some of them developed real expertise, particularly in the more technical fields. For Deng, the party should exercise overall control and set policy, but the details of implementation should be left to the government. Zhao Ziyang would try to flesh out this distinction between party and state, never very clear in Leninist systems, at the Thirteenth Party Congress in 1987 (see below).

Of course, Deng was very emphatic about the role of the party and upholding socialism – he was not advocating a weakening of the role of the party. As he put it, "The purpose of reforming the system of party and state leadership is precisely to maintain and strengthen Party leadership and discipline, and not to weaken or relax them."[13] But he did envision a division of labor in which the party would set overall policy but not do everything itself, which Deng saw as the cause of bureaucratism and inefficiency.

Deng was also quite clear about the need for the party to step away from detailed economic management. Deng favored strengthening the

---

Deng Xiaoping wenxuan, disan juan (Selected Works of Deng Xiaoping, Vol. 3) (Beijing: Renmin chubanshe, 1993), p. 37.

[12] "Senior Cadres and the Party's Fine Tradition," *Selected Works of Deng Xiaoping (1975–1982)*, p. 213.

[13] Deng Xiaoping, "On the Reform of the System of Party and State Leadership," p. 324.

role of plant director or manager. Thus, in his speech on reform of the party and state systems, he called for party committees to get rid of routine affairs so they could concentrate on ideological and political work. This paragraph was not included in the speech as it was first published in Deng's *Selected Works* in 1983, but it was restored when the speech was republished in *People's Daily* on July 1 (the anniversary of the founding of the party) in 1987. Its deletion from the first published version of the speech suggests significant opposition to Deng's proposal, whereas its reinsertion in 1987 reflects a determined Deng concerned that party organizations were interfering with economic efficiency.

Finally, as the remarks quoted above suggest, Deng envisioned the development of a legal system. Rules needed to be developed, promulgated and followed, but in saying this Deng had no vision of a separate court system, certainly not one that could constrain the party. Rather, he sought a set of rules that would allow consistent implementation of policy. Deng did not elaborate, but it seems likely that he had in mind reducing the arbitrary abuse of power that so many party cadres exercised in the absence of rules and law. Doing so would, to some degree, depersonalize the exercise of authority and strengthen the party as a system.

It is clear that in wanting to limit the involvement of the party in the day-to-day operation of the running of the administrative system and the economy, in instituting a retirement system and in developing and enforcing rules for running the party, Deng had no intention to weaken the party, much less any intention to move toward some form of democracy, but rather he intended to make the party stronger and more efficient. It seems unlikely that he ever considered that his intended reforms would come into conflict with the Leninist nature of the party – its monopoly over political power, its domination of the economy, its mobilizational nature, or its basic structure. After all, as Vogel points out, "If anything was sacred for Deng, it was the Chinese Communist Party. He bristled instinctively at criticism of the party."[14]

The Era of Deng Xiaoping

We often date the start of "reform and opening" from the Third Plenary Session of the Eleventh Central Committee, or, more concisely,

---

[14] Vogel, *Deng Xiaoping*, p. 262.

as simply the "Third Plenum." The Third Plenum, held in December 1978, does demarcate political eras better than most dates given to us by history, but the inauguration of the Deng era was hardly as simple as the convening of one meeting. It was instead a process that started well before the Third Plenum and continued after that meeting.

In retrospect it seems that pushing aside the younger and less experienced Hua Guofeng was inevitable, but Hua did have several things going for him, none more important than the simple fact that Mao had designated him as successor. This was in an era when decisions made by Mao were not easily overturned, even after the Chairman had passed from the scene, no matter how many disagreed with the decision. It was at a party Work Conference in March 1977 that veteran party leader Chen Yun and veteran military leader Ye Jianying argued that Deng Xiaoping should be allowed to return to work. In July 1977 at the Third Plenary Session of the Tenth Central Committee, Deng was formally restored to all his posts: PBSC, party vice chair, vice premier of the State Council, vice chair of the CMC, and chief of staff of the PLA. The following month, the party held its Eleventh Party Congress.

There was obvious hesitation in turning power over to Deng. Careers, policy, and ideology were all at stake. As Vogel puts it: "With Deng Xiaoping, however, there was reason to be concerned. He was so confident, so decisive, so sure-footed that they [leaders like Ye Jianying] worried he might become too much like his mentor, Mao Zedong."[15] Ye Jianying had pushed for Deng's return, but Ye was reluctant to overturn Mao's decision to designate Hua as successor and he preferred that the party establish a collective leadership. Li Xiannian had similar feelings. In 1976, Li had called both the Gang of Four and Deng Xiaoping "insufferably arrogant" (*buke yishi*).[16] Both were wary of a new dictatorship.[17] Deng would have to proceed slowly.

When one looks at the leadership between the Eleventh Party Congress and right before the Twelfth Party Congress in 1982 (and indeed after it), one sees perhaps more continuity than one might expect for congresses that represent two different eras in Chinese politics. That continuity is found first and foremost in the military,

---

[15] Ibid., p. 247.
[16] Quoted in Teiwes and Sun, *The End of the Maoist Era*, p. 588.
[17] Vogel, *Deng Xiaoping*, p. 248.

which underscores that Deng's political strength was rooted in his long-term role as a military leader. When one looks at the PB of the Twelfth Central Committee, of the twenty-nine full and alternate members, fourteen were former military leaders, including Deng. Many of these, including Wei Guoqing, Li Desheng, Yang Dezhi, Yu Qiuli, and others had fought alongside Deng. Most of these had been on the PB of the Eleventh Central Committee, so they provided much of the continuity between the two eras.

Discussion on "Practice as the Sole Criterion of Truth"

What made the Third Plenary Session so fascinating as a political event was that it was preceded by an ideological debate on "Practice as the Sole Criterion of Truth." The only other ideological campaign associated with leadership change was the 1942–1944 Rectification Campaign, which intended to solidify Mao Zedong's leadership, not to challenge a previous leader. In contrast, the debate on practice in 1978 was used to erode the foundations of Hua Guofeng's leadership and legitimize the rise of Deng. Such a discussion could only have taken place during extraordinary times. In 1978 the party's leadership was made up of diverse forces, the military was more loyal to Deng than to Hua (despite Hua being head of the CMC), and policy direction was far from certain. The sort of relatively open atmosphere that prevailed at the time, when party leaders and their advisers questioned many of the truths handed down from the Maoist era, was not to return.

This truth criterion discussion started at the Central Party School after it was restored in March 1977. Hua Guofeng, as chairman of the party, was appointed president of the party school pro forma. His deputy, Wang Dongxing, who headed the General Office of the party and had dispatched the Central Guard unit to arrest the Gang of Four, was first vice president, but his other duties precluded him from paying attention to the party school. That meant that Hu Yaobang, the executive vice president, ran the school's affairs on a day-to-day basis.

In the months of reorganization that were necessary before the school could welcome back "students" – high-level officials who would be in charge of implementing party policy in the months and years to come – Hu had many discussions on what to teach. One could not teach documents from the Cultural Revolution, but what should replace them? In the course of these discussions, Hu suggested setting

up an internal journal to discuss some of the most important ideological issues of the day. This journal, *Lilun dongtai* (Theoretical
Trends), was inaugurated on July 15 with a discussion on "continuing
the revolution" – one of the key themes of the Cultural Revolution.

As Hu Yaobang and others discussed topics, the issues of "practice"
and "truth" came up with some frequency, with some arguing that
practice should be the criterion for judging truth. Others demurred,
saying that Mao Zedong Thought was another criterion for judging
truth. This was the origin of the title of an article in *Lilun dongtai*,
which insisted that practice alone could be the criterion for judging
truth. *Lilun dongtai* ran the article internally on May 8, then the paper
Enlightenment Daily ran it as a Commentator article on the
following day, and *People's Daily* ran it as a "Special Commentator"
article on May 10. By running the article as authored by a special
commentator, *People's Daily* was taking advantage of a loophole in
China's censorship system. If it had been run as a "Commentator
Article" or "Editorial," it would have had to been sent to Wang
Dongxing, who was in charge of ideology. So the paper did an end
run around Wang Dongxing, and the angry head of the General Office
called Hu Jiwei, the chief editor of *People's Daily*, to complain vocifer-
ously. With that phone call, a nationwide discussion on practice was
ignited.

At the time that *People's Daily* published this article, the PLA was
preparing a conference. There were those who argued in favor of
upholding Hua Guofeng's "Two Whatevers" ("We will resolutely
uphold *whatever* policy decisions made, and unswervingly follow
whatever instructions Chairman Mao gave") – a formulation that
would make it impossible to carry out reform. Hearing this, Deng
declared that he would speak at the conference.[18] Deng was his typical,
blunt self, declaring: "The principle of seeking truth from facts is the
point of departure, the fundamental point, in Mao Zedong
Thought."[19] With Deng's speech, it was apparent that Deng had the
support of the military. Thereafter, various party leaders began to
weigh in and the atmosphere in the party began to change dramatically.

---

[18] Shen Baoxiang, *Zhenli biaozhun wenti taolun shimo* (The Whole Discussion of
the Issue of the Criterion of Truth) (Beijing: Zhongguo dangshi chubanshe,
2008), p. 91.

[19] Deng Xiaoping, "Speech at All-Army Conference on Political Work," in
Selected Works of Deng Xiaoping (1975–1982), p. 128.

In November 1978, the party called a Work Conference to prepare for the Third Plenum, scheduled for December. Building on the atmosphere created by the discussion on Practice as the Sole Criterion of Truth, this Work Conference brought political change to the highest level. Originally called to discuss economic issues, the conference quickly began to focus on political issues, particularly Hua Guofeng's unwillingness to reverse the verdict on the 1976 Tiananmen incident when people had gone to the square to mourn the death of Zhou Enlai. As mentioned above, Mao had later dismissed Deng as the "black hand" behind the incident, and Hua had let this charge linger over Deng. On November 12, Chen Yun addressed the small group that he was part of and demanded the rehabilitation of the Group of 61, a group of CCP members, including senior economic specialist Bo Yibo, who had been released from Guomindang (GMD) jails after denouncing – with CCP permission – the CCP. This issue had been brought up during the Cultural Revolution, sending Bo and others to prison. Now it was time to reverse this verdict, Chen said. He also demanded that the 1976 Tiananmen incident be reversed and that Peng Dehuai, the minister of defense Mao had purged at the 1959 Lushan Plenum, be posthumously rehabilitated. As one of the most respected senior leaders of the CCP, Chen's speech imparted new momentum to the demands for political change.

In the end, Hua Guofeng accepted the views of the delegates that the verdict on the Tiananmen incident should be reversed. He also agreed that Peng Dehuai and others should be rehabilitated, and the conference affirmed the criterion of practice. Hua Guofeng's "Two Whatevers" were voted down, beginning Hua's slide into obscurity.[20]

The Third Plenary Session

On the last day of the Work Conference, December 15, Leonard Woodcock, the US representative in China, went to meet with Deng Xiaoping a final time before normalization of diplomatic relations. Under instructions from President Carter, Woodcock explained that the US would continue to sell weapons to Taiwan. Deng Xiaoping was obviously displeased, but, in the end, he decided to announce the

---

[20] Vogel, *Deng Xiaoping*, pp. 229–240; Yu Guangyuan, *Deng Xiaoping Shakes the World.*

establishment of diplomatic relations as planned. Knowledge that he had successfully negotiated the recognition of the People's Republic of China could only have bolstered him as he went into the Third Plenary Session of the Eleventh Central Committee.

The watershed Third Plenum opened on December 18 and confirmed the decisions made at the Work Conference. In a historic change, the plenum denied the Maoist theses of "taking class struggle as the key link" and "continuing the revolution under the leadership of the proletariat"; instead it endorsed turning the main focus of party work to the economy. The plenum criticized the "Two Whatevers" and "highly appraised" the discussion on Practice as the Sole Criterion of Truth.

The Third Plenum did not remove Hua Guofeng, but it did add Chen Yun to the PBSC and it promoted Hu Yaobang, Deng Yingchao (Zhou Enlai's widow), and Wang Zhen (who had also supported Deng Xiaoping's return to work in March 1977) to the PB. In addition, it added nine veteran party members, including Deng's long-time associate Song Renqiong, to the Central Committee. Finally, it restored the party's CDIC, naming Chen Yun as its head and Hu Yaobang as its third secretary. So the Third Plenum was a major turning point, but senior party leaders were still reluctant to grant full power to Deng. That would have to wait.

The Fourth and Fifth Plenums and the End of Hua Guofeng

Deng's quest to be paramount leader continued at the party's Fourth Plenary Session of the Eleventh Central Committee in September 1979. In addition to passing a resolution on accelerating agricultural development, this plenum added twelve veteran cadres, including Peng Zhen, Yang Shangkun, and Bo Yibo, to the Central Committee. It then elevated Peng Zhen to the PB and similarly promoted Zhao Ziyang from alternate member of the PB to full membership. Such personnel changes obviously augmented the strength of Deng's coalition.

Personnel changes were continued some months later when the Fifth Plenum was held in February 1980. This meeting was critical because it ousted the so-called "little Gang of Four" – Wang Dongxing, Wu De, Chen Xilian, and Ji Dengkui. Wang Dongxing was a member of the PBSC and head of the Central Guard. The other three were members of the PB. These four were supporters of Hua Guofeng, and with their ouster, Deng and his allies were in control.

Figure 1.2 Third Plenum leadership: Politburo Standing Committee following the Third Plenary Session of the Eleventh Central Committee in December 1978. From left to right: Chen Yun, Deng Xiaoping, Hua Guofeng, Ye Jianying, Li Xiannian, and Wang Dongxing (Bettmann via Getty Images)

Zhao Ziyang, who had pioneered economic reform in Sichuan province, was now further promoted from regular membership in the PB to membership in the PBSC. Wan Li, who had fought under Deng Xiaoping and had pioneered the agricultural reforms in Anhui province, was likewise added to the PBSC as well as to the Secretariat. In the spring, he was named a vice premier and also added to the Financial and Economic Leadership Small Group in charge of agriculture. These changes prepared the way for implementing reform, particularly in agriculture.

In November 1980, Deng Xiaoping, meeting with Chen Yun and Li Xiannian, decided that Hua Guofeng should step down. A PB meeting concluded:

In the past four years, Comrade Hua Guofeng has done some beneficial work, but he obviously lacks the necessary political ability and organizational ability to be chairman of the Central Committee. That he is incapable of fulfilling the responsibilities of chairman of the Military Commission is known by everyone.[21]

There was one more step to be taken before the Twelfth Party Congress was convened and that was taken at the Sixth Plenary Session of the Eleventh Central Committee, which was held June 27–29, 1981. The Sixth Plenum is known primarily for passing the "Resolution on Some Problems in Our Party since the Founding of the Country," better known as the "History Resolution."

However, the plenum was also important for making further leadership adjustments. The plenum formally approved Hua Guofeng's "request" to resign as party chairman and appointed Hu Yaobang as party chairman to replace Hua. Hu would take the more familiar title "general secretary" at the Twelfth Party Congress. Hua was given the title "deputy chairman" to ease the hurt, but he was removed from the PBSC. These leadership changes are summarized in Table 1.1.

The period between congresses is normally one without major leadership purges, but obviously the five years following the Eleventh Party Congress was one of constant changing of elites, paralleling the dramatic changes in ideology. Party leadership changed as Chen Yun and

---

[21] "Zhonggong zhongyang zhengzhiju huiyi tongbao" (Communique of the Meeting of the Political Bureau of the CCP Central Committee), in *Sanzhong quanhui yilai zhongyao wenxian xuanbian* (Guangzhou: Renmin chubanshe, 1982), Vol. 1, pp. 596–600.

Table 1.1 *Leadership changes after the Eleventh Party Congress*

11th Party Congress, 1st Plenum (Aug. 19, 1977)	3rd Plenum (Dec. 18–22, 1978)	4th Plenum (Sept. 25–28, 1979)	5th Plenum (Feb. 23–29, 1980)	6th Plenum (June 27–29, 1981)
Standing Committee	**Standing Committee**	**Standing Committee**	**Standing Committee**	**Standing Committee**
Hua Guofeng	Hua Guofeng	Hua Guofeng	Hua Guofeng	Hu Yaobang
Ye Jianying	Ye Jianying	Ye Jianying	Ye Jianying	Ye Jianying
Deng Xiaoping	Deng Xiaoping	Deng Xiaoping	Deng Xiaoping	Deng Xiaoping
Li Xiannian	Li Xiannian	Li Xiannian	Li Xiannian	Zhao Ziyang
Wang Dongxing	Wang Dongxing	Wang Dongxing	Chen Yun	Li Xiannian
	Chen Yun	Chen Yun	**Hu Yaobang**	Chen Yun
			Zhao Ziyang	Hua Guofeng
Politburo	**Politburo**	**Politburo**	**Politburo**	**Politburo**
Wei Guoqing	Wei Guoqing	Wei Guoqing	Wei Guoqing	Wei Guoqing
Ulanhu	Ulanhu	Ulanhu	Ulanhu	Ulanhu
Fang Yi	Fang Yi	Fang Yi	Fang Yi	Fang Yi
Liu Bocheng	Liu Bocheng	Liu Bocheng	Liu Bocheng	Liu Bocheng
Xu Shiyou	Xu Shiyou	Xu Shiyou	Xu Shiyou	Xu Shiyou
Ji Dengkui	Ji Dengkui	Ji Dengkui	Su Zhenhua	Su Zhenhua
Su Zhenhua	Su Zhenhua	Su Zhenhua	Li Desheng	Li Desheng
Li Desheng	Li Desheng	Li Desheng	Yu Qiuli	Yu Qiuli

Table 1.1 (*cont.*)

11th Party Congress, 1st Plenum (Aug. 19, 1977)	3rd Plenum (Dec. 18–22, 1978)	4th Plenum (Sept. 25–28, 1979)	5th Plenum (Feb. 23–29, 1980)	6th Plenum (June 27–29, 1981)
Wu De	Wu De	Wu De	Zhang Tingfa	Zhang Tingfa
Yu Qiuli	Yu Qiuli	Yu Qiuli	Chen Yonggui*	Chen Yonggui
Zhang Tingfa	Zhang Tingfa	Zhang Tingfa	Geng Biao	Geng Biao
Chen Yonggui	Chen Yonggui	Chen Yonggui	Nie Rongzhen	Nie Rongzhen
Chen Xilian	Chen Xilian	Chen Xilian	Ni Zhifu	Ni Zhifu
Geng Biao	Geng Biao	Geng Biao	Xu Xiangqian	Xu Xiangqian
Nie Rongzhen	Nie Rongzhen	Nie Rongzhen	Peng Chong	Peng Chong
Ni Zhifu	Ni Zhifu	Ni Zhifu	Deng Yingchao	Deng Yingchao
Xu Xiang Qian	Xu Xiangqian	Xu Xiangqian		
Peng Chong	Peng Chong	Peng Chong		
	Deng Yingchao	Deng Yingchao		
	Hu Yaobang	Hu Yaobang		
		Zhao Ziyang		
		Peng Zhen		
Alternates	**Alternates**	**Alternate**	**Alternate**	**Alternate**
Chen Muhua	Wang Zhen	Chen Muhua	Chen Muhua	Chen Muhua
Zhao Ziyang	Zhao Ziyang			
Saifuding	Peng Zhen			

Notes: Bold type designates those promoted.

* In September 1980, Chen Yonggui was removed as vice premier.

Deng Yingchao, Hu Yaobang, and Wang Zhen were added as members of the PB, and nine people were added to the Central Committee: Huang Kecheng, Song Renqiong, Hu Qiaomu, Xi Zhongxun, Wang Renzhong, Huang Huoqing, Chen Zaidao, Han Guang, and Zhou Hui.

The CDIC was established with Chen Yun as chair, and Deng Yingchao and Hu Yaobang as second and third secretaries respectively.

At the Fourth Plenum, Zhao Ziyang was promoted from alternate member to full member of the PB. Peng Zhen was promoted from the Central Committee to the PB. In addition, twelve veteran members of the CCP were added to the Central Committee: Wang Heshou, Liu Lanbo, Liu Lantao, An Ziwen, Li Chang, Yang Shangkun, Zhou Yang, Lu Dingyi, Hong Xuezhi, Peng Zhen, Jiang Nanxiang, and Bo Yibo.

The Fifth Plenum re-established the Secretariat. Hu Yaobang was elected as general secretary (head of the Secretariat), and Wan Li, Wang Renzhong, Fang Yi, Gu Mu, Song Renqiong, Yu Qiuli, Yang Dezhi, Hu Qiaomu, Yao Yilin, and Peng Chong as members. It passed "Some Principles Regarding Political Life inside the Party," and rehabilitated Liu Shaoqi. It also removed Wang Dongxing, Ji Dengkui, Wu De, and Chen Xilian from the PB.

The Sixth Plenum passed the "Resolution on Some Historical Issues in the Party since the Founding of the State." It approved Hua Guofeng's resignation as chairman and elected Hu Yaobang to replace him. Xi Zhongxun was elected to the Secretariat.

then Hu Yaobang and Zhao Ziyang joined the PBSC, and others, such as Peng Zhen, joined the PB. Eventually, the "little gang of four" was dropped from the PBSC and PB and Hua Guofeng resigned as party chairman. At the same time, a number of changes were made in the composition of the Central Committee. Of the original 169 members, sixteen were either dropped or died before the end of their term, and twenty-one people were added to the Central Committee, two of whom died before the end of their terms. So the body that would meet at the Twelfth Party Congress in 1982 was substantially different – and more supportive of Deng and reform – than the group that had emerged from the First Plenum of the Eleventh Central Committee in 1977.

It should also be noted that important changes were made in the critical positions. In December 1977, Hu Yaobang replaced Guo Yufeng as head of the Organization Department. Guo had been brought up by Kang Sheng, the notorious member of the Central Case Examination Group and member of the PBSC, and he was a staunch opponent of reform, whereas Hu was obviously close to Deng and, as head of the Organization Department, undertook to review and reverse many cases, including the Group of 61 that rehabilitated Bo Yibo. A year later, shortly after the Third Plenum, Hu Yaobang replaced Zhang Pinghua as head of the Propaganda Department. At the beginning of the discussion on Practice as the Sole Criterion of Truth, Zhang had toured the Northeast urging local officials to support the "Two Whatevers."[22] So removing Zhang and putting Hu in his place "flipped" an important position to Deng's side. Hu passed control of the Organization Department to Song Renqiong, a staunch supporter of Deng, so the position remained in the hands of reformers. In 1978, after the Third Plenum, Wang Dongxing gave up control of the General Office to Yao Yilin, a protégé of Chen Yun. With the Sixth Plenum and the reorganization of the PBSC, the reformers were thus in a position to substantially remake the political elite at the Twelfth Party Congress.

The Twelfth Party Congress

Overall, the Twelfth Party Congress has to be considered a great success for Deng and his associates. The radicals who had made their

---

[22] Vogel, *Deng Xiaoping*, p. 227.

careers during the Cultural Revolution were all but eliminated. The new Central Committee consisted of 210 full members and 138 alternate members. Of the 210 full members, 128 were new (61 percent), a historically high number. Of those 128 new members, 113 were directly promoted; that is, they had not previously served on the Central Committee as either full or alternate members. Only fifteen were promoted from the alternate list. As noted above, the rehabilitation process had been going on for some time, so if one looks at the eighty-seven who were on the Eleventh Central Committee (as full members) and continued to serve on the Twelfth Central Committee, it includes such important cadres as Hu Yaobang, Zhao Ziyang, Wan Li, Yao Yilin, and Deng Xiaoping himself. The Cultural Revolution never impacted the military very seriously, except in the aftermath of the Lin Biao incident, so many of the military cadres who were selected to the Twelfth Central Committee had survived the Cultural Revolution, including Wang Zhen, Wei Guoqing, Li Desheng, Yang Dezhi, Yu Qiuli, Zhang Tingfa, and Xu Xiangqian, all of whom served on the Politburo of the Eleventh Party Congress. All in all, the Twelfth Party Congress has to be considered a great success for the Dengists.

The Twelfth Party Congress also established the Central Advisory Commission (CAC), which was a transitional body (eliminated in 1992), to encourage older cadres to retire from their official positions to make way for younger cadres. Deng Xiaoping took the lead by chairing the new body (though without giving up his position on the PBSC or his chairmanship of the CMC). Altogether 172 old cadres joined this body in 1982, but even with this success, the Twelfth Party Congress did not achieve the rejuvenation that Deng had wanted.

As Deng had said, if the Congress could not select fifty people under the age of fifty, it would not be considered a success. Of course, the Congress did not come close to achieving this goal. If one looks at the full members of the Central Committee, then there were only fifteen who were younger than fifty – a substantial rejuvenation but well short of Deng's goal. If one relaxes the age requirement to younger than fifty-five, another nine people make the cut, for a total of twenty-four. Deng's use of the figure fifty for the age he was aiming at does not appear arbitrary. Deng was looking not only for rejuvenation but also for long-term stability. A person appointed to the Central Committee at the age of fifty, or even fifty-five, could expect to serve two terms and thus secure the reforms Deng was driving to achieve. Wang Hongwen

Figure 1.3 Vice Chairman Deng Xiaoping meets with foreign news reporters, January 1979 (Bettmann via Getty Images)

had threatened that the radicals would make a comeback in ten years' time, and Deng would do whatever he could to prevent that from happening. Rejuvenation was certainly about bringing in people with a different mind-set, better education, and greater skills, but it was also about preserving reform.

The CCP Representative Meeting of 1985

Deng's urgency to secure his reform is seen clearly in the convocation of a Party Representative Meeting in 1985. This was a format that the party had used only once before in its history, in 1955 following the Gao Gang and Rao Shushi affair. The format of the 1985 Party Representative Meeting closely followed the procedures of a party congress, and for all intents and purposes it was an additional congress wedged in between the Twelfth and Thirteenth Party Congresses. The major difference was that the party did not elect delegates and select an entirely new Central Committee. Rather the meeting was attended by the entire Central Committee (full members and alternates) and "only" recommended the promotion of fifty-five people for promotion from alternate status to full membership on the Central Committee while accepting the resignation of sixty-four aged Central Committee members, fifty-four of whom were full members. Seven of these new members were fifty or younger, while another twenty-four were fifty-five or younger. Added to the number of those aged fifty-five years or younger who had been elected in 1982, there were now fifty-five full members who were fifty-five or younger. So Deng's goal was basically met.

After the 1985 Party Representative Meeting, there were only fifty-two people who had served on the Eleventh Central Committee as full members, a remarkable remaking of the political elite over the course of seven years. Of those fifty-two people, ten were members of the PB (including one as an alternate). These ten, of course, included Deng Xiaoping, Hu Yaobang, and Zhao Ziyang. The Party Representative Meeting was not so much about weeding out neo-Maoists (they were mostly gone by the Twelfth Central Committee) but about securing the future of reform. Almost all those promoted to full membership would go on to serve on the Thirteenth Central Committee, and many of them would serve on the Fourteenth Central Committee and beyond. Among the names on the list were such people as Hu Jintao, future general secretary; Qian Qichen, future foreign minister; and Jia Chunwang, long-term head of the Ministry of Public Security. Jiang Zemin and Li Peng had already joined the Central Committee in 1982. In short, between the younger members of the Twelfth Central Committee and those promoted at the Party Representative Meeting, one can see the coming together of the core leadership that would rule China into the twenty-first century. The next decade would be politically tumultuous, including the fall of Hu Yaobang and Zhao Ziyang, but there would be remarkable continuity in the broader political elite.

Balances

Deng certainly had definite ideas about how the party should work and what it should do. It is tempting to call him an "institutionalist," except for the proviso outlined in the Introduction that one cannot institutionalize a Leninist party without fundamentally changing the nature of the party, and Deng had no intention of doing that. Moreover, he was a practical politician who clearly recognized the different forces in the party. Those different forces stretched from conservatives like economic specialist Chen Yun and ideologue Hu Qiaomu, both of whom saw a need for reform but were leery of moving too far away from their notions of socialism, to reformers like Hu Yaobang and Zhao Ziyang who were more tolerant of the expression of different ideas and welcomed the introduction of market forces. This complexity of ideas and forces is what people mean when they speak of the "Dengist coalition."

One can think of the difference between this approach and that of Mao in ideological terms. With Mao there was a single ideology ("Mao Zedong Thought") around which everything was supposed to revolve (even if the content of Mao Zedong Thought changed). Deng was not an ideologue, so he set up boundaries and demanded that discussion remain within those boundaries. On the one side, he used "Truth from Facts" to rein in those who would stray too far to the "left," while on the other side he used the "Four Cardinal Principles" to rein in those on the right who would go too far in a "liberal" direction. These boundaries define a "middle course," which could tolerate differences of opinion but only up to a point.[23]

This middle course reflects the realities of politics in the 1980s. If Deng was the dominant figure of the era, and he was, then Chen Yun was clearly number two. Chen had served at higher levels in the party from an earlier point in time than Deng. He had served on the Provisional PB in the Jiangxi Soviet from September 1931 to January 1934 (this would have been under the leadership of Bo Gu, which probably did not endear Chen to Mao). More importantly, Chen served on the PB of the Seventh Central Committees (June 1945) and as a member of the PBSC of the Eighth Central Committee (elected in September 1956). Deng Xiaoping had entered the PBSC with Chen in 1956. Chen's service as head of the State Planning Commission and thus as chief liaison to the Soviet Union during the First Five-Year Plan, his work following the Great Leap Forward, and his work following the Cultural Revolution made him China's most senior economic policy maker. Deng Xiaoping obviously had extensive military, party, and diplomatic experience, which made him number one, but Chen's work in the party, including heading the Organization Department from 1937 to 1944, and his experience in economic work, made him a major figure in the leadership. Those in the propaganda sector seemed

---

[23] Tang Tsou, "Political Change and Reform: The Middle Course," pp. 219–258 in Tang Tsou, *The Cultural Revolution and Post-Mao Reforms* (Chicago: The University of Chicago Press, 1986).

to gravitate toward Chen's leadership, particularly after Deng Liqun gave a series of talks at the Central Party School in 1980 on Chen's economic thought.[24] In terms of running the party and the economy, Deng relied primarily on Hu Yaobang and Zhao Ziyang, who did not always see eye to eye, but Chen was a force in his own right. Whereas conservatives relied on the State Council bureaucracy and the propaganda system, Hu and Zhao solicited advice from much smaller and far less institutionalized groups of advisers, "establishment intellectuals" in Hu's case, and think tanks like the Institute of Economic Structural Reform (*tigaisuo*) in Zhao's case.

What this distribution of power did was set up a series of balances that can be depicted as in Figure 1.4. This balancing of the situation seemed normal in the early 1980s. It allowed a range of people with different organizational and ideological backgrounds to work together, and, perhaps not coincidentally, it forced major decisions to the top – that is, to Deng. It allowed for veteran cadres to manage much of the economy and maintain a degree of orthodoxy ideologically even as Zhao Ziyang and others explored new, more market-oriented approaches to reform and as younger and more open-minded

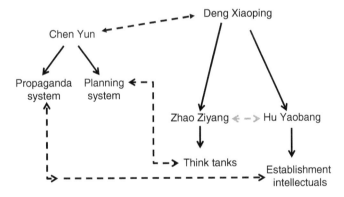

Figure 1.4 Political balances in the 1980s
Note: Solid lines indicate relationships of subordination; dotted lines indicate relationships with tension.

---

[24] Richard Baum, *Burying Mao: Chinese Politics in the Age of Deng Xiaoping* (Princeton, NJ: Princeton University Press, 1994), p. 111.

intellectuals explored more innovative understandings of Marxism and explored controversial themes, such as humanism, in literature.

Balances, however, are not institutions, and they can break down for any number of reasons – ideological divergence, policy differences, the death of a critical player. In China's case, there were three main issues that upset this balance: ideological/cultural conflicts, economic policy differences, and the issue of succession. The ideological area is very large and has been explored in depth elsewhere;[25] suffice it to say that deep differences existed within the party on the question of how to evaluate Mao Zedong, the degree to which China should open up, and how much China should loosen controls over the cultural sphere. The cultural area illustrates how issues – issues of perspective, of organization, and of influence – can spiral from one level to another, ending in deep political cleavage.

In 1980 the author Bai Hua wrote a novella called "Unrequited Love." It was about an intellectual who was persecuted by the "Gang of Four." In the end, chased across the countryside, the intellectual falls on a snowscape, with a drop of blood below his twisted body, forming a question mark. The question Bai Hua put in the words of the scholar's daughter: "You love your country, but does this country love you?" The question deliberately raised the distinction between "country," which was the object of patriotic loyalty, and the "state," which controlled and punished the actions of patriotic Chinese who were trying to bring about a better and more humane China. Bai Hua's question expressed the torment of thousands of intellectuals coming out of the Cultural Revolution.

Attacking the same issue from a different angle, on the centenary of Marx's death in March 1983, Zhou Yang, the former cultural czar who persecuted many intellectuals before the Cultural Revolution but lived to regret his previous actions, gave a moving speech on alienation. The speech was drafted by Wang Ruoshui, the philosopher and deputy chief editor of *People's Daily*, who had been exploring the Marxist concept of alienation, noting painfully that the advent of socialism had hardly eliminated alienation. This was too much for China's ideologues. Deng Liqun, then head of the Propaganda Department, responded with

---

[25] Merle Goldman, *Sowing the Seeds of Democracy in China: Political Reform in the Deng Xiaoping Era* (Cambridge, MA: Harvard University Press, 1994); Liu Binyan, A Higher *Kind of Loyalty: A Memoir by China's Foremost Journalist* (New York: Pantheon, 1990).

a speech attacking "spiritual pollution." This theme was picked up by the Second Plenary Session of the Twelfth Central Committee in the fall of 1983, where Deng Xiaoping, ever the hardliner on ideology, attacked "some comrades who are fond of talking about the value of man, humanism, and so-called alienation." Such people, Deng said, "are not interested in criticizing capitalism but in criticizing socialism." Such spiritual pollution, he said, should be eliminated from the ideological front.[26]

This was one of the major turning points in the reform movement. The Campaign against Spiritual Pollution started out vigorously, as Deng's harsh remarks suggest, but it alarmed reformers who were concerned it would hurt China's economy and spread through the countryside. After complaints from Hu Yaobang and Zhao Ziyang, Deng allowed the movement to wither away after only thirty-eight days. The ensuing resentment among conservatives marked the deepening of the split within the party.

An even more dramatic turning point occurred the following year when the Fourth Congress of the Writers' Association was held in December 1984. Many of the younger and more liberal writers were still resentful of the Campaign against Spiritual Pollution and of those, including the leadership of the Writers' Association, who had supported it. Normally, the Organization Department would pick a slate to run the Writers' Association, which inevitably would be the old guard, and that would be it – the writers would be forced to vote for them. This time, however, Hu Yaobang decided that the Organization Department should not intervene and that the membership of the Writers' Association should be allowed to vote for whomever they wanted. As a result, the old guard was thrown out and the younger leaders were voted in. The resentment of the old guard reverberated in the Propaganda Department and conservative ideologues such as Deng Liqun and Hu Qiaomu, already angered by the curtailing of the Campaign against Spiritual Pollution, reflected their feelings upward to Deng Xiaoping.[27]

---

[26] Deng Xiaoping, "Dang zai zuzhi zhanxian he sixiang zhanxianshang de poqie renwu" (The Party's Urgent Tasks on the Organizational and Ideological Fronts), pp. 36–48.

[27] Zhao Ziyang, *Gaige licheng* (The Course of Reform) (Hong Kong: Xin shiji chubanshe, 2009), p. 185.

Hu Yaobang's action was one of his major missteps. Deng clearly felt that Hu was not tough enough to manage the party. As Zhao Ziyang put it, "You simply cannot sing a tune contrary to Deng's."[28] Two years later the issue was still simmering. In the summer of 1986, with leaders gathered at Beidaihe to relax and slowly sort through policy issues, Deng told Yang Shangkun and others that he had made a serious mistake in terms of his judgment about Hu Yaobang and that Hu would step down at the Thirteenth Party Congress. Deng told Hu of this decision, but apparently presented it as part of a rejuvenation of the leadership. But the fact that Deng had told others of this decision changed the behavior of senior leaders, including Yang Shangkun and Bo Yibo. Knowledge of Deng's decision played into the conservatives' demand for Hu's ouster at

Figure 1.5 Hu Yaobang was appointed party chairman in 1981, general secretary in 1982. Known as relatively open in intellectual matters, he would be purged in January 1987. His death in 1989 set off the student protests that spring (NERCIAT/AFP via Getty Images)

[28] Ibid., p. 185.

the end of the year when demonstrations erupted in Shanghai and elsewhere.[29] Hu was accused of being "lax on bourgeois liberalization," subjected to intra-party criticism at a five-day long "intra-party life meeting," and ousted as general secretary on January 16, 1987.

At the same time as antagonisms developed in the ideological and cultural spheres, similar resentments were building in the economic realm. In economic circles, there had been constant debate since the beginning of the reform period over the importance of the market. Chen Yun was famous for his "birdcage" theory of economics, which advocated expanding the cage enough to give the bird room to fly but still keeping it caged. This was a metaphor for the economy: the plan was primary and the market was secondary. But, as market-oriented reformers pointed out, one could not really separate the planned economy from the market economy; prices were the key to the efficient allocation of goods and reform required greater efficiency. Moreover, the reformers argued, the failure to integrate plan and market had been behind the economic cycles that China had repeatedly experienced in the past. If the economy were decentralized and the plan loosened, the economy would overheat; if centralization and the plan were tightened, the economy would be stifled. This was expressed in the saying, "when things are loosened, chaos ensues; when things are tightened, the economy dies" (*yifang, jiuluan, yishou, jiusi*). Integrating plan and market, which really meant allowing the market to operate in the planned economy – was the key to deepening reform.

These debates lay behind the drafting of the "Decision on Economic Structural Reform" which was adopted by the party at the Third Plenary Session of the Twelfth Central Committee in 1984. The key to this economic document lay in obscure Marxist argot. In Marxist economics, a "commodity" is something that, when exchanged, transferred ownership. That is to say, if a factory produces a commodity and sells it to another factory (or store), ownership is transferred. This is how markets work. But the goal of socialism was to move away from markets. Ownership would not reside in individuals or in factories but in the "whole people." So when a state-owned enterprise (SOE) produced something, say steel, and sold it to another factory, say an automobile plant, ownership was not transferred because both factories were owned by the whole people. In Marxist terminology, what was being transferred was not a "commodity" but a "product." Thus, the

---

[29] Ibid., pp. 187, 191–192.

Chinese economy was described as a "product economy." Lower-level economic units – collectives – could produce and sell "commodities"; SOEs transferred "products."

All this seems very arcane, but it went to the heart of the economic debates during this period. Since the late 1970s, one of China's premier economists, Xue Muqiao, had been developing his theory of a "commodity economy." He had published this theory in an important book in 1980 that laid out much of the thinking that went into the economic reforms.[30] The irony is that Xue Muqiao had worked closely with Chen Yun for many years, but now Xue was breaking with Chen's economic thinking.

It was this ideological barrier that the 1984 Decision on Economic Structural Reform broke. In declaring that China was building a "commodity economy" (albeit a socialist one), that decision made a break with years of economic orthodoxy. China was not yet prepared to call itself a "market economy," but the declaration that it was a commodity economy was already a major step in that direction. When Xue Muqiao saw Chen Yun on the Tiananmen rostrum at the October 1 National Day celebration in 1984, he went over to greet his old superior, but Chen looked at him coldly and said, "Who are you? I don't recognize you."[31] From Chen's perspective, Xue had betrayed him and had turned his back on socialism.

The main thrust of the Third Plenary Session of the Twelfth Central Committee decision was to shift the focus of reform to the cities and to invigorate urban enterprises with market incentives. As a programmatic document, it did not go into much detail about how to do this. More specifically, the task – perhaps an impossible task – was to introduce market mechanisms without disrupting the planned economy. The "Decision" talked about straightening out prices, about separating enterprises from the ministries that supervised them, and about enterprise managers taking charge while party committees stepped back, but reformers faced a fundamental constraint: if they tried to reform the SOEs, they faced real risks of disrupting the economy and the certainty of staunch opposition from the bureaucrats who managed the plan. The

---

[30] Xue Muqiao, *Dangqian woguo jingji ruogan wenti* (Some Problems in China's Contemporary Economy) (Beijing: Renmin chubanshe, 1980).
[31] Interview.

task was to find a way to introduce market mechanisms without disrupting the planned economy.

That was the problem tackled by the Moganshan conference in late 1984. Moganshan is a scenic mountain outside Shanghai that had been used as a retreat by the rich and powerful for many years (both Chiang Kai-shek and Green Gang leader Du Yuesheng had villas there). It was also away from the prying eyes of people in Beijing. It was there that a group of youth, originally part of the Agricultural Reform Group, gathered as the newly established Institute of Economic Structural Reform (known as the *tigaisuo*). Talking late into the night, they hit upon what would become known as the "dual-track mechanism." The dual-track mechanism refers to having two (or more) prices for the same product. One price would be the in-plan price, and the other price would be the higher, out-of-plan price. The out-of-plan price did not have to be a market price (if a market price could be determined) but it was a movement in that direction.

The idea of a dual-price mechanism grew out of the reality of reform. As village and township enterprises (TVEs) arose, they needed energy, but they were not part of the plan, so they could not secure coal. Out of necessity, they sent people to the coalfields of Shanxi and elsewhere to buy coal. But one could not buy coal from the large SOEs that dominated the energy sector, so they talked to the people in the villages and the village party secretaries near the coalfields. Peasants, of course, often found smaller seams of coal – not large enough for the SOEs to bother with – and they could exploit those seams for their own use or for limited commercial purposes. Thus, supply and demand came together. Energy-hungry TVEs could buy coal from villages and villages could open new, and often very dangerous, coal mines. Of course they sold the coal at higher market prices, and the TVEs were willing to pay the higher prices because it was the only way they could secure energy for their machines.

For the market-oriented young economists, this reality became a strategy to introduce market mechanisms into the economy. The TVEs could purchase energy at market prices and they could sell their goods at market prices because their products were not part of the plan. For instance, one popular product at this time was simple electric fans. No one had yet produced them for the consumer market, so there was no state-set price. Therefore, they could be sold at market prices. The trick of introducing market prices into SOEs was similarly clever. SOEs were still required to produce for the plan, but if they could produce more, the government allowed them to sell this above-quota amount at a certain premium (at first, only 5 percent) above the planned price. But factories loved the extra revenue stream, so they started to produce some of their products for the market. As the margins slowly expanded so did their conformity with market pressures. SOEs were slow to follow the market and never developed the flexibility of private firms, but they did begin to feel and respond to market pressures.

While the dual-track mechanism was an ingenious solution to a seemingly impossible problem, it did have a downside, as quickly became evident. With two or more prices for products becoming widely available, the temptation to engage in arbitrage – corruption – was irresistible.

The other problem that quickly developed, one that really should never have become a problem, was that as the economy developed, localities became wealthier vis-à-vis the center. This was the product of two things. On the one hand, there were "extrabudgetary" revenues that had to be kept separately from the revenues that needed to be shared with the central government. Sometimes such revenues took a shadier form of becoming "little treasuries" (*xiao jinku*); that is, financial reserves that could be used for local expenses or corruption. On the other hand, the tax system that had been adopted in 1980, local contracting (*difang baogang*), had guaranteed that the localities could keep all revenues during a specified length of time. This system was adopted because localities were afraid that if they generated greater revenues, the central government would simply up their quotas and demand yet more revenue the following year, a phenomenon known as "whipping the fast ox." It did not pay to work hard and develop the local economy if the central government simply took the revenues. Local contracting was a way to avoid that dilemma. But the result was that the localities became relatively wealthy while the central government felt poor, something the Ministry of Finance complained about incessantly. From the perspective of the central planners, market-oriented reform was weakening the authority of the central government and undermining the plan.

So, over time, there were very real pressures that drove the "reformers" and the "conservatives" farther apart as the reforms deepened. That is why the succession loomed so large, particularly at the Thirteenth Party Congress. Both conservatives and reformers each hoped to claim the future, an issue made ever more urgent by the purge of Hu Yaobang.

Figure 1.6 Zhao Ziyang in 1980 (François Lochon/Gamma-Rapho via Getty Images)

The Thirteenth Party Congress, 1987

The Thirteenth Party Congress is mostly remembered for Zhao Ziyang's bold report that states that China was in the "primary stage of socialism." He called for political reform by separating party from state and by creating a dual cadre structure consisting of "professional cadres" on the one hand, who would resemble civil servants in other countries, and those doing "political work"; that is, the party cadres who would set policy. It was an attempt to copy the separation between politics and administration that exists in the economically developed countries.[32] Had Zhao's proposal really been implemented it might indeed have led to the institutionalization of the State Council system, but that was not to be.

[32] Zhao Ziyang, "Advance along the Road of Socialism with Chinese Characteristics," *Beijing Review*, Vol. 30, No. 45 (November 9–15, 1987): 419–436.

Rereading Zhao's proposals today is jarring, if only because we are more aware of the tensions that were roiling politics behind the scene. After all, the Thirteenth Party Congress was held only ten months after Hu Yaobang's unceremonial dismissal as general secretary, after which there had been a virulent campaign directed against "bourgeois liberalization." Perhaps because the Campaign against Spiritual Pollution had been curtailed, the 1987 Campaign against Bourgeois Liberalization unfolded with unprecedented ferocity (for the reform era). It took as its main target three intellectuals: the crusading journalist Liu Binyan, the astrophysicist Fang Lizhi, and the writer Wang Ruowang, all of whom were denounced repeatedly in the media. Zhao Ziyang made strong efforts to limit the scope of the campaign by trying to confine it to within the CCP and keep it out of the countryside, efforts that reveal how far the campaign was reaching. Of course, Zhao's efforts only antagonized the conservatives, who argued that the talk of "some people" (a reference to Hu Yaobang) reflected bourgeois liberalization, but "others" (a reference to Zhao Ziyang) engaged in bourgeois liberalization. The Campaign against Bourgeois Liberalism continued to dominate the political arena until May, when Zhao Ziyang reported to Deng Xiaoping on his concerns about the atmosphere in which the Thirteenth Party Congress would be held. With Deng's blessing, Zhao gave a major speech on May 13 that was summarized in two editorials in *People's Daily* in May. On July 1, the day on which the party commemorates its founding, *People's Daily* republished Deng Xiaoping's 1980 speech on the reform of the party and state leadership system, on which Zhao's report was explicitly based.[33]

Behind the scenes, moreover, there were at least two issues that reflected continuing tensions within the party. One concerned Deng Liqun, the head of the Propaganda Department from 1982 to 1985 and stalwart defender of Marxist orthodoxy. Born into a wealthy landlord family in Hunan in 1915, Deng attended Peking University for one year in 1935–1936. He was active in the December 9th Movement (a movement directed against Japanese aggression in north China) in 1935 and joined the CCP the following year. In the 1950s he served as secretary to Wang Zhen, who was then in charge of establishing Communist rule in Xinjiang, a task accomplished with great violence. Later he became secretary to Liu Shaoqi and was deputy editor in chief of the party's theoretical journal, *Red Flag*.

---

[33] Stanley Rosen, "China in 1987: The Year of the Thirteenth Party Congress," *Asian Survey*, Vol. 28, No. 1 (January 1988): 35–51.

He was jailed as a counterrevolutionary during the Cultural Revolution, re-emerging in 1974 as a member of the Political Study Office, which would serve as a think tank for Deng Xiaoping. Although a supporter of Deng Xiaoping, he allied himself with the conservative wing of the CCP and was active in the Campaign against Spiritual Pollution in 1983 and the Campaign against Bourgeois Liberalization in 1987. For more liberal-minded people in the party, Deng Liqun was a bête noire.

In preparations for the Thirteenth Party Congress, leaders had decided to allocate a PB seat to Deng Liqun. That would give him an important position but not necessarily power. But that year, for the first time, the party introduced a system in which there would be more candidates than seats, a modest step in the direction of political reform. Under this new voting system, Deng Liqun failed to receive enough support to join the Central Committee, and thus he could not join the PB. In his memoir, Deng Liqun makes clear that he blamed Zhao Ziyang for his not securing enough votes.[34]

Deng Liqun got his revenge by securing positions for several of his close followers in important positions in the bureaucracy. His anger no doubt reflected a broader anger at the role Zhao Ziyang had played to push market-oriented reform forward so quickly.[35]

The other issue to be tackled was who should be premier. When Deng Xiaoping had dismissed Hu Yaobang the previous January, he had not made preparations for reorganizing the leadership. Deng clearly wanted Zhao Ziyang to succeed Hu Yaobang, appointing Zhao "acting general secretary" following Hu's ouster. Deng's idea was to appoint Wan Li to replace Zhao as premier. This would have given the CCP a strongly reformist leadership at the top, and Zhao, born in 1919, could no doubt have gone on to serve one or more terms as general secretary, had the 1989 Tiananmen events not intervened.

When Wan Li went to the other elders to solicit their support for his becoming premier, he found none. He had contributed enormously to the rural reforms that ushered in the relative prosperity in the country-side, but he had also been a staunch opponent of the Campaign against Spiritual Pollution in 1983 and the Campaign against Bourgeois Liberalization in 1987. Conservatives did not want such a liberal as

---

[34] Deng Liqun, *Deng Liqun zishu: Shi'erge chunqiu* (Deng Liqun's Memoir: Twelve Springs and Autumns) (n.p., n.d.).
[35] Ibid.

premier, especially with Zhao Ziyang as general secretary. So the choice fell to Li Peng, the foster son of Zhou Enlai, who had risen quickly up the party ranks with the support of Chen Yun, Deng Yingchao (Zhou Enlai's widow), and others. In 1983 Li Peng had been named a vice premier, and at the 1985 Party Representative Conference he had been added as a member of the PB. As an engineer, albeit one trained in hydroelectric power, he seemed a likely candidate for premier. But, reflecting serious doubts about Li Peng's understanding of economics, Zhao Ziyang was named to head the Financial and Economics Leadership Small Group, the first time in party history that a party head led that group (though the general secretary has continued to lead that group ever since).

The naming of Li Peng to the PBSC was an effort to balance political forces. Other PBSC members were Qiao Shi, the former head of the Organization Department and then head of the Political and Legal Affairs Commission who had been brought up by Hu Yaobang and had worked well with Deng Xiaoping, and Hu Qili, who was Hu Yaobang's protégé in the CYL. Another member was Yao Yilin, then a vice premier and former head of the State Planning Commission. An ally of Chen Yun's, he represented conservative interests, particularly the state-owned economy. Given the divisions within the party, the appointment of Li Peng balanced interests in the party.

However, this balance represented not so much an effort to build a coalition as a reflection of the barely concealed tensions within the party. Conservatives had made clear their opposition to Zhao Ziyang in the course of the Campaign against Bourgeois Liberalization (and Deng Liqun confirms it in his memoir). With the ouster of Hu Yaobang, the conservatives had a certain momentum. When Deng's effort to promote price reform in the summer of 1988 led to inflation, it was Zhao who inevitably became the scapegoat. Li Xiannian began a campaign to oust Zhao in the fall of 1988 – all these tensions bursting out before a single student had gone to Tiananmen Square. Li Peng was the obvious candidate to succeed as general secretary if Zhao stumbled.

Despite these tensions, the Thirteenth Party Congress was obviously intended to pass power on to a new generation. Deng Xiaoping, Chen Yun, and Li Xiannian all left the PBSC for the CAC. Deng's loyal military associates, Yang Dezhi and Yu Qiuli, left the PB. They were replaced by such people as Jiang Zemin, Li Peng, Li Tieying, Li Ruihuan, and Li Ximing. These people were all in their fifties or early sixties, a decade or more younger than those who were retiring. Hu Yaobang, unceremoniously removed in January, was nevertheless able to retain a seat on the PB, albeit without power, to try to dampen the tensions in the party. The congress was not a complete transition – senior military leaders Yang Shangkun and Qin Jiwei remained on the PB, and Deng remained as head of the CMC (his doing so necessitated a change in the constitution) – but it looked like a step-by-step transition from the revolutionary generation to a postrevolutionary generation.

Table 1.2 *Comparison of the Politburos following the Twelfth Party Congress, the CCP Representative Meeting, and the Thirteenth Party Congress*

Twelfth Politburo, 1982	Party Representative Meeting, 1985	Thirteenth Politburo, 1987	
Standing Committee	**Standing Committee**	**Standing Committee**	Position following Thirteenth Party Congress
Hu Yaobang	Hu Yaobang	Zhao Ziyang	General secretary
Ye Jianying	Deng Xiaoping	Li Peng	Premier
Deng Xiaoping	Zhao Ziyang	Qiao Shi	Politics and Law Commission, Secretariat
Zhao Ziyang	Li Xiannian	Hu Qili	Secretariat
Li Xiannian	Chen Yun	Yao Yilin	Vice Premier, head, State Planning Commission
Chen Yun			
Politburo	**Politburo**	**Politburo**	
Wan Li	Wan Li	Wan Li	NPC
Xi Zhongxun	Xi Zhongxun	Tian Jiyun	Vice premier
Wang Zhen	Fang Yi	Jiang Zemin	Party secretary, Shanghai
Wei Guoqing	Tian Jiyun	Li Tieying	Economic Structural Reform Commission

Table 1.2 (*cont.*)

Twelfth Politburo, 1982	Party Representative Meeting, 1985	Thirteenth Politburo, 1987	Position following Thirteenth Party Congress
Standing Committee	**Standing Committee**	**Standing Committee**	
Ulanhu	Qiao Shi	Li Ruihuan	Party secretary, Tianjin
Fang Yi	Li Peng	Li Ximing	Party secretary, Beijing
Deng Yingchao (f)	Yang Shangkun	Yang Rudai	Party secretary, Sichuan
Li Desheng	Yang Dezhi	Yang Shangkun	CMC
Yang Shangkun	Wu Xueqian	Wu Xueqian	Foreign minister
Yang Dezhi	Yu Qiuli	Song Ping	Organization Dept.
Yu Qiuli	Hu Qiaomu	Hu Yaobang	d. 1989
Song Renqiong	Hu Qili	Qin Jiwei	CMC
Zhang Tingfa	Yao Yilin		
Hu Qiaomu	Ni Zhifu		
Nie Rongzhen	Peng Zhen		
Ni Zhifu			
Xu Xiangqian			
Peng Zhen			
Liao Chengzhi			
Alternates	**Alternates**	**Alternates**	
Yao Yilin	Qin Jiwei	Ding Guan'gen	Vice chair, State Planning Commission
Qin Jiwei	Chen Muhua (f)		
Chen Muhua (f)			

Despite all the tensions, the Thirteenth Party Congress reflected the high point of reform in China, assuming that "reform" means the adoption of market-oriented economic measures and at least modest political reform. The boldness of the Thirteenth Party

Figure 1.7 Zhao Ziyang at Tiananmen Square, May 19, 1989. To the right of Zhao is Wen Jiabao, then head of the General Office (Chip HIRES/Gamma-Rapho via Getty Images)

Congress reflects the degree to which Leninist institutions can be flexible – but only under a leader as strong as Deng Xiaoping. The eruption of inflation in the summer of 1988 and of student protests in the spring of 1989 meant that Zhao's proposals would never be implemented, so we do not know how far they might have gone. Had the Tiananmen protests never occurred and Zhao remained as general secretary, he certainly would have faced enormous difficulties. Could he have dampened Chen Yun's opposition to his market-oriented reforms? Could he have secured the support of the PLA? Could he have controlled the critical positions that are so important to maintaining one's position? Perhaps Zhao could have converted the CCP into non-Leninist authoritarian system, but the odds were against him.

Conclusion

When one looks at the decade from the Eleventh Party Congress in 1977 to the Thirteenth Party Congress in 1987, it really was a remarkable decade. Deng had the unenviable task of pushing aside the person Mao had designated as his successor. Doing so was not easy. There were still people who were unwilling to break with many of Mao's decisions, including his designation of Hua as successor. There were others, like Li Xiannian, who thought that Deng was "insufferably arrogant." And still others, like Ye Jianying, who hoped, despite the experience of the entire twentieth century, that a "collective" leadership could emerge. Deng had to push patiently, if urgently. He engineered the removal of opponents while promoting the careers of veteran cadres, slowly changing the balance in the Central Committee. He supported a discussion on Practice as the Sole Criterion of Truth, to challenge Hua Guofeng's embrace of the "Two Whatevers." And he was able eventually to secure the endorsement of the Third Plenary Session of the Eleventh Central Committee in 1978. Deng's advocacy of political reform in his historic talk "On the Reform of the Party and State Leadership Structure" in 1980 further undermined Hua Guofeng's position. Hua had to yield his position as party chairman to Hu Yaobang and his position as premier to Zhao Ziyang. In hindsight, Deng's emergence as the paramount leader seems inevitable, but behind this leadership change was old-time power politics. Supported by the military, Deng promoted his own people and ousted those opposed to him.

With Deng ensconced in power there seemed a real chance that Chinese politics might finally become institutionalized. Deng had laid out many of his ideas in his talk "On the Reform of the Party and State Leadership Structure." Even if that speech had been conceived as a way to undermine Hua Guofeng's position, it did lay out a program for rationalizing party rule. Older cadres should retire, expertise should be brought to bear, party and state should be separated, party and enterprise management should be separated, and power should be less concentrated. The document "Several Principles of Intra-party Life," promulgated in 1980, tried to restore "normal" party life, demanding an end to factionalism, implementation of collective leadership, and an end to labeling people and persecuting them. The gradual implementation of a retirement system, starting with the creation of the CAC as a way to ease older cadres out of their positions and to make room for younger cadres, was an important step forward.

However, when we look more closely we see aspects of the political system that suggested that this "institutionalization" was more apparent than real. Even when Deng was clearly dominant, indeed because he was dominant, the structure that he set up was based on balances, not just the hierarchical principles of Leninism. This system recognized the importance of certain interests and people in the party, including Chen Yun, who continued to have major influence over economic policy, and Hu Qiaomu, whose influence in the propaganda system reflected his long service as Mao's personal secretary. At the same time, younger leaders like Hu Yaobang and Zhao Ziyang could take over formal control of the party and the state apparatus respectively. Intentionally or not, however, it set up competing hierarchies that had the benefit, from Deng's perspective, of reflecting policy differences to the top of the system; that is, to Deng. But competing hierarchies had the negative consequence of exacerbating intra-party differences. For instance, Zhao Ziyang, the premier, whose job was to manage the economy, had no ability to appoint the head of the State Planning Commission, the most important bureaucracy in the planned economy, so his desire to implement market-oriented reforms were always constrained by the State Counsel system (hence the need for clever end-arounds, such as the dual-track price system). Similarly, Hu Yaobang, in charge of ideology, found himself in competition with Hu Qiaomu and Deng Liqun. Such conflicting interests, particularly under the pressure of succession, led to destructive struggles over power and influence, including the ouster of Hu Yaobang in January 1987 and the ensuing Campaign against Bourgeois Liberalization. Later, the campaign to remove Zhao Ziyang in the fall of 1988 would feed into the tensions that led to the tragedy of Tiananmen.

If one mark of political institutionalization is a decision-making rule on the promotion and selection of party leaders, then the decision to remove Hu Yaobang reflects the lack of institutionalization. This was, as far as we know, a one-person decision. Deng decided that Hu was not tough enough to manage the party, particularly with regard to ideological issues. When he told Yang Shangkun and others of this decision, Deng was intending to make the change at the Thirteenth Party Congress, which would have made it appear to be more of an institutional process. As matters turned out, student demonstrations in the fall of 1986 angered Deng and led to Hu's immediate removal. In either case, the decision would have been by one person who stood above the party.

In this decade, power and policy differences were dealt with through personnel changes (such as the Party Representative Meeting), subterfuge (orchestrating Deng Liqun's failure to be elected to the Central Committee in 1987), campaigns (such as those against spiritual pollution and bourgeois liberalization), and Deng Xiaoping's personal decisions. His decisions were often good, gaining the praise of Chinese and foreigners alike, but sometimes they exacerbated tensions, as when his decision to push ahead with price reform in 1988 set off an inflationary spiral. The combination of a structure of balances and personal decision making undermined the likelihood of institutionalization.

2 | *Succession and the Art of Consolidating Power*

The escalating tensions within the party, outlined in the previous chapter, were ultimately about two things. One was the nature of the party. Could it evolve from a hierarchical Leninist party into something more open? Could it adapt to a more pluralist society and allow the legitimacy of societal voices? Could it accept interest groups as legitimate? And, if the party could make such adaptations, could it maintain its hierarchical, disciplined nature? Hu Yaobang failed in his efforts to balance those pressures. The second was the issue of succession. In 1989, Deng Xiaoping was eighty-four years old, Chen Yun was eighty-five, Li Xiannian was eighty, and Yang Shangkun was eighty-two. Yang Shangkun, as president of the PRC, was the only one of these elders to still have a position on the Central Committee. The other three were all retired. In the mid-1980s, the obvious frontrunners for leader of the party were Hu Yaobang (age seventy-four in 1989), Zhao Ziyang (age seventy), and Li Peng (age sixty-one). The purge of Hu Yaobang in January 1987 obviously took him out of the running as a potential successor, and the retirement of Deng Xiaoping from the Central Committee (but not the Central Military Commission!) in 1987 put the issue of succession front and center. The Thirteenth Party Congress seemed to settle that issue by naming Zhao Ziyang as general secretary, but it reflected the deep cleavages in the party by simultaneously naming Li Peng as premier. When Deng Xiaoping put the issue of price reform on the agenda in the summer of 1988 at a time of rising inflationary pressures, he inadvertently set off panic buying and a new round of intra-party struggle. By the fall of 1989, Zhao was no longer notified of meetings of the Economic and Financial Leadership Small Group, which he formally headed, and Li Xiannian was leading a "dump Zhao" movement.[1] The student demonstrations

---

[1] Zhao Ziyang, *Gaige licheng* (The Course of Reform) (Hong Kong: Xin shiji chubanshe, 2009), pp. 261–265.

following the death of Hu Yaobang in April 1989 had inadvertently reopened the succession issue in spades.

Chinese politics demands two things that often stand in tension with each other: loyalty to the party and loyalty to one's superior. Deng, as an old revolutionary and old soldier, demanded absolute loyalty. When, on the afternoon of May 16, 1989, Zhao Ziyang told Mikhail Gorbachev that at the Thirteenth Party Congress the party had made a decision to turn to Deng for all important questions, Deng certainly believed that Zhao was putting pressure on him to step down. When Zhao, on the morning of May 17 at Deng's house, asked Deng to take back the language he had used in the infamous April 26 editorial, accusing the students of undertaking a "planned conspiracy" to "negate the leadership of the CCP and the socialist system," it was further evidence that Zhao was distancing himself from Deng. No doubt Deng saw this as betrayal, and like similar leadership struggles in party history, it was settled by someone winning and someone losing. Zhao was put under house arrest and the two leaders never saw each other again.

Although the literature on the "institutionalization" of politics in the PRC does not go into this important episode, it does raise the question of how quickly a political system can become institutionalized. There are reasons why institutionalization can happen, but it is a process that usually takes years. Neither organizations nor humans normally change their behavior very quickly, and, as we shall see, China did not institutionalize in the way some have claimed.

Following Zhao's purge and house arrest, the leadership had to choose a new party head. One might have expected the party to call a plenary session of the Thirteenth Central Committee, but all indications are that discussions were closely held in private. On May 31, three days before the bloody denouement of the Tiananmen demonstrations, Deng called in Li Peng and Yao Yilin and told them:[2]

The people see reality. If we put up a front so that people feel that it is an ossified leadership that cannot reflect the future of China, then there will be constant trouble and there will never be a peaceful day.

---

[2] Deng Xiaoping, "Zucheng yige shixing gaige de you xiwang de lingdao jiti" (Organize a Leading Collective That Will Carry Out Reform and Be Hopeful), in *Deng Xiaoping wenxuan, disan juan* (Selected Works of Deng Xiaoping, Vol. 3), p. 296.

Figure 2.1 Jiang Zemin meets with the press shortly after becoming general secretary (Forrest Anderson/The LIFE Images Collection via Getty Images)

Having dashed Li Peng's hopes of becoming the next general secretary, Deng told these conservatives that he had discussed with Chen Yun and Li Xiannian about the formation of a new, third generation of leadership, giving a pretty good idea of who Deng thought needed to be consulted. Deng told them that they had decided on Jiang Zemin to be the "core" of the third generation of leadership. It is difficult to construe a conversation between three party leaders (no doubt conducted through their secretaries) as an "institutional procedure," so Milan Svolik is no doubt correct when he writes that when institutional procedures are not used, it is a good indicator that "formal institutions are most likely epiphenomenal or at least secondary to potentially violent, noninstitutional methods of resolving political conflicts."[3] But this was an accepted practice in the CCP, and it was not surprising that the Fourth Plenum, which met in Beijing on June 23–24, accepted Deng's recommendations.

The choice of Jiang seemed to be an odd one. He was not a member of the PBSC, but Deng had clearly vetoed Li Peng and Yao Yilin. Hu Yaobang's protégé Hu Qili had taken himself out of the race by

---

[3] Svolik, *The Politics of Authoritarian Rule*, p. 39.

siding with Zhao at the decisive May 17 meeting at Deng's house. That left Qiao Shi as the only member of the five-person PBSC left. Qiao seemed a probable choice. He had rich experience working at the central level. Starting in 1983, he had served as head of the General Office and simultaneously as head of the Organization Department under Hu Yaobang. He had entered the PB and Secretariat in 1985; the following year, he was named a vice premier. But he had made it clear during the demonstrations that he had opposed the use of military force to crack down. In the end, he abstained from voting on whether to send the military into Tiananmen Square.

According to the *Tiananmen Papers*, Deng proposed Li Ruihuan, the party secretary of Tianjin who had risen from the ranks of the working class to supervise the building of the Great Hall of the People, to become general secretary of the party. But the provenance of the *Tiananmen Papers* is weak, so that story is uncertain.[4] Certainly Li's lack of education and international experience would have counted against him. Similar objections could have been raised against most of the other members of the PB. Jiang Zemin had the advantage of being in the right age range – sixty-three – of being well educated (he had graduated from Jiaotong University in Shanghai and had studied engineering in the Soviet Union), of having risen through the ranks to be party secretary of China's most economically important city, and of having some international experience. In addition to his time spent in the Soviet Union, he had accompanied Hua Guofeng on his important tour of Eastern Europe in 1978 and he had served as secretary general of the State Administration Commission on Foreign Investment from 1980 to 1982.

At the time, there was much skepticism in the West about Jiang being able to hold on to power, surrounded as he was by grizzled revolutionaries who had just demonstrated very different political stances. Such skepticism was justified. Jiang had served as minister of electronic

---

[4] The *Tiananmen Papers* quotes Bo Yibo speaking at the critical May 17 meeting at Deng Xiaoping's house that decided to declare martial law, saying, "We have no room for any retreat." See Andrew J. Nathan and Perry Link, eds., *The Tiananmen Papers: The Chinese Leadership's Decision to Use Force against Their Own People – in Their Own* Words (New York: PublicAffairs, 2001), p. 188. However, according to *Zuihou de mimi: Zhonggong shisanjie sizhong quanhui [liu si] jielun wenjian* (The Last Secret: The Final Documents from the Fourth Plenary Session of the Thirteenth Central Committee [June Fourth]) (Hong Kong: Xin shiji ji chuanmei youxian gongsi, 2019), p. 225, Bo Yibo was sick at the time and thus not at the meeting. Also personal correspondence with Bao Pu.

industries from 1982 to 1985, before being appointed mayor of Shanghai, but being a minister of the State Council, particularly in what was then a relatively minor ministry, was a long way from being at the top of the system. If Zhao Ziyang was not always clear about what the party elders were thinking after having served as premier for seven years and as general secretary for almost two years, then one can imagine the gulf that separated Jiang from the top leaders above him. This gap was reduced by his familiarity with Chen Yun and Li Xiannian, frequent visitors to Shanghai, to whom Jiang extended every possible courtesy. And Zeng Qinghong, Jiang's top aide, could introduce Jiang to the rest of the party elite. Zeng's father, Zeng Shan, had been close to Mao during the Jiangxi period and had gone on to become minister of the interior. So Zeng had grown up as a part of the "red aristocracy." Perhaps the most critical connection that Zeng helped Jiang make was to Bo Yibo, the conservative economic leader who was close to Chen Yun and part of the so-called "eight immortals" – the group of elders who dominated Chinese politics despite their being largely retired.[5]

Figure 2.2 Jiang Zemin conferring with former president Yang Shangkun in 1991 (Mike Fiala/AFP via Getty Images)

[5] Deng Xiaoping had left the Central Committee in 1987 but had retained the chairmanship of the CMC. Yang Shangkun remained on the Central Committee,

Although he succeeded to the top position in the party, Jiang's hold on power was anything but secure. Obviously his two predecessors had not been able to hold on to their positions, and Jiang had absolutely no military experience or connections with the PLA. Li Peng was certainly cold to Jiang, and Qiao Shi no doubt resented Jiang for jumping over him to take the top spot.[6] It was not an easy position to be in, and moving from an insecure position to a dominant force in Chinese politics was not simple. Skillful maneuvering and luck were both involved.

When Jiang was named general secretary in 1989, elite politics were beset by a number of balances. These were not the balances of the Deng period when his dominance permitted him to allow different groups to coexist (until the tensions finally exploded).

Most obviously the PBSC was dominated by people not well disposed to Jiang's leadership – Li Peng, Yao Yilin, and Qiao Shi – though both Li Peng and Yao Yilin were close to Chen Yun, who supported Jiang. The elders balanced those in formal office, and the military leadership was an important part of the system that remained loyal to Deng Xiaoping, not to Jiang Zemin. Surviving in this mix of contending politicians, all of whom were more experienced than Jiang, was not easy. The route to dominance could only come through fending off the threats that surrounded him. Centralization of power is not only part of the organizational culture of the CCP; it is a means to survive.

When Jiang took office in June 1989, China was in the throes of yet another ideological campaign. The Fourth Plenum criticized Zhao harshly. Li Peng declared that "bourgeois liberalization" had "spread rampantly" under Zhao and that the party should "carry out the struggle against bourgeois liberalization for a long time to come rather than to do it perfunctorily or give it up halfway as in the past" – an apparent reference to the campaigns against spiritual pollution in 1983 and against bourgeois liberalization in 1987.[7] Li Xiannian, who had led the charge against Zhao, called him the "root cause of the riots and

---

served as president of the PRC, and was vice chairman of the CMC. Chen Yun headed the Central Advisory Committee (CMC), and Bo Yibo was retired, as were Li Xiannian, Peng Zhen, Wang Zhen, and Song Renqiong.

[6] Willy Wo-lop Lam, *The Era of Jiang Zemin* (Singapore and New York: Prentice Hall, 1999).

[7] Cited in Joseph Fewsmith, *China since Tiananmen: From Deng Xiaoping to Hu Jintao*, 2nd ed. (Cambridge: Cambridge University Press, 2008), p. 30.

rebellion" while Peng Zhen accused Zhao of "attempting to topple the Communist Party."[8]

The need for Jiang to proceed cautiously was evident, but as the immediate crisis passed, Deng grew increasingly anxious about reform. On January 28, 1991, Deng Xiaoping went to Shanghai to pass the Spring Festival. Unlike the other times he had gone to Shanghai for the Spring Festival, this year he was extremely busy, conducting inspections, visiting firms, and listening to reports about opening up Pudong (the east side of Shanghai, across the river from the main part of the city). Over the course of three weeks (Deng left Shanghai on February 18), Deng gave a number of talks that were summarized in four commentaries, published in *Liberation Daily*, written under the pen name "Huangfu Ping," which can be translated as "Shanghai Commentary"or "Helping Deng Xiaoping." Huangfu Ping was the pen name of Zhou Ruijin, the deputy editor in chief of the Shanghai party paper, *Liberation Daily*. Zhou worked closely with Deng's entourage, and the publication of his articles was overseen by Deng's daughter, Deng Nan, and Shanghai mayor Zhu Rongji.[9]

These commentaries criticized "ossified thinking" and repeatedly called for a new round of "emancipating the mind." The second article, which Zhou regarded as the most important, was called "Reform and Opening Require New Thinking," and it directly conveyed Deng's belief that planning and markets were two different methods of distributing resources and did not reflect the difference between capitalism and socialism. This thesis was, of course, a direct refutation of arguments then circulating in Beijing.[10]

By this time, spring of 1991, Deng had given up all his positions and was merely an ordinary party member, so his words did not convey the same degree of importance. Of course, his primary opponents, Chen Yun and Deng Liqun, were also retired, but these retirements did not lessen the importance of the debate that followed. Chen Yun

[8]   Ibid., p. 31.
[9]   Wei Yung-cheng, "Reveal the Mystery of Huang Fu Ping," *Ta kung pao*, October 7, 1992, trans. FBIS-CHI-92–201, October 16, 1992, p. 19; and Gao Xin and He Pin, *Zhu Rongji zhuan* (Biography of Zhu Rongji) (Taipei: Xinxinwen, 1993).
[10] Zhou Ruijin, "Record of How the Series of 'Huangfu Ping' Essays Came About," May 7, 2008, available at www3.nd.edu/~pmoody/Text%20Pages% 20-%20Peter%20Moody%20Webpage/Huangfu%20Ping.pdf, accessed September 15, 2020.

complained that Deng created his own "one-voice chamber" (*yiyan-tang*) and suggested that a leader should consult with others, "espe-cially those who hold views opposite from our own."[11] The conservative journal *Dangdai sichao* (Contemporary Thought) chimed in with a harsh commentary warning that "bourgeois liberalization" could never be confined to the ideological sphere because it inherently involved the issue of whether the country was taking the capitalist or the socialist road.[12]

This debate, concerning the most fundamental issues then facing China, was the background to Deng's famous "Southern Tour" in January and February 1992, to Wuhan, Shenzhen, and Zhuhai, during which Deng gave a full-throated defense of reform and declared that the "left" was currently the main danger facing reform. Those who opposed reform, he said, should "step down."

This declaration reflected Deng's frustration and impatience. The debates had been going on for three years (counting from Tiananmen) and all of them were occurring above Jiang's head. Being general secretary was not enough.

Deng's impatience was reflected when Yang Baibing, vice chair of the CMC, declared at the spring 1992 meeting of the NPC that the PLA would "protect and escort" (*baojia huhang*) reform. Yang Baibing apparently did not clear his action with Deng, making this PLA inter-vention in civilian politics truly extraordinary (though Deng did not stop Yang). It was, of course, a challenge to Chen Yun and other conservatives in support of Deng's personal authority.

Having thought about dismissing Jiang, Deng now backed him wholeheartedly. When the Fourteenth Party Congress met in October 1992, an unusual lineup emerged. Yang Baibing was given a seat on the PB, but Liu Huaqing was given a seat on the PBSC. Liu Huaqing, then age sixty-nine, was a veteran of Deng's 129th Division. He had retired from the Central Committee at the Party Representative Conference in 1985, but had nevertheless retained his position as head of the navy. After the Thirteenth Party Congress he joined the CMC, so his "retirement" was more nominal than real. Nevertheless, joining the PBSC at that age and without having served on the PB was unusual.

---

[11] *Renmin ribao*, January 18, 1991.
[12] "Why Must We Unremittingly Oppose Bourgeois Liberalization?," *Renmin ribao*, April 24, 1991, p. 5. Trans. FBIS-CHI-91–081, April 26, 1991, pp. 18–21.

Figure 2.3 Zeng Qinghong, Jiang Zemin's closest adviser, October 2002 (GOH CHAI HIN/AFP via Getty Images)

The reason Liu Huaqing was appointed to the PBSC soon became clear. In intervening so blatantly in party affairs, having used the Yang brothers to reinforce his authority, Deng now dismissed them. Deng understood that without dismissing the Yang brothers, Jiang would never be able to establish his own authority over the PLA. Deng had known Yang Shangkun since the 1930s and Yang Baibing had fought in Deng's own 129th division. But, as with Hu Yaobang, Deng did not allow personal feelings to get in the way of what he thought was necessary. The *PLA Daily* ran a series of articles on the need to prevent factionalism as people associated with the Yang brothers were purged. Liu Huaqing was there to maintain Deng's personal authority over the military, to stabilize the PLA as its leadership was reorganized, and to tutor Jiang Zemin in the ways of the PLA.[13]

Also added to the PB was Zhang Zhen, then aged seventy-one. Like Liu Huaqing, Zhang had left the Central Committee in 1985, but he

---

[13] You Ji, "Jiang Zemin's Command of the Military," *China Journal*, No. 45 (January 2001), pp. 131–138.

had continued to be active, becoming the first head of National Defense University. In 1992, he was suddenly re-elected to the Central Committee and named to the CMC to help stabilize the PLA and guide Jiang Zemin.

Jiang could never compete with Deng Xiaoping in his ability to control the military but he could win support by advocating larger budgets. Whereas prior to Tiananmen, Deng could hold military budgets down (compensating by allowing greater military involvement in enterprises and engaging in arms sales). Jiang, in contrast, argued that military budgets should increase in step with the economy. In his first five years as party head, Jiang had increased the wages of officers and soldiers on three separate occasions, winning much support from the PLA.[14] At least at first, Jiang took a "reign but not rule" approach to the military, issuing broad directives rather than detailed instructions, which, along with the budget increases, slowly increased Jiang's support within the PLA.[15]

If we look more deeply at the composition of the party elite emerging from the Fourteenth Party Congress, we see that Jiang's power was still limited (see Table 2.1). Li Peng, who had resented Jiang's appointment, remained premier. Qiao Shi was hardly respectful of Jiang, and Li Ruihuan likewise was not an ally. Zhu Rongji had been appointed the previous year at the NPC by Deng Xiaoping. Although Zhu and Jiang had worked together in Shanghai and would again soon work well together in Beijing, Zhu was not dependent on Jiang.

The most interesting appointment was that of Hu Jintao. Hu Jintao was then only forty-nine years old. No one that young had been appointed to the PB, much less the PBSC, since Wang Hongwen was made vice chairman of the party in 1973. Hu had risen quickly in the party. After graduating from Tsinghua University's Water Conservancy Engineering Department, he had spent a year as an instructor at Tsinghua before being sent to the interior province of Gansu as a worker. Discovered by Song Ping, then serving as provincial party secretary, Hu rose quickly and was promoted to secretary of the Gansu branch of the CYL. In 1982 he became first secretary of the CYL in Beijing and that fall was named to the Twelfth Central Committee. In 1985 he was sent to Guizhou as provincial party secretary, and in 1988 he was transferred to Tibet as party secretary, just as major

---

[14] Ibid., p. 134.   [15] Ibid., pp. 136–137.

Table 2.1 *Comparison of the Fourteenth and Fifteen Politburos*

Fourteenth Politburo (1992)			Fifteenth Politburo (1997)		
Name	Position	Age	Name	Position	Age
PBSC			**PBSC**		
Jiang Zemin	General secretary	66	Jiang Zemin	General secretary	71
Li Peng	Premier	64	Li Peng	NPC	69
Qiao Shi	NPC	68	Zhu Rongji	Premier	69
Li Ruihuan	CPPCC	58	Li Ruihuan	CPPCC	63
Zhu Rongji	Vice premier	64	Hu Jintao	Party School	55
Liu Huaqing	Vice chairman, CMC	76	Wei Jianxing	CDIC	66
Hu Jintao	Secretariat, Party School	50	Li Lanqing	Vice premier	65
Politburo			**Politburo**		
Ding Guan'gen	United Front Work Department; Propaganda (1992); Secretariat	63	Ding Guan'gen	Propaganda Department, Secretariat	68
Tian Jiyun	Vice chairman, NPC	63	Tian Jiyun	Vice chairman, NPC	68

Table 2.1 (*cont.*)

Fourteenth Politburo (1992)			Fifteenth Politburo (1997)		
Name	Position	Age	Name	Position	Age
Li Lanqing	Vice premier	60	Li Changchun	Henan party secretary; Guangdong party secretary (1998)	48
Li Tieying	State councilor	56	Li Tieying	Head, Chinese Academy of Social Sciences (CASS)	61
Yang Baibing	None	72	Wu Bangguo	Vice premier	56
Wu Bangguo	Shanghai party secretary	51	Wu Guanzheng	CDIC	54
Zou Jiahua	Vice premier	66	Chi Haotian	Vice chairman, CMC	68
Chen Xitong	Beijing party secretary	62	Zhang Wannian	Vice chairman, CMC	69
Jiang Chunyun	Shandong party secretary; added to Secretariat in 1994	62	Luo Gan	Politics and Law; Secretariat	62
Qian Qichen	Ministry of Foreign Affairs	64	Jiang Chunyun	Vice chairman, NPC; Secretariat	69
Wei Jianxing	CDIC; Secretariat	61	Jia Qinglin	Beijing party secretary	66
Xie Fei	Guangdong party secretary	60	Qian Qichen	Minister of foreign affairs	69
Tan Shaowen	Tianjin party secretary	64 (died 1993)		Foreign minister	

Name	Position	Age
Huang Ju	Mayor, Shanghai	54
Alternates		
Wen Jiabao	Head, General Office; Secretariat	50
Wang Hanbin	Chair, Law Committee, NPC	67

Name	Position	Age
Huang Ju	Shanghai party secretary	59
Xie Fei	Vice chairman, NPC	65 (died 1999)
Alternates		
Zeng Qinghong	Head, General Office; Secretariat;	58
Wu Yi (f)	Ministry of Foreign Trade and Economic Co-operation	54

demonstrations and riots erupted in that minority region on the eve of the 30th anniversary of the Tibetan uprising. Some argue that Hu's use of decisive force impressed Deng Xiaoping.

Deng Xiaoping, no doubt supported by Song Ping, appointed the young Hu Jintao to the PBSC with the intention that Hu would replace Jiang Zemin ten years later, in 2002. Having supported Jiang by purging the military, Deng was now declaring that Jiang should not serve for life and should not appoint his own successor. Having declared in 1989 that he would retire and not interfere in management of the party, Deng was nevertheless trying to decide on party arrangements for the foreseeable future. Apparently Deng's analysis of the structural flaws of the party had not changed; he continued to view the overconcentration of power as a serious structural problem. In 1980, he had told the Italian journalist Oriana Fallaci that it was "feudal" for a leader to select his own successor,[16] and even though Deng had selected three successors, two of whom had failed, he was nevertheless trying to prevent Jiang from determining his own successor. This arrangement may have been as close as the CCP ever came to "institutionalizing" party succession, but in doing so, Deng was fighting the natural human tendency to want to extend one's rule, or at least to influence the choice of one's successor. He was also going against the party's long history of concentrated power. Rules-based succession was simply not compatible with democratic centralism.

When one looks at the critical positions, one of the anomalies that shows up is that Zeng Qinghong, despite not being a member of the Central Committee, took over as head of the General Office and as secretary of the Work Committee of the Central Committee. This Work Committee oversees the discipline inspection work of organs under the party center and approves the appointment of party secretaries in those organs, so it is extremely powerful. Normally the heads of these organs are members of the Central Committee, so Jiang was able to exercise his authority to arrange for perhaps his closest aide to move into these positions. When one looks at the rest of the PB, it is apparent that Jiang was able to promote some protégés – such as Wu Bangguo, Li Lanqing, and Jiang Chunyun – but there were also quite a few people

---

[16] Deng Xiaoping, "Answers to the Italian Journalist Oriana Fallaci," in *Selected Works of Deng Xiaoping (1975–1982)* (Beijing: Foreign Languages Press, 1983), p. 328.

who were less than wholehearted supporters, people like Chen Xitong, whom Jiang would purge in 1996, and Li Tieying, the son of party elder Li Weihan. Similarly, membership of the Secretariat was split. Jiang had survived his first three years in power, but he was still far from consolidating power.

The Turning Point

Part of politics is luck. When one looks at the critical period following the 1989 Tiananmen events, it is apparent that if the elders had died in a different order, the political outcome would have been quite different. Imagine, if you will, Deng dying shortly after the student demonstrations. One cannot say with certainty what the result would have been, but surely Chen Yun and Li Xiannian would have carried greater weight, the 1992 Southern Tour would never have occurred, and the personnel arrangements at the Fourteenth Party Congress would have been significantly different.

However, as events unfolded, the conservative leaders departed from the scene first. Li Xiannian died in June 1992, Hu Qiaomu died in September 1992, and Chen Yun died in April 1995. Their deaths marked the true passing of the revolutionary generation.[17] As Chen Yun was passing, Deng was entering his dotage. On October 1, 1994, *People's Daily* published a picture of Deng Xiaoping watching the National Day fireworks with a blank look on his face. The photo was a clear signal to the Chinese people that Deng would soon join his revolutionary comrades at Babaoshan (the crematory/cemetery for deceased leaders).

With the purge of the Yang brothers and the passing of these elders, the PBSC was less balanced by senior and retired party leaders and Jiang finally had a chance to secure his own authority – five years after becoming general secretary. The turning point came in September 1994, when the Fourth Plenary Session of the Fourteenth Central Committee made clear that power had passed to Jiang Zemin. As an authoritative editorial in *People's Daily* declared, the party's "second-generation leading collective

---

[17] The "eight immortals" is a sardonic reference to eight party elders, none of whom
      retained a position on the Central Committee, but who nevertheless played
      a guiding role during the Tiananmen protests. The group consisted of Deng
      Xiaoping, Chen Yun, Li Xiannian, Peng Zhen, Yang Shangkun, Bo Yibo, Wang
      Zhen, and Song Renqiong. Hu Qiaomu was not part of this group, but as Mao's
      former secretary, he was a highly influential articulator of conservative ideology.

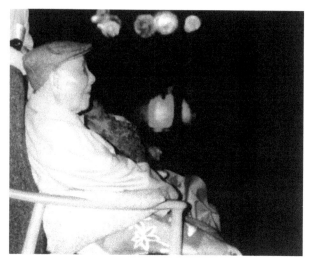

Figure 2.4 Deng Xiaoping watching fireworks on October 1, 1994 (FILES/ Stringer/AFP via Getty Images)

has been successfully relieved by its third-generation leading collective." This declaration was reinforced by personnel changes that strengthened Jiang's position. Huang Ju, one of Jiang's closest protégés in Shanghai, was promoted to the PB, and two other close followers, Wu Bangguo and Jiang Chunyun, both PB members, were added to the Secretariat.

Given his reinforced position, Jiang acted quickly to consolidate power. In 1995 Jiang launched his campaign to "study politics" (*jiang zhengzhi*), a campaign designed to reinforce his own authority. This campaign followed up on the "Decision on Some Major Issues on Strengthening Party Building" that was passed by the plenum.[18] The military came out in strong support of Jiang. Zhang Wannian, who would replace Liu Huaqing at the Fifteenth Party Congress, enthusiastically supported Jiang's speech, and in November, *PLA Daily* published a picture of Jiang reviewing a naval parade. Behind Jiang was the entire leadership of the PLA, an unprecedented show of support for the new core.[19]

---

[18] "Guanyu jiaqiang dang de jianshe jige zhongda wenti de jueding" (Decision on Some Major Issues on Strengthening Party Building), *Renmin ribao*, September 28, 1994.

[19] You Ji, "Jiang Zemin: In Quest of Post-Deng Supremacy," pp. 1–28, in Maurice Brosseau and Suzanne Pepper, eds., *China Review 1996* (Hong Kong: Chinese University Press, 1996).

In April 1995 Jiang had Chen Xitong, the party secretary of Beijing, arrested on charges of corruption. Chen was guilty primarily of *lèse majesté*, of not respecting Jiang. He was also extremely well connected. A product of the Beijing party machine, Chen was well connected with Peng Zhen and Wan Li as well as Deng Xiaoping. It was actually Hu Yaobang who had "discovered" him, and Li Peng had known Chen since Chen was a secretary to Liu Ren, a second party secretary in Beijing in the 1960s and a cousin of Li Peng. Chen had also provided much support for Li Peng in 1989. So getting rid of Chen was no easy matter, and Jiang's ability to do so was testament to his skill as a politician as well as his new political strength.[20] Jiang's power was no longer so dependent, or circumscribed, by the elders, and the leadership was no longer so collective.[21]

Deng died in February 1997. His death ended the sort of strongman politics he had embodied; no matter how politically skilled Jiang was, he would never be able to exercise power the way Deng did. No doubt this end of strongman politics played into the notion that politics was becoming increasingly institutionalized. However, we have already seen that the purge of the Yang brothers, the mixed results at the Fourteenth Party Congress in October 1992, and finally the promotion of important allies at the Fourth Plenum in September 1994, followed by the purge of Chen Xitong in 1995, outlined the contours of a struggle for power that Jiang won rather than a smooth passage of power, as is sometimes depicted in the literature.

Toward the Fifteenth Party Congress

The importance of balances, informal politics, and the resulting negotiations can be seen in the Fifteenth Party Congress, held in September 1997. Jiang would "win" these negotiations, in the sense that he improved his position. But he had to make concessions as well. There were at least three negotiations that were important, and in two of them Jiang had the help of Bo Yibo, one of the three "immortals" then still living. One issue was the position of the military on the PB. Liu Huaqing had taken a position on the PBSC to "escort and protect" Jiang Zemin after the Yang brothers were purged. The military had demonstrated support for Jiang in 1995, so now it seemed that it was time for Jiang to take firmer control over the military. Bo Yibo suggested that, under the principle of "the party controls the

[20] Ibid., pp. 14–15.   [21] Fewsmith, *China since Tiananmen*, pp. 162–165.

gun," no uniformed military persons should sit on the PBSC. So Zhang
Wannian, the designated successor to Liu Huaqing, took up a seat on the
PB, but not on the PBSC. His fellow CMC vice chair, Chi Haotian, likewise
sat on the PB. Thus, the tradition that the uniformed military has two seats
on the PB but none on the PBSC was born and has been continued to
this day. Whether this is a good idea is another matter. It can be argued that
having a senior military person on the PBSC would better co-ordinate
matters on national security and that not having a military person on the
PBSC contributes to the bifurcation between the civilian leadership and the
military.[22] But it was conducive to Jiang's consolidation of power.

The second issue on which Bo Yibo's help was essential was in pressur-
ing Qiao Shi to retire. The relations between Jiang Zemin and Qiao Shi
were not good. As noted at the beginning of this chapter, Qiao Shi had
long worked at high levels in the party while Jiang was working his way
up in Shanghai. Qiao had joined the PBSC in 1987, but Jiang was named
general secretary and "core" of the third generation of leadership in 1989.
It is thus only natural that Qiao would resent Jiang skipping over him.

When Jiang launched the campaign to "talk politics" in 1995 to
strengthen his leadership, Qiao Shi, head of the NPC, continued to talk
about "rule of law." It is not difficult to see that Qiao was trying to offset
Jiang's ambitions and his desire for personal leadership (as opposed to
collective leadership) with discussions about law. Bo Yibo went to see Qiao
and said that Jiang wanted to implement a retirement system at the
upcoming Fifteenth Party Congress and set the retirement age at seventy.
This was a bit awkward because Jiang was seventy-one, but Bo said that
Jiang had taken power at a critical time and the party needed his leadership.

Qiao made only two demands in response. One was that Wei
Jianxing take over as head of the CDIC. Wei had emerged from Hu
Yaobang's network and would keep that critical position out of the
hands of a Jiang protégé. But that was a small price to pay to remove
Qiao. The other request was even easier to meet, namely retaining Tian
Jiyun, a noted reformer brought up by Zhao Ziyang, as vice chairman
of the Standing Committee of the NPC.

But before he retired Qiao Shi revealed a secret, namely that Deng
Xiaoping and the other elders, the PBSC, and the PB as a whole, had

---

[22] James Mulvenon, "Straining against the Yoke? Civil–Military Relations in
China after the Seventeenth Party Congress," in Cheng Li, ed. *Chinese Politics in
the Xi Jinping Era: Reassessing Collective Leadership* (Washington, DC:
Brookings Institution Press, 2016), pp. 267–279.

decided that Hu Jintao would succeed Jiang as general secretary as the core of the fourth generation. Li Ruihuan and Wan Li on different occasions made similar remarks. Making this knowledge "public" to high-ranking party members would make Jiang's life difficult. Whether Jiang hoped to extend his leadership of the party or whether he hoped to designate a close follower, presumably Zeng Qinghong, as his successor is not clear, but it is clear, from his later actions as well as from reports that have been leaked, that he did not want to turn power over to Hu Jintao.[23] Qiao's remarks made it impossible for Jiang to reject Hu's succession without directly challenging Deng's will.

Whether Jiang liked it or not, the Fifteenth Party Congress positioned Hu Jintao and Wen Jiabao for their subsequent succession to the leadership, thus becoming the model for institutionalized politics. But the story of the Fifteenth Party Congress is more complicated. Li Peng, having served two terms as premier, might have been expected to retire, but given his sensitive role in the suppression of the Tiananmen demonstrations, his retirement might well have been taken as a sign that the regime was considering a re-evaluation of the verdict on Tiananmen. Any hint in that direction could have opened up vigorous debate within the party and perhaps have led to new demonstrations. Li Peng was sixty-nine years of age at the time. This may well explain why Jiang set the retirement age at seventy – an age that would force Qiao to retire but would allow Li Peng to serve one more term. But he could not serve another term as premier for he had already served the constitutionally limited two terms.

Moving Li Peng to lead the NPC was thus a solution; it also underscored the fact that the "Jiang–Li structure" that had dominated Jiang's early years had now become a Jiang-centric structure. Moving Li to the NPC also had the advantage of providing another rationale for persuading Qiao Shi, then head of the NPC, to retire. Li would not be as powerful as he had been as premier, but he would be allowed to stay in the leadership. Normally the number-two leader on the PBSC is the premier – as Li Peng had been on the Thirteenth and Fourteenth Central Committees, and as Zhao Ziyang had been once Ye Jianying retired at the 1985 Party Representative Conference. But demoting Li Peng from his number two position

[23] "Jiang Zemin zai Qiao Shi tuixiu de qianhou" (Jiang Zemin before and after Qiao Shi's Retirement"), Aboluo News Network (July 11, 2019), available at www.aboluowang.com/2019/0711/13133895.html, accessed September 16, 2020.

would have been controversial, so he was allowed to keep his position as the second-ranked member of the PBSC, and Zhu Rongji, the new premier, took the number three position. Jiang's protégé Li Lanqing, vice premier in charge of foreign trade, was promoted to the PBSC. But Jiang's nemesis Qiao Shi was ousted, becoming the first "victim" of the new retirement rule.

When one looks at the rest of the leadership, it is apparent that Jiang had significantly improved his position. There were at least seven Jiang allies on the PB, while the inclusion of protégés of Deng Xiaoping (Ding Guangen), Li Peng (Luo Gan), and Qiao Shi (Tian Jiyun) displayed the sort of magnanimity that avoids making enemies. Jiang's close aide, Zeng Qinghong, was made an alternate member of the PB and continued to run the General Office and the Central Work Committee. He also joined the powerful Secretariat. Considering that Zeng had not been a member of the Central Committee five years earlier, this was a significant jump.

Jiang supporters Zhang Wannian and Chi Haotian became vice chairs of the CMC, and CMC leaders of the future, Guo Boxiong and Xu Caihou, joined the CMC. From not having any military experience when he became general secretary, Jiang had secured the support of the PLA. Indeed, the PLA had become his power base.[24]

Many analysts have regarded the Jiang Zemin period as one in which politics was institutionalized, or at least moving in the direction of institutionalization. It is certainly true that Jiang could not rule as a strongman. To the extent that "institutionalization" conveys a sense that a person exercises the powers of a given position and that institutional arrangements constrain those powers, that was certainly not true. As we have noted, Jiang had to share power with Li Peng at the beginning of his term; had to rely on Deng Xiaoping and Liu Huaqing to begin to gain control over the military; needed Bo Yibo's help to push Qiao Shi aside; was lucky that the party elders had died, shifting the balance of power and necessitating the Fourth Plenum to confirm Jiang's "core" status; and finally used that core status to oust (carefully) Chen Xitong. In other words, Jiang's power increased over time not so much because of institutionalization but because careful maneuvering and important support shored up his power until one could say that his position was "consolidated."

Part of this consolidation of power did involve the division of labor as different members of the PBSC focused on different portfolios and

---

[24] You Ji, "Jiang Zemin: In Quest of Post-Deng Supremacy."

collective decision making. But one should not mistake this for institutionalization. Had opponents been able to coalesce, as under different circumstances they might have, Jiang's power might well have proven ephemeral. Collective decision making was as much a product of Jiang's innate caution and personality as it was a reflection of institutionalization.

There were, however, times when Jiang seemed to move toward institutionalization. Jiang did not have the revolutionary legitimacy that Deng and his generation had and he could never achieve the strongman status that Deng had. There are good reasons for reaching toward institutionalization. Revising CCP ideology could perhaps provide the party with new legitimacy. That is what Jiang attempted to do in advancing his doctrine of the "Three Represents" – that the party represents the advanced productive forces, the advanced cultural forces, and the interests of the broad mass of the Chinese people. Jiang did this because the party, in a fit of conservative pique following the Tiananmen events, prohibited "capitalists" from joining the party.[25] That measure put the party in a bind because "capitalists," however defined, were essential to the economy and to China's future. As Li Junru, vice president of the Central Party School and close adviser to Jiang Zemin put it, "One lesson of political parties that have lost their ruling positions in the late twentieth and early twenty-first centuries is that they have lost the support of youthful entrepreneurs and young intellectuals." In other words, excluding the most dynamic sectors of Chinese society from the party could only lead to the collapse of the party.[26] The CCP had to find a way to bring in this segment of society. The Third Plenum that had inaugurated reform in 1978 had dramatically downgraded class struggle; now, Jiang was explicating allowing entrepreneurs into the party. This was a tacit admission that revolutionary legitimacy was all but gone.

This jettisoning of class struggle was paralleled by the notion that the party was transitioning from a "revolutionary party" (*gemingdang*) to a "ruling party" (*zhizhengdang*), and presumably a ruling party would operate differently than a revolutionary party. The answer seemed to come at the Fifteenth Party Congress when Jiang talked about "rule of

---

[25] Of course, many capitalists had already joined the party. See Bruce Dickson, *Red Capitalists in China: The Party, Private Entrepreneurs, and Prospects for Political Change* (Cambridge: Cambridge University Press, 2003).

[26] Li Junru, "Zhengque lijie he jianchi dangde jiejixing" (Correctly Understand and Uphold the Party's Class Nature), *Lilun dongtai*, July 20, 2001, p. 3.

law" (*fazhi*) and "democracy," a term he used thirty-two times in his report. With Qiao Shi out of the way, Jiang felt free to adopt his emphasis on law. Indeed, Jiang talked in terms of "rule of law" instead of the usual "rule by law." Unfortunately the term for "rule of law" is pronounced the same as the term for "rule by law" (*fazhi*) but the characters are different, so the different meanings were clear to the Chinese reader. The former term implies that the party itself would be subject to the law, whereas the latter term implies the party would use law to control others.

The other area that might have led to institutionalization, but did not, was Jiang's effort to expand "intra-party democracy." Under the lead of Zeng Qinghong, starting in 1998 the CCP began experimenting with intra-party elections at the township level. The purpose was not to democratize China or the CCP but rather to deal with local party organizations, which had become increasingly autonomous of central party control. The intent was to deal with complaints about the fairness of promotions, to deal with bloated party organizations, and to break up local networks in a way that would enhance Beijing's control.

These very limited experiments clearly revealed the tensions between institutionalization and Leninist order. To the extent that these township elections depended on specific rules and procedures, one can argue that they embodied the rudiments of institutionalization (even though they were carried out under strict party supervision). But they aroused the concern of the Organization Department (despite the fact that it was running the experiments) because such elections went against the fundamental principle that the party controls the cadres (*dangguan ganbu*) – that higher-level party organizations appoint the cadres at the lower level. Thus, these experiments ceased after Zeng Qinghong was moved out of the Organization Department in 2002.[27]

Conclusion

Jiang Zemin will always be known as the "accidental general secretary." He had not been groomed as a future leader, and he had no visible faction supporting him prior to taking office. He had no military experience, and the Yang brothers were not fans. Given the tensions in the leadership in the wake of Tiananmen, Jiang had to tread carefully. He had the support

---

[27] Joseph Fewsmith, *The Logic and Limits of Political Reform in China* (New York: Cambridge University Press, 2013).

of Chen Yun and Li Xiannian, but Deng was not a firm supporter and seriously considered replacing him in 1991. But once Deng asserted himself, going on his "Southern Tour," and the military came out in support of Deng, Jiang swung into line, strongly supporting Deng and reform. By the time the Fourteen Party Congress came around in the fall, Jiang was in a better, though by no means secure, position. Finally in 1994, as Deng lay ill, the Fourth Plenum strongly endorsed Jiang. Jiang's position may have been secure, but he was hardly a dominant leader.

It was too much to expect that institutions could significantly constrain power, given the history of the CCP and Chinese history in general. Although Jiang's rise had initially been backed by Chen Yun and Li Xiannian, it was Deng who provided the essential boost that allowed Jiang to secure power. Revealing once again how important control of the military was for the maintenance of political power, Deng ousted the Yang brothers, and purged their followers, following the 1992 Fourteenth Party Congress. In their place, he installed seventy-eight-year-old Zhang Zhen and seventy-six-year-old Liu Huaqing. Neither had political ambitions of his own and both seemed willing to mentor Jiang as he began to build up support in the military.

With the arrest of Chen Xitong, the ouster of Qiao Shi, and the promotion of Zhang Wannian and Chi Haotian, Jiang finally had a chance to secure his own authority.

Even the passing of Li Xiannian, Hu Qiaomu, and Chen Yun benefited Jiang because there were no longer party elders to balance against the PBSC. Jiang was no longer *primus inter pares*; he was *yibashou* (number one).

We do not know what was on Jiang's mind, but his actions suggest that he understood (or learned) that in order to survive he needed to triumph. If in the beginning of his era, the system could be characterized as a "Jiang–Li system" (*Jiang–Li tizhi*), then by 1995 it was clearly a Jiang system. Jiang continued to rule by consensus, but his voice had become firmer and more certain. Like any other ruler with such power, he sought to extend his influence into the Hu Jintao period, even though he could not stop Hu's accession.

3 | Hu Jintao and the Limits of Institutionalization

In many ways, the Hu Jintao era (2002–2012) has been taken as the *sine qua non* of the institutionalization of elite politics in China. It is not unimportant that this was the first time in the history of the CCP that power – or at least the highest formal position in the political system – was transferred peacefully. But even that seeming breakthrough should raise questions in the observer's mind. Political systems tend to evolve only slowly; the underlying "rules of the game" usually reflect great inertia.

Before looking at why the Hu Jintao era did not mark a transition to institutionalization, it is only right to recognize that the political system was evolving and that there were pressures in the direction of institution-alization. First and foremost, the retirement system, introduced in 1980, had become increasingly effective. There were occasional exceptions, but provincial- and ministerial-level officials were almost always held to a retirement age of sixty-five. And rarely was an official appointed to such a position when over the age of sixty-three. Over time, the retirement system was extended upward, even if for some very uninstitutionalized reasons. As we have seen, Jiang Zemin extended the retirement system to the PB in 1997 when he demanded the resignation of all PB members aged seventy or older, even though Jiang himself was seventy-one at the time. The purpose was clearly to oust Qiao Shi, a political rival. Five years later, at the Sixteenth Party Congress in 2002, Jiang called for the age limit be lowered to sixty-eight. This revision of the retirement rule forced the retirement of Li Ruihuan, former Tianjin party secretary and later head of the CPPCC. Jiang was ridding himself of another rival while opening up a seat for one of his supporters.

Despite the obvious political machinations apparent in the adoption of this retirement age, it has stuck, at least up until the present. At the moment, signs suggest that Xi Jinping will serve a third term as general secretary when the Twentieth Party Congress convenes in 2022. Born in 1953, Xi will be sixty-nine in 2022 and thus will violate this norm if he serves a third term.

A corollary of this retirement rule is that once an official becomes a full or alternate member of the Central Committee, he or she is almost never asked to retire before reaching the retirement age. A review of the biographies of officials suggests several people whose careers became untracked either because they proved less competent than initially thought or because a patron had been lost but he nevertheless stayed on the Central Committee. Such people were often shunted to lesser positions but they were not asked to retire. The party has often declared that cadres must be allowed to be promoted or demoted according to their abilities, but in practice instances of demotion, such as losing a position on the Central Committee, are few and far between. This unwritten rule has generally been adhered to, though, as we shall see, Xi Jinping's campaign against corruption has removed many people before their retirement age.

The implementation of the retirement system and the unwillingness to demote officials provide for stability within the party. Retirement opens up positions for those moving up in the system and the unwillingness to demote officials prevents new leaders from taking revenge against "losers." There are nevertheless exceptions to this practice. When a major official is found guilty of a serious crime, it is likely that some – and sometimes a lot – of his or her followers will be removed from office.

Another norm that has been adhered to is that no one serves more than two terms at a given level. Again, this norm allows for the circulation of elites as higher-level officials either need to be promoted or step down after two terms. It was this norm that brought about Li Tieying's retirement in 2002. As noted in the previous chapter, Li Peng served two terms as premier, but was retained on the PBSC in 1997 by moving him to head the NPC.

One also observes in this period the greater professionalization of the PLA. That is not to say, however, that the PLA had become unimportant in the struggle for power. As we have seen, the PLA became an important basis for Jiang Zemin's power, and, as will be argued below, Hu Jintao's inability to control the PLA accounts, in part, for his political weakness. In more recent years, we have seen Xi Jinping reorganize the PLA high command, confirming that the PLA remains important for political control.

All these trends reflect the end of "strongman politics." With the passing of Mao and Deng, there was no one who could dominate the political system in the same way. Other than "ruthless struggle" and "merciless blows," the only way forward was to develop norms and institutions. But – and it is an important but – personal relations remained an important part of Chinese politics. As we saw in the previous chapter, Jiang was able to increase his political strength by placing his followers in critical positions. Deng's decision dictated that Jiang yield his position as general secretary to Hu Jintao in 2002, but it was obvious that Jiang was reluctant to go. As shown below, Jiang tried to retain influence by placing his protégés in critical positions. So rather than having the harmonious, incremental, and institutionalized passing of power usually presented, what developed was a decade of tension between Hu Jintao trying to assert himself by relying on institutions and his own network of followers, and Jiang Zemin trying to retain influence by relying on personal relations. By the time of the Seventeenth Party Congress, convened in 2007, we see some strengthening in Hu's political position. However, his overall political weakness was reflected in the rapid ouster of his followers after the end of his term. Whatever progress had been made toward institutionalization was not sufficient to constrain the struggle for power.

The Sixteenth Party Congress

The Sixteenth Party Congress, which met in Beijing on November 8–14, 2002, is often regarded as a milestone in the institutionalization of the Chinese political process. Cheng Li, for instance, optimistically thinks that the Sixteenth Party Congress showed that "strongman politics" was giving way to a new politics of power sharing, political compromise, and factional negotiation.[1] Even when Jiang Zemin held onto his position as chairman of the CMC, some took this as a sign of a gradual transfer of power rather than the stifling of Hu Jintao's power, which it really was.

Preparations for the Sixteenth Party Congress, as always, started early. In March 2002, Jiang Zemin presided over separate meetings of the PBSC and the entire PB to make arrangements to set up a special group, directly under the supervision of the PBSC, to take charge of nominating and evaluating candidates for the Central Committee and the CDIC. When

---

[1] Cheng Li and Lynn White, "The Sixteenth Central Committee of the Chinese Communist Party: Hu Gets What?" *Asian Survey*, Vol. 43, No. 4 (August 2003): 553–597; Cheng Li, "The 'New Deal:' Politics and Policy of the Hu Administration," *Journal of Asian and African Studies*, Vol. 38, No. 4–5 (2003): pp. 329–346.

Figure 3.1 Premier Wen Jiabao (l) and General Secretary Hu Jintao (r) in 2012 (Lintao Zhang via Getty Images)

the congress met in November, delegates were given a list of 208 candidates for full membership and another 167 names for alternate membership. In a primary, the delegates whittled down these lists marginally, selecting 198 people for full membership (dropping only ten people – or 4.8 percent) and 158 for alternate membership (eliminating nine people – or 5.3 percent). This margin of elimination was the same as it had been fifteen years earlier when the party first started nominating more candidates than seats (*cha'e xuanju*), so "intra-party democracy" had made little, if any, progress, even though the work report of the congress called intra-party democracy the "lifeblood of the party."[2]

Despite this long and apparently careful process, presumably intended not only to select the best-qualified candidates but also to build consensus, evidence suggests that bargaining was long and difficult. The annual Beidaihe meeting, held in the early part of August, was apparently contentious. According to seasoned observer Ching Cheong, the conference reached a "tacit understanding" that there would be "no changes" in the third-generation leadership, in the party's "core," or in the military leadership. Chen Shui-bian, president of Taiwan, on August 3, just as the Beidaihe conference was convening, issued his provocative call for "one country on each side of the Strait," adding support to the argument that Jiang should stay on as head of the military. But Cheong adds that a show of hands showed that Jiang did not have a clear majority.[3] Later events would show that even though Jiang received support to stay on as head of the CMC, many people, including in the military, were not happy.

On October 22, the Xinhua News Agency reported that Huang Ju, party secretary of Shanghai, and Jia Qinglin, party secretary of Beijing, would be "transferred to the center." As the world would later learn, "to the center" meant that both would enter the PBSC. Apparently this arrangement had not been agreed at Beidaihe, hence the late announcement. Since the party secretaries of Beijing and Shanghai are routinely given PB seats, the transfers of Huang and Jia opened up an additional two seats for Jiang's allies. These seats would be taken by Liu Qi, who moved over from the mayor's office in Beijing to party secretary, and Chen Liangyu, the mayor of Shanghai, who replaced Huang Ju as party secretary. Although Cheng Li reports

---

[2] He Ping and Liu Siyang, "Jianfu qi jiwang kailai de zhuangyan shiming – dangde xinyijie zhongyang weiyuanhui dansheng ji" (Shouldering the Serious Mission of Inheriting from the Past and Opening the Future – An Account of the Birth of the Party's New Central Committee), Xinhua, November 15, 2002, available at http://zqb.cyol.content/2002-11/15/content_564726.htm, accessed September 16, 2020; and Gang Lin, "Leadership Transition, Intra-party Democracy, and Institution Building in China," *Asian Survey*, Vol. 44, No. 2 (March–April 2004): 255–275.

[3] Ching Cheung, "China's New Leadership May Rule under Jiang's Shadow," *Straits Times*, August 22, 2002. It seems the decisive votes in the military were held by vice chairs, Guo Boxiong and Xu Caihou, and they supported Jiang staying on. See Chien-wen Kou, "Xi Jinping in Command: Solving the Principle-Agent Problem in the CCP–PLA Relations?" *China Quarterly*, No. 232 (December 2017): 866–885. The contentious nature of this meeting and Hu Jintao's less than clear mandate may explain why in 2003 he decided not to hold any future conclaves.

that Jiang suffered for this power play, it is not apparent that he did.[4] After all, Jiang emerged from the Congress in a stronger political position than before the congress met.

When the new PBSC was unveiled following the First Plenary Session of the new Sixteenth Central Committee, it was revealed that the new PBSC had been expanded from the usual seven members to nine members, the largest it has been in the reform era. One other surprise at the top of the system was that Zeng Qinghong, Jiang Zemin's loyal lieutenant, had been promoted from alternate member of the PB to member of the PBSC. No other alternate has ever been promoted two levels like this in the reform era, adding credibility to the rumor that Jiang demanded the elevation of Zeng as a condition of his (Jiang's) stepping down. The PBSC is presented in Table 3.1.

Of this group, only Wen Jiabao could be counted as a stalwart supporter of Hu Jintao. Wu Bangguo, Jia Qinglin, Zeng Qinghong, Huang Ju, and Li Changchun can be counted as members of Jiang

Table 3.1 *Sixteenth Central Committee Politburo Standing Committee,* *2002*

Name	Position	Age in 2002	Previous position
Hu Jintao	General secretary	60	Politburo; Vice chairman, CMC
Wu Bangguo	Vice premier; Secretary, Central Enterprise Work Committee	61	Politburo; Central Work Committee of Large Enterprises
Wen Jiabao	Premier	60	Politburo; Secretariat; Vice premier, secretary of Financial Work Committee
Jia Qinglin	Chair, CPPCC	62	Party secretary, Beijing
Zeng Qinghong	President, Central Party School	63	Alternate member, Politburo; Head, General Office

---

[4] Cheng Li, "the 'New Deal'," p. 333.

Table 3.1 (*cont.*)

Name	Position	Age in 2002	Previous position
Huang Ju	Executive vice premier; Head, Financial and Economics Leadership Small Group	64	Party secretary, Shanghai
Wu Guanzheng	Secretary, CDIC	64	Politburo; Party secretary, Shandong
Li Changchun	Chairman, CCP Central Guidance Commission for Spiritual Civilization	58	Politburo; Party secretary, Guangdong
Luo Gan	Politics and Law Commission	67	Politburo; Secretariat; State councilor; Secretary general, State Council; Deputy secretary, Politics and Law Commission

Zemin's network. Wu Guanzheng was not clearly associated with any group, making him acceptable to all groups as secretary of the CDIC. Luo Gan was a protégé of Li Peng. Looked at in this way, the sudden promotion of Jia Qinglin and Huang Ju to the PBSC was critical; it gave Jiang Zemin's group a clear majority.

Looking at the remainder of the PB, one sees that Hu Jintao was only a bit more successful (Table 3.2).

Of these fifteen people, both Wang Lequan and Wang Zhaoguo had careers in the CYL, but both had made their careers independently of Hu Jintao. Liu Qi, Liu Yunshan, Zhang Dejiang, Chen Liangyu, Zhou Yongkang, He Guoqiang, and Guo Boxiong can be counted as allies of Jiang Zemin, despite the fact that Liu Yunshan also emerged from the CYL. Zhang Lichang is closely associated with Li Ruihuan, and Zeng

Table 3.2 *Sixteenth Central Committee Politburo, 2002*

Name	Position	Age (in 2002)	Previous position
Wang Lequan	Party secretary, Xinjiang	58	Party secretary, Xinjiang; political commissar of the Production and Construction Corps
Wang Zhaoguo	All China Federation of Trade Unions (ACFTU); Vice chair, CPPCC	61	Head, United Front Work Department
Hui Liangyu (Hui nationality)	Vice premier	58	Party secretary, Jiangsu
Liu Qi	Party secretary, Beijing	60	Mayor, Beijing
Liu Yunshan	Head, Propaganda Department; Secretariat	55	Deputy secretary, Propaganda Department
Wu Yi (f)	Vice premier; State councilor	64	Alternate member, Politburo; State councilor
Yu Zhengsheng	Party secretary, Hubei	57	Minister of construction
Zhang Lichang	Party secretary, Tianjin	63	Party secretary, Tianjin
Zhang Dejiang	Party secretary, Guangdong	56	Party secretary, Zhejiang
Chen Liangyu	Party secretary, Shanghai	56	Deputy secretary, Shanghai
Zhou Yongkang	Secretariat; State councilor; Minister, Public Security	60	Minister, Land and Natural Resources; Party secretary, Sichuan
He Guoqiang	Secretariat; Head, Organization Department	59	Governor, Fujian; Party secretary, Chongqing
Guo Boxiong	Vice chairman, CMC	60	Commander, Lanzhou Military Region

Table 3.2 (*cont.*)

Name	Position	Age (in 2002)	Previous position
Zeng Peiyan	Vice premier; Chair, Development and Planning Commission	64	Deputy chairman, Development and Planning Commission
Alternate			
Wang Gang	Secretariat; Head, General Office (since 1999)	60	Deputy head, General Office (1994–1999)

Peiyan was a technocrat. As a veteran of the oil industry, Wu Yi's closest relationship was probably Zeng Qinghong. Yu Zhengsheng is a princeling and could no doubt work with Zeng Qinghong, also a princeling, as well as with Jiang Zemin. Wang Gang was the only member of the Sixteenth Central Committee PB who had not been a full member of the Fifteenth Central Committee, normally a prerequisite for membership on the PB. Wang Gang's appointment is interesting because previously he had served as Zeng Qinghong's deputy in the General Office and, after the Sixteenth Party Congress, he succeeded Zeng as head of the General Office. He also joined Zeng as a member of the Secretariat. Together they were only two of Jiang's allies on the Secretariat; others included Liu Yunshan, Zhou Yongkang, He Guoqiang, and Xu Caihou.

At the Sixteenth Party Congress, Zhang Wannian (aged seventy-four) and Chi Haotian (aged seventy-three), vice chairmen of the CMC, finally retired. At the same time, five other members of the CMC retired, leaving only Cao Gangchuan (aged sixty-seven), Guo Boxiong (aged fifty-five), and Xu Caihou (aged fifty-four) as the only military officers retained on the CMC. Cao remained a vice chairman, while Guo was promptly promoted to vice chairman of the CMC (along with Hu Jintao). Xu was promoted to the Secretariat and named head of the General Political Department (GPD). Both were named to the PB, replacing Zhang Wannian and Chi Haotian. Liang Guanglie, Liao Xilong, and Li Jinai were added to the CMC, as the size of the CMC fell from eleven to eight. Li Jinai had been deputy head of the GPD when Xu Caihou was assistant to Yu Yongbo (Xu's mentor), who was head of the GPD. Liao Xilong has no known connection to either Xu Caihou or Guo Boxiong (or Jiang Zemin), but he took over as head of the General Logistics Department. Liang Guanglie also had no known relationship with Guo Boxiong or Xu Caihou (but he did have a relationship with Song Ping and possibly Bo Xilai).

Altogether the Sixteenth Central Committee was composed of 198 full members. Of these, eighty-eight were retained from the Fifteenth Central Committee. That number includes the twenty-nine who were party or state leaders (PB, Secretariat, or CMC). Of the remaining fifty-nine people, very few had obvious CYL ties. Hu Jintao's most obvious ally was Li Keqiang, then still a provincial party secretary (in Henan). Also on the Central Committee were people like Zhou Qiang, then first secretary of the CYL, and Chen Kuiyuan, who had served with Hu in Tibet and was appointed to head the CASS in 2002.

There were sixty-five full members of the Central Committee who were promoted directly (without first having served as alternate members of the Central Committee), twenty-one of whom were in the military, reflecting the ongoing effort to promote younger and better-educated officers. One might suspect an effort to plant supporters in the military, but fourteen of these twenty-one would retire five years later at the Seventeenth Party Congress, so any such effort would have been minimal. Similarly, twenty-four members of the State Council were appointed directly to the Central Committee, but thirteen retired at the Seventeenth Party Congress.

Perhaps most telling, if we look at critical positions – Propaganda, Organization Department, the CDIC, the Political and Legal Commission, State Security, Public Security, the Work Office for Offices Directly under the Central Commission (*zhongyang zhishu jiguan gongwei*) – these were all in the hands of Jiang supporters. Most important, Jiang Zemin decided to stay on as chairman of the CMC. He did step down as general secretary – and that is important – but one of his conditions was that he be able to appoint Guo Boxiong and Xu Caihou to be vice chairmen of the CMC. And this move reduced Hu Jintao "to a mere figurehead."[5] When Hu Jintao ordered

---

[5] Chien-wen Kou, "Xi Jinping in Command," p. 869. See also Ye Bing, "Xu Caihou shangjiang luoma (1): yi she quandou ji bozhuo mimou (The Fall of

the PLA to investigate and deal with the disastrous Wenchuan earthquake in 2008, it took the military eight hours to respond. In addition, the PB reportedly decided to refer important decisions to Jiang Zemin, especially on important personnel decisions.[6] Jiang was still "core."

So it can be concluded that Hu Jintao, although he gained the title of "general secretary," emerged from the congress in a weak political position.

The Impact of Institutionalization

It is easy to see that the Sixteenth Party Congress did not, in and of itself, pass power on to Hu Jintao. Jiang Zemin continued to hold many of the keys to power, including retaining the chairmanship of the CMC. There may well have been a sense that the transfer of power should take place in phases, as many observers have argued, but it is also clear that there were frictions between Jiang and Hu. Jiang did not give up his influence easily. So what tools were available for Hu to enhance his control?

One has to start with a negative. Despite Jiang's impressive show of force, he was not a universally liked figure in the party. As Cheng Li points out, Jiang's bodyguard, You Xigui, received the fewest number of votes of anyone named as an alternate member of the Central Committee. Similarly, Jiang's former personal secretary and then party secretary of Shenzhen, Huang Liman, received the third-fewest votes. Chen Zhili, a close ally and former deputy secretary of Shanghai, failed to make the PB, and Xiong Guangkai, head of the PLA's Second Division in charge of intelligence and reputedly close to Jiang, did not even make the Central Committee as an alternate.[7]

Moreover, as pointed out above, the role of the military in domestic politics had been reduced. It was still a powerful institution, but its scope of power and influence was more restricted. As Kiselycznyk and

---

General Xu Caihou (1): The Probable Involvement in Power Struggles and the Bo and Zhou Plot), *Voice of America*, August 11, 2015, retrieved from www .voachinese.com/content/top-general-investigated-20140701/1948242.html.

[6] Guo Xuezhi, *The Politics of the Core Leader in China: Culture, Institution, Legitimacy, and Power* (Cambridge: Cambridge University Press, 2019), pp. 64, 306.

[7] Li, "The 'New Deal'."

Saunders put it, there was a growing bifurcation between the civilian side of the party and the military.[8] Guo Boxiong and Cao Gangchuan (later Xu Caihou) may have been loyal to Jiang Zemin, but they were not about to challenge the civilian leadership.

On the positive side, Hu Jintao was general secretary. Whatever desire Jiang might have had to change the succession arrangements made by Deng, he did not or could not effect such a change. Institutions may not, in and of themselves, be strong enough to allow a general secretary to exert power, but they do confer a degree of strength. One of the powers of a general secretary is the right to set the "party line," and one of the requirements for any new general secretary is to define a new party line that is both distinct from that of his predecessor but also consistent with the previous line. So one of the first things Hu Jintao did was to shift the emphasis in Jiang's "Three Represents" (the party represents advanced productive forces, advanced culture, and the fundamental interests of the vast majority of the Chinese people) from the first principle that the party represents advanced productive forces to the third principle that of the fundamental interests of the vast majority of the Chinese people. Doing so allowed Hu to present himself as more of a "man of the people." This more populist approach was endorsed by the Second Plenary Session of the Sixteenth Central Committee, which declared that it was necessary to "take people as the basis (*yiren weiben*); establish a concept of comprehensive, co-ordinated, sustainable development; and promote comprehensive economic, social, and human development."[9] Hu's shift reflected the increasing sense that tensions in the countryside were presenting a growing threat to social order – by 2002, there were some 50,000 mass incidents throughout the country. This notion became the basis for formulating Hu's chief ideological innovation, the "scientific development concept."[10] Of course, the notion that one should follow

---

[8] Michael Kiselycznyk and Phillip C. Saunders, "Civil–Military Relations in China: Assessing the PLA's Role in Elite Politics," *INSS China Strategic Perspectives*, No. 2 (August 2010): 5–8.

[9] "Zhongguo gongchandang dishiliujie zhongyang weiyuanhui disanci quanti huiyi gongbao" (Communiqué of the Third Plenary Session of the Sixteenth Central Committee of the Chinese Communist Party), Xinhua News Agency, October 14, 2003, available at http://cpc.people.com.cn/GB/64162/64168/64569/index.html, accessed October 22, 2020.

[10] Joseph Fewsmith, "Promoting the Scientific Development Concept," *China Leadership Monitor*, No. 11 (Summer 2004), available at www.hoover.org/resea rch/promoting-scientific-development-concept, accessed September 16, 2020.

"scientific development" suggested that one's predecessor had not done so.

What the scientific development concept meant in practice was a readjustment to budgetary priorities as the central government funneled more resources to the inland areas. In his first government work report, Premier Wen Jiabao told the NPC that agriculture was the most important problem (*zhongzhong zhi zhong*) and promised to increase investment, reduce taxes, and increase subsidies to agriculture. At the same time, the Hu–Wen administration increased investment in the West and the Northeast, trying to stimulate growth in regions that had clearly fallen behind. These priorities marked an important shift from Jiang Zemin's emphasis on the east coast and his single-minded focus on economic growth. Some started calling Hu's approach a "new deal."

But there was nothing liberal about this Chinese version of the new deal. At the same time as Beijing was adopting policies intended to address the growing inequalities in Chinese society, it took steps to tighten control over ideology – steps that would carry over into the Xi Jinping administration. Shaken by the "color revolutions" in Georgia in 2003, Ukraine in 2004, and Kyrgyzstan in 2005, China became visibly more fearful of "peaceful evolution." In the summer of 2003, even before these events, the center approved the establishment of a Study Group on Neoliberalism at CASS. This group worked to show that liberalism did not work in general and was inappropriate for China in particular. Within three months the group started producing reports to send to the center.

Jiang's Resignation from CMC

Although Jiang's retention of his CMC post seems to have had the support of the military leadership in 2002, there were obvious tensions between Jiang and Hu. Jiang's high profile in the months following the Sixteenth Party Congress must have rankled the new party head. For instance, when the NPC met in March 2003, *People's Daily* ran a picture of Jiang leading the leadership into the meeting. Jiang was perhaps four or five steps in front of Hu Jintao. Of course, Jiang was still president at the beginning of the meeting, but no such explanation is available for why a month later in April, Jiang was at the center of a photograph of the party leadership planting trees.

There were also clear disagreements over the handling of SARS, which broke out in spring 2003. Hu Jintao was obviously more supportive of handling the epidemic openly whereas Jiang quietly supported subtle efforts by the military to keep it quiet.

Furthermore, in 2003, the PLA budget increase was held under 10 percent for the first time since 1989, provoking serious complaints from the PLA. It was in this context that the issue of the "two centers": came to the fore.

On March 11, 2003, the day after Jiang Zemin had given a major speech at the NPC meeting, *Liberation Army Daily* carried a most curious article. Written by Wang Wenjie, deputy director for reporting, the article suggested difficulties at the policy-making level. "Should the military try to avoid or confront 'bottleneck problems' that produce constraining effects on our military's organizational structure, functioning mechanisms, and policy systems?" the article asked. The article then goes on to record the complaints of two military delegates attending the NPC meeting. They complained, "Having one center is called 'loyalty,' while having two centers will result in 'troubles.'" This was a clever wordplay on two Chinese characters that are made up of the character for "center" and the character for "heart." When the character for heart is placed under the character for center, it means "loyalty," but when the character for heart is placed under two "centers" stacked on top of each other, it means "trouble" or "disaster." [11] As military analyst James Mulvenon notes, this article appeared to be a thinly veiled attack on the divided leadership over the military in which Hu Jintao was "general secretary of the party and state president nonetheless subordinate to Jiang (who is not even a member of the Central Commission)." [12]

The article continued:

---

[11] "Jundui renda daibiao xuexi Jiang Zemin zhuxi zai jundui daibiaotuan zhongyao jianghua zongshu (A Free Discussion of Military Delegates to the NPC Studying Jiang Zemin's Important Talk to the Military Delegation), accessed from http://mil.news.sina.com.cn/2003-03-11/111304.html, October 22, 2020.

[12] James Mulvenon, "Reduced Budgets, the 'Two Centers,' and Other Mysteries of the 2003 National People's Congress," *China Leadership Monitor*, No. 7 (Summer 2003), www.hoover.org/research/reduced-budgets-two-centers-and-other-mysteries-2003-national-peoples-congress, accessed January 15, 2021.

"Leading cadres are organizers of efforts to implement the 'Three Represents,' and should personally practice the 'The Represents.' Leading cadres now should firmly remember the 'two musts' [humility and prudence[13]], and work hard to do a good job of serving as the 'five models.'[14] It is necessary to dare to take the lead, to reach the level of ideological advancement characterized by not being vainglorious .... "[15]

This complaint suggested real pressure from within the military for Jiang to follow Deng's example and retire after two years. Jiang took the hint and finally retired at the Fourth Plenum in 2004.[16] Jiang's retirement, however, did not mean that Hu Jintao had firm control of the military; after all, Guo Boxiong and Xu Caihou were still vice chairmen of the CMC.

Pushback

There were two points at which one can see a real pushback against Hu Jintao's populist agenda. The first came in the midst of an acrimonious debate over marketization. It was a debate that reflected the degree to which "New Left" forces had gained strength. In summer of 2005, a virulent debate opened up about a draft of the property rights law that was to be considered by the NPC at its annual meeting in the following March. On August 12, Peking University law professor Gong Xiantian fired off a venomous letter accusing the draft law of being a violation of the constitution. The draft law, Gong wrote, did not affirm that "socialist public property is sacred and inviolable" and thus acted to

---

[13] The "two musts" were first raised by Mao Zedong at the Second Plenary Session of the Seventh Central Committee in March 1949, held in Xibaipo, as the Communist Party prepared to enter Beijing. In 2002, just after the Sixteenth Party Congress, Hu Jintao led the PBSC to Xibaipo and reminded people of Mao's "two musts."

[14] The "five models" are (1) be a model of hard study, (2) be a model of party discipline and state law, (3) be a model seeking truth and practicality, (4) be a model of diligent government for the people, and (5) be a model of keeping up with the times.

[15] "Jundui renda daibiao xuexi Jiang Zemin zhuxi zai jundui daibiaotuan zhongyao jianghua zongshu (A Free Discussion of Military Delegates to the NPC Studying Jiang Zemin's Important Talk to the Military Delegation), accessed from http://mil.news.sina.com.cn/2003-03-11/111304.html, October 22, 2020.

[16] James Mulvenon, "Reduced Budgets, the 'Two Centers,' and Other Mysteries of the 2003 National People's Congress."

protect private property, not socialism. Gong accused those who wanted to reform the state-owned economy by selling off SOEs of "pursuing the capitalist road" and of being "under the influence of Western liberal economic studies and the 'Washington Consensus'." He asked rhetorically, "Is not privatization the greatest cause of the current social instability in China?" Gong declared that the "masses" were saying that the "Communist Party" had become a "private-property party."[17]

Gong's letter set off a heated debate. "Nonmainstream" economists – those supportive of greater state ownership – came out in support of Gong, while "mainstream" – more market-oriented – economists fired back. In November, the influential financial journal *Caijing* carried an article by senior market-oriented economists Wu Jinglian, Gao Shangquan, and others pointing out that the populist effort to level the social system would have dire consequences for the economy and society.[18] As the reform-minded *Nanfang zhuomo* (Southern Weekend) pointed out:

The key difference in understanding in the argument is that one side holds that the problems are caused by the marketizing reforms, and so it is necessary to turn back in an all-round fashion; while the other side holds that problems are caused by the fact that the reforms are not thorough and are incomplete. Hence it is necessary to speed up promotion of the reforms, and there can be no wavering over the direction.[19]

Given the virulent disagreements among social activists, Hu Jintao backed off. At the March 2006 NPC meeting, which decided to postpone consideration of the property rights law, Hu Jintao embraced the "mainstream" position by saying, "We should unswervingly adhere to the reform orientation, further strengthen our determination and

[17] Gong Xintian, "Yibu weibei xianfa he beili shehui zhuyi jiben yuanze de 'wuquanfa' (cao'an)," (The Property Law (Draft) Violates the Constitution and Violates the Basic Principles of Socialism), available at www.boxun.com/news/gb/pubvp/2005/08/200508201243.shtml, accessed September 16, 2020.

[18] Wu Jinglian, "Xiang furen kaiqiang hui daozhi hen yanzhong de shehui houguo" (Opening Fire on the Wealthy Will Bring about Dire Social Consequences), March 12, 2009, available at www.taoke.com/article/8278.htm, accessed September 16, 2020.

[19] Li Liang and Xu Toghui, "2004–2006 'disanci gaige lunzheng' shimo" (The Whole Story of the 2004–2006 "Third Argument against Reforms") *Nanfang zhoumo*, March 16, 2006, available at http://news.sina.com.cn/c/2006-03-16/10 379365018.shtml, accessed September 16, 2020. These three paragraphs in the text have been borrowed, with some modification, from my *China since Tiananmen: From Deng Xiaoping to Hu Jintao*, 2nd ed. (Cambridge: Cambridge University Press, 2008), pp. 265–266.

confidence in the reforms, repeatedly perfect the socialist market economy structure, and fully exercise the basic role of the market in the allocation of resources."[20] Similarly, Wen Jiabao told reporters, "we should unswervingly push forward the reform and opening up … Although in our way ahead there will be difficulties, we cannot stop; retrogression offers no way out."[21]

Clearly Hu and Wen had backed off from the populism that their "new deal" rhetoric had set off.

The second point at which Hu suffered a setback came with an apparent victory, namely his purge of Shanghai party secretary Chen Liangyu. The purge of Chen was really about two issues. On the one hand, Chen repeatedly resisted orders from Beijing to restrain investment in line with Hu Jintao's efforts to invest more in the hinterland to address regional inequalities. At one point, Chen argued strongly against Wen Jiabao's macroeconomic control policies, saying that they would hamper the country's growth, especially the real-estate market. Chen apparently told the premier that he should take "political responsibility" for the negative impact of these policies.[22]

The other issue was plain old factional politics. Chen was a stalwart member of the so-called Shanghai Gang. Purging him, it seemed, would strengthen Hu, just as Jiang's purge of Chen Xitong in 1995 had helped solidify Jiang's position. When Chen Liangyu fell in September 2006, everyone, including the current author, believed that Hu had scored a major victory over Jiang and the Shanghai Gang. The expectation was that the purge of Chen would allow Hu to move up one of his

[20] "Hu Jintao, Wu Bangguo, Wen Jiabao, Jia Qinglin, Wu Guanzheng, Li Changchun, Luo Gan fenbie canjia shenyi he taolun" (Hu Jintao, Wu Bangguo, Wen Jiabao, Jia Qinglin, Wu Guanzheng, Li Changchun, Luo Gan Participate in Examination and Discussion), March 8, 2006, available at www.china-embassy.or.jp/chn/zgxw/t239160.htm, accessed September 15, 2020.

[21] "Wen Jiabao zongli da zhongwai jizhe wen" (Premier Wen Jiabao Answers the Questions of Chinese and Foreign Reporters), *Renmin ribao*, March 14, 2006, retrieved from www.gov.cn/2007lh/content_520478.htm, accessed October 22, 2020.

[22] Cheng Li, "Was the Shanghai Gang Shanghaied? The Fall of Chen Liangyu and the Survival of Jiang Zemin's Faction," *China Leadership Monitor*, No. 20 (Winter 2007), available at www.hoover.org/research/was-shanghai-gang-shanghaied-fall-chen-liangyu-and-survival-jiang-zemins-faction, accessed September 16, 2020.

followers at the Seventeenth Party Congress that was due to take place the following year.[23] However, things did not work out as expected.

The Seventeenth Party Congress

The Seventeenth Party Congress met in Beijing on October 15–21, 2007. This meeting marked the beginning of Hu Jintao's second and final term as general secretary, so it was his final opportunity to put in place some of his followers and to extend his influence into the future, much as Jiang Zemin had done beforehand. But Hu's ability to do so was constrained by the age distribution of those in critical positions. As noted above, the Chinese system rarely forces leaders to retire before their mandated retirement age. On balance, this informal norm has benefited stability in elite politics by limiting purges, but it has also prevented new leaders from putting their own followers into strategic positions. So part of the game of politics has been to promote people who are young enough to stay in position long after the leader has retired. And Jiang had played this game extremely well.

When we look at the PB as a whole, we see surprising continuity between the leadership that emerged from the Sixteenth Party Congress and that coming out of the Seventeenth Party Congress. At the PBSC level, Jiang Zemin lost two strong supporters: Huang Ju, who died in June 2007, and Zeng Qinghong, who was forced to retire for reasons of age. In addition, Wu Guanzheng and Luo Gan also retired. Xi Jinping and Li Keqiang took two of the empty seats as heirs apparent (they would take up their roles as general secretary and premier, respectively, at the Eighteenth Party Congress in 2012). But Jiang's close protégé Zhou Yongkang jumped from the position of minister of public security and full member of the Central Committee to the PBSC and took over as head of the powerful Political and Legal Affairs Commission. Similarly, He Guoqiang moved from being head of the Organization Department (which was taken over by Hu Jintao's close ally Li Yuanchao) to head of the CDIC. So despite significant losses, Jiang still had five supporters on the PBSC.

Jiang suffered significant losses on the Secretariat as Zeng Qinghong, He Guoqiang, Wang Gang, and Xu Caihou all stepped down. The departure of Xu Caihou from the Secretariat marked the last time

---

[23] Tony Saich, "China in 2006: Focus on Social Development," *Asian* Survey, Vol. 47, No. 1 (January–February 2007): p. 37.

Table 3.3 *Seventeenth Central Committee Politburo Standing Committee,*
2007–2012

Name	Position	Age in 2007	Previous position
Hu Jintao	General secretary	65	General secretary
Wu Bangguo	Head, NPC	66	Head, NPC
Wen Jiabao	Premier	65	Premier
Jia Qinglin	Head, CPPCC	67	Head, CPPCC
Li Changchun	Chairman, Central Guidance Commission for Building Spiritual Civilization	63	Chairman, Central Guidance Commission for Building Spiritual Civilization
Xi Jinping	President, Central Party School	54	Party secretary, Shanghai
Li Keqiang	Executive vice premier	52	Party secretary, Liaoning
He Guoqiang	CDIC	64	Head, Organization Department; Secretariat
Zhou Yongkang	Political and Legal Affairs Commission	65	Minister of Public Security; Secretariat

(until now) that a member of the military has served on the Secretariat, suggesting that the military would have a narrower, more focused mission as defender of Chinese sovereignty. This was not unambiguously good, as we have noted before, because it marked a further bifurcation between the party and the military.[24]

These Jiang supporters were replaced by Xi Jinping, Li Yuanchao, Ling Jihua, and Wang Huning. Wang Huning had been brought to Beijing by Jiang Zemin, but he stayed on, loyally serving Hu Jintao (and has now been promoted to the PBSC by Xi Jinping). This configuration

---

[24] Li Cheng and Scott W. Harold, "China's New Military Elite," *China Security*, Vol. 3, No. 4 (Autumn 2007): p. 65.

Table 3.4 *Full members of the Politburo, 2007–2012*

Name	Position	Age in 2007	Previous position
Wang Gang	Vice chair, CPPCC	65	Alternate member, Politburo; Secretariat
Wang Lequan	Party secretary, Xinjiang (until 2010)	63	Party secretary, Xinjiang (since 2002)
Wang Zhaoguo	Vice chair, NPC; Head, ACFTU	66	Vice chair, NPC; Head, ACFTU
Wang Qishan	Vice premier	59	Mayor, Beijing
Hui Liangyu (Hui nationality)	Vice premier	63	Vice premier
Liu Qi	Party secretary, Beijing	65	Party secretary, Beijing
Liu Yunshan	Head, Propaganda Department	60	Head, Propaganda Department
Liu Yandong (f)	State councilor	62	Vice chair, CPPCC
Li Yuanchao	Head, Organization Department; Secretariat	57	Party secretary, Jiangsu
Wang Yang	Party secretary, Guangdong	52	Party secretary, Chongqing
Zhang Gaoli	Party secretary, Tianjin	61	Party secretary, Shandong
Zhang Dejiang	Vice premier	61	Politburo; Party secretary, Guangdong
Yu Zhengsheng	Party secretary, Shanghai	62	Politburo; Party secretary, Hubei
Xu Caihou	Vice chair, CMC	64	Politburo; PLA, GPD; Secretariat
Guo Boxiong	Vice chair, CMC	65	Politburo; Vice chair, CMC
Bo Xilai	Party secretary, Chongqing	58	Politburo; Minister of commerce

suggests that during his second term Hu Jintao had a more supportive Secretariat than he did during his first term.

A comparison of the full members (those not on the Standing Committee) of the Sixteenth and Seventeenth PBs shows remarkable continuity. Of course, Chen Liangyu had been purged, but only Wu Yi and Zeng Peiyan were forced to retire for reason of age (both were sixty-nine). The new PB dropped the position of alternate member but added two seats to the full membership. Wang Gang, previously an alternate member of the PB, was promoted to full status, but he was removed from the Secretariat and made a vice chair of the CPPCC – a powerless position. Wang Qishan, a close friend of Xi Jinping, was added to the PB, as were Liu Yandong, a prominent "princeling" as well as a CYL leader, and Bo Xilai, son of party elder Bo Yibo and rival to Xi Jinping – a rivalry that would explode within several years.

When one looks at the CMC, the main difference is first that Cao Gangchuan, a relatively apolitical expert on armaments, had to retire from his position as vice chairman, leaving Guo Boxiong and Xu Caihou as the two vice chairmen. A structural change was made as the heads of the two other general departments and the commanders of the navy and air force were brought onto the CMC: Chen Bingde (chief of the general staff), Chang Wanquan (director of the General Armaments Department), Wu Shengli (commander of the navy), and Xu Qiliang (commander of the air force). In general, this change seemed to accord with the further professionalization of the military as well as with the belated effort to give the navy and air force greater weight in an organization long dominated by the army.

This structural change may well have been an effort to dilute Jiang's supporters in the military, but the two vice chairs remained Jiang loyalists, and Xu Qiliang was reportedly close to Jiang.[25] The broader turnover of military representation on the Central Committee may well have been intended to reduce Jiang's influence, but the more important factor appears to have been the professionalization of the military as people with better education and technical training were promoted. Moreover, anyone being promoted to a critical position would have had to have the approval of Guo Boxiong and/or Xu Caihou. Given later revelations of corruption, they may also have had to pay for their promotions.

[25] Ibid., p. 70.

Figure 3.2 Ling Jihua, former head of the General Office and secretary of the Secretariat (Lintao Zhang via Getty Images)

It must be said that Hu Jintao played the age game well. One of the advantages of the CYL is that careers advance more quickly than in the regular party bureaucracy, so at the Seventeenth Party Congress Hu was able to appoint a number of young officials who would go on to serve on the Eighteenth Central Committee. Altogether there were twenty-nine people with CYL affiliations named to the Seventeenth Central Committee (15 percent); twenty-two of them would be retained on the Eighteenth Central Committee. One should not assume that all people with CYL affiliations were necessarily Hu loyalists (Liu Yunshan seemed to work well with Jiang Zemin), and there were also people that Hu had met in Tibet who were part of his network (e.g. Guo Jinlong and Hu Chunhua), but if we use CYL affiliation as a rough indicator of Hu's political strength, we are probably not too far off. Some of these people were in important positions. Apart from Li Keqiang being premier-in-waiting, there also were Li Yuanchao, head of the Organization Department; Shen Yueyue, deputy head of the Organization Department; and Ling Jihua, head of the General Office. But there also were quite a few who were provincial party secretaries and governors. Whether this group of supporters could move into more important positions and display their influence at the Eighteenth Party Congress remained to be seen.

Conclusion

Over the course of the decade in which Hu served as general secretary he was able to make doctrinal changes, begin to deal with the growing regional divides by channeling more money into agriculture and begin to develop the health care system. He was also able to modify Jiang Zemin's Taiwan policy and pressure North Korea to join the Six Party Talks. These were changes he could make by virtue of being general secretary. But he had difficulty moving his people into critical positions. He had stronger control over the Secretariat after the Seventeenth Party Congress – his close aide Ling Jihua was promoted to head the General Office, replacing Zeng Qinghong, and another close follower, Li Yuanchao, took over the Organization Department. Such appointments certainly strengthened his hand.

But some critical positions remained in the hands of Jiang Zemin sup- porters. Most notably Zhou Yongkang took over the Political and Legal Affairs Commission. Another Shanghai Gang member, Meng Jianzhu, took over the Ministry of Public Security, and He Guoqiang took over the CDIC. These are the three party bodies with investigative powers, so it was unlikely that any other follower of Jiang Zemin would be purged as Chen Liangyu had been in 2006. Rather than signaling consolidation of Hu's power, the purge of Chen Liangyu deepened the riff between Jiang and Hu.

The very tracing of these personnel appointments reflects the degree to which political power and control over policy remained dependent on personal relations rather than on institutions. Cheng Li has written about "one party and two factions" and hoping that the two factions were codependent and therefore would evolve in a more democratic direction. But close inspection of these personnel movements and the advantage of hindsight suggest that the power transition from Jiang to Hu was neither smooth nor institutionalized. The transition was more conflictual than harmonious, and Hu was never able to dominate the system. He was never given the informal but symbolically important title of "core," and there was a reason for that.

4 | *The Pathologies of Reform Leninism*

The turn to reform marked what Jowitt calls the "inclusionary" phase of Leninist development. As outlined in the Introduction, Jowitt sees Leninist systems as developing in three phases, starting with the "transformation" of society. This is the phase in which the party tries to remake society in the party's own image. In China this consisted of land reform, the criticism of landlords and other "bad elements," the mobilization of peasant activists, and eventually the formation of the communes (in 1958). During this phase, the party sets itself apart from society, seeing itself as exclusive, ruling over society. The second phase of "consolidation" is when the party rules over a transformed society. There was never really a consolidation phase in China because Mao repeatedly launched political campaigns, including the Anti-Rightist Movements (1957 and 1959), the Great Leap Forward (1958–1961), the Socialist Education Movement (1963–1966), and the Cultural Revolution (1966–1976). It looked briefly as if the Eighth Party Congress in 1958 might mark the start of a consolidation phase, emphasizing as it did the end of class struggle, but later that year Mao called for the Great Leap Forward, restarting the mass mobilizations that would continue throughout the Maoist era. With the death of Mao in 1976 and the arrest of the "Gang of Four" soon thereafter, the need to end mass mobilization was obvious. Even the much-maligned Hua Guofeng hoped to moderate the policies of the Cultural Revolution, and it was Hua who began to explore "opening up" by going to Yugoslavia and Romania in 1978 and to France and the United Kingdom in 1979.[1]

Therefore, China really skipped the consolidation phase and directly entered the "inclusionary phase." The inclusionary phase occurs when the Leninist party seeks to "integrate itself with, rather than insulate

---

[1] See www.youtube.com/watch?v=4eJBh5h4kqI&t=97s, accessed September 16, 2020.

itself from, its host society"; in other words, it begins to recognize the legitimacy, however tentatively, of societal interests.[2] In China, this meant a whole host of measures, starting with a new focus on the economy. It also meant rehabilitating thousands of cadres, including Liu Shaoqi, China's deceased vice chair and former president. Since Liu was the chief target of the Cultural Revolution, rehabilitating him meant reversing one of Mao's most important and visible decisions, thus bringing an end to the cult of Mao. Husbands and wives, frequently assigned to different workplaces, were allowed to rejoin each other, and some semblance of normal life was restored. Although the *danwei* (work unit) system continued to dominate urban life and communes continued to rule the countryside (until 1983), the party began to retreat from constant interference in everyday life. Mass mobilizations ended and a "zone of indifference" was created between society and government in which, over time, private life could resume, rural commerce was allowed, and space was created in which TVEs could emerge. Cultural activities, including, briefly, the publication of "scar" literature, which probed the pain of the Cultural Revolution years, began to flourish.[3]

This normalization of life, however, exposed both pain and confusion. The faith that people once had in Mao Zedong and Mao Thought was shattered, but there was nothing to replace it. People talked about the "three crises": a spiritual crisis (*jingshen weiji*), a cultural crisis (*wenhua weiji*), and a crisis of faith (*xinyang weiji*). For much of the 1980s, ideological fights were about how to fill this gap, with liberals arguing for some form of humanism and leftists arguing for upholding Marxism, albeit without the radical populism of the Cultural Revolution. These fights, as noted in Chapter 1, were reflected in the political tensions that led to the Tiananmen events.

This inclusionary phase meant some sort of reconciliation between party and society, but a reconciliation that could go only so far. Creating a zone of indifference did not mean the collapse of the Leninist system, but it did create new challenges for the party to

---

[2] Jowitt, "Inclusion and Mobilization in European Leninist Regimes," 72.
[3] "Zone of Indifference" is Tang Tsou's term. See Tang Tsou, *The Cultural Revolution and Post-Mao Reforms* (Chicago: The University of Chicago Press, 1986). On scar literature, see E. Perry Link, ed., *Stubborn Weeds: Popular and Controversial Chinese Literature after the Cultural Revolution* (Bloomington: Indiana University Press, 1983).

maintain its organizational coherence while "reconciling" with society. With the collapse of the Cultural Revolution and the realization that years of exhausting labor had actually left China poorer, Chinese leaders developed a new respect for "objective reality." In 1978, Deng Liqun, who later emerged as a conservative opponent of liberal reform, led a delegation to Japan, where he was clearly amazed at the economic progress Japan had made. The fact that their young guide and interpreter changed clothes every day surprised Deng; and that merchants could leave some of their wares outside their shops at night without fear that they would be stolen confused him: how could a capitalist society have such high moral standards, whereas China, a socialist society, did not?[4] An authoritative expression of this new appreciation of the limits of ideological efforts to transform reality came in Hu Qiaomu's 1978 report to the State Council, titled, "Act in Accordance with Economic Laws, Step Up the Four Modernizations." The central thesis of this report was that economic laws are objective. "Politics itself," the report states, "cannot create a law beyond the objective economic laws and impose it on economics." This statement marked an important expression of what Tang Tsou calls the "sociological postulate," namely that different fields of knowledge have their "special characteristics" (*tedian*) that cannot be overridden by politics without paying a severe price.[5] Although acknowledgment of economics as a field of study had its own "special characteristic" marking an important step away from the centrality of Marxist ideology, it raised the awkward question of who could interpret these special characteristics – party specialists in Marxism–Leninism or those trained in economics – and, if the latter, what type of economics?[6]

This inclusionary phase was welcomed by the Chinese people, who soon began exploring, and sometimes pushing, the bounds of the party's new tolerance. The Dengist reforms had been inaugurated by a discussion on Practice as the Sole Criterion of Truth, but when liberal intellectuals began arguing that Mao Zedong was the cause of so many

[4] Deng Liqun, *FangRi guilai de sisuo* (Thoughts on Returning from a Visit to Japan) (Beijing: Zhongguo shehui kexue chubanshe, 1979).
[5] Tang Tsou, "Political Change and Reform."
[6] See Julian Gewirtz, *Unlikely Partners: Chinese Reformers, Western Economists, and the Making of Global China* (Cambridge, MA: Harvard University Press, 2017), for the impact of Western economics on China.

mistakes in the party's history – from the Great Leap Forward through the Cultural Revolution – Deng responded with his speech "Uphold the Four Cardinal Principles."[7] Guo Luoji, a professor in the Philosophy Department of Peking University, responded by asking that if practice were the sole criterion of truth, how could the party declare Marxism to be truth? Did it not need to be tested? Deng was angry and quickly exiled Guo to Nanjing University.[8] The CCP's ideology was no longer the mobilizing ideology of the Mao period, but there were certain limits beyond which critics would not be permitted to go. But where were the limits? As we saw in Chapter 1, this was one of the major questions facing the 1980s.

Launching reform is difficult for Leninist systems. Inclusion is not easy because a Leninist system wants to reconcile with society without giving up its exclusivity, and society inevitably wants to reconcile on the basis of constraining the arbitrary powers of the Leninist party. Reform also creates difficulties for the Leninist system itself. As noted above, there are tensions built into Leninism that reform unleashes. In particular, the role of cadres changes. No longer the object of mass political campaigns to control their behavior or able to use political campaigns to control the behavior of others, local cadres pursue economic development and often self-enrichment. Doing so often requires developing close relations with other cadres and developing ties with economic actors in society. Local networks and corruption are an inevitable consequence of reform. In short, a degree of party dysfunctionality is a part and parcel of reform. Local cadres become less responsive to higher-level commands and conflict with society is a by-product of politically directed economic reform. That reform erodes control and discipline in Leninist systems is wholly predictable. The impact of reform on Leninism was visible from the start.

---

[7] Deng Xiaoping, "Uphold the Four Cardinal Principles," March 30, 1979, pp. 166–191, in *Selected Works of Deng Xiaoping (1975–1982)* (Beijing: Foreign Languages Press, 1983).

[8] Guo Luoji, "Zhengzhi wenti shi keyi taotande" (Political Issues Can Be Discussed), *Renmin ribao*, November 14, 1979. See also William Alford, "Double-Edged Swords Cut Both Ways: Law and Legitimacy in the People's Republic of China," *Daedalus*, Vol. 122, No. 2 (Spring 1993), available at http s://go.gale.com/ps/i.do?p=AONE&id=GALE%7CA13802438&v=2.1&it=r&si d=zotero&userGroupName=mlin_b_massblc&isGeoAuthType=true, accessed September 16, 2020.

In the economy, rural reform led the way. The Household Responsibility System emerged from the bottom up, though with some help from sympathetic cadres and some well-connected intellectuals.[9] By 1983, the communes had been replaced by the townships. One of the changes that came along with this administrative reform was the exaction of taxes. In the days of the communes, peasants turned their grain over to officials who took it to the grain stations and returned to the village with cash. After funds were deducted for the cost of fertilizer and perhaps farming implements (such as hoes), the remaining sum (not very much) was given to peasants. As the communes were replaced by the townships and as the peasants were allowed to take their own grain to the market, the cadres' salaries became a point of contention. Cadres at and above the township level were paid out of state coffers, but those at the village level were paid out of village funds. The breakup of the communes and implementation of the Household Responsibility System transformed what had been a hidden tax into a very visible tax – and peasants were none too happy to pay taxes for the upkeep of cadres who had done little to produce the crop. Tensions between the party and society were an inevitable part of reform.

It was these issues – the fear of serious local conflict and the desire to hold village cadres accountable – that prompted otherwise conservative officials – Peng Zhen, Bo Yibo, Song Ping – to support village elections. There was no intention to implement democracy, with the possible exception of some officials at the Ministry of Civil Affairs. By implementing village elections, it was hoped, social tensions could be eased. As long as elections were kept below the township level, they would not directly disrupt the Leninist system.[10]

In the urban areas, private enterprises began to develop. In some places, particularly Wenzhou, private workshops were developed to make shoes and other products. Although these workshops were small by later standards, they quickly raised the question whether

[9] Joseph Fewsmith, *Dilemmas of Reform in China: Political Conflict and Economic Debate* (Armonk, NY: M. E. Sharpe, 1994), Chapter 1.
[10] Li Lianjiang and Kevin J. O'Brien, "The Struggle over Village Elections," pp. 129–144, in Merle Goldman and Roderick MacFarquhar, eds., *The Paradox of China's Post-Mao Reforms* (Cambridge, MA: Harvard University Press, 1999); Tianjian Shi, "Village Committee Elections in China: Institutionalist Tactics for Democracy," *World Politics*, Vol. 51, No. 3 (April 1999): 385–412.

"capitalists" were "exploiting" workers – a question that would come up again in the wake of the Tiananmen events. Conservatives argued that there should be no private capitalists, whereas reformers argued that a limited number of small-scale enterprises would not mark a "restoration of capitalism." The issue was settled, in theory at least, by limiting the number of employees, on the basis of a letter Marx had once written, to under eight. This limit was soon exceeded, but it showed the inevitable tension that would develop between the party as a Leninist organization and "objective reality." Inclusion was not easy.

Tensions between a still unconstrained political system and the emerging "rights" of citizens came to a head in 2003, when a college graduate by the name of Sun Zhigang went to Guangzhou in search of work. He was arrested by police who thought he was a migrant worker and he did not have papers on him to prove otherwise. Under the custody and repatriation system then in place, the police had the right to arrest him and send him back home. For whatever reason, the arresting officers beat Sun, and by the next morning he was dead. Sun's case became a *cause célèbre* when three young PhDs in law – Yu Jiang, Teng Biao, and Hu Yuzhi – penned an open letter to the NPC arguing that the custody and repatriation system violated China's constitution. The NPC agreed and abolished the system. This marked the beginning of the rights-protection movement (*weiquan yundong*).

This movement tried to use the law to constrain the party and, over time, hundreds of lawyers took on human rights cases. Sometimes they won, but even when they lost, the strategy put pressure on the party. On July 9, 2015, the party would crush the rights-protection movement, arresting over 300 lawyers. No action more clearly illustrated the limited tolerance under Jiang Zemin and Hu Jintao and the turn to harsh repression under Xi Jinping.

This crackdown, however, was a later matter. In the meantime, the emergence of the rights-protection movement clearly reflected the simple fact that the inauguration of reform had changed the relationship between the party and society. Under reform, society, long suppressed, began to come back to life. In China, social life is often called *minjian shehui* (literally, "society among the people"). This is not the equivalent of the term "civil society" in the West, because civil society has the implication of interacting with the state, whether to support or to protest government policy. In China, *minjian shehui* has the connotation of being free of state control. But that was something the Leninist party found difficult to tolerate, especially when a *minjian* movement such as the rights-protection movement tries to effectively constrain the party.

Impact on the Party System

The shift to the inclusionary phase had major effects on the political system. As we have seen in the previous chapters, the party adopted a variety of norms (*not* institutions) in an effort to constrain political power. The retirement system, the regular holding of party congresses, and the staggered filling of PB and other seats every five years as some retired, did create something of a system of "checks and balances." However, as we have seen, the personal desire to consolidate and extend power as well as the natural tendency of democratic centralism to centralize power allowed Jiang Zemin to manipulate the rules and to extend his influence.

Below the top party and state leadership – that is, the members of the PB and CMC who ultimately run China – the development of reform had profound effects on the cadre system. As the tensions of the Cultural Revolution wound down, bureaucrats found themselves having no choice but to try to get along with each other. They had to. After all, many had to return to organizations that had criticized them severely, while others had to watch as people whom they had criticized returned to positions higher than theirs. Rather than engage in serious criticism and self-criticism – a long-standing practice in party organizations – people tried to minimize their criticisms so as not to offend. After all, the whole point of focusing on the economy was to get something done, and ideological battles were precisely what had prevented economic progress in the past. Given this new atmosphere, people tried to avoid criticism. Higher-level party organizations complained that cadres wanted to be "good old boys" (*laohaoren*), and that this atmosphere weakened ideological awareness and fostered weak discipline.[11] They were right, but that was the cost of reform.

---

[11] This is an ongoing campaign. A recent article in *Zhongguo jijian jiancha zazhi* (Journal of Chinese Inspection and Supervision) declares that there will be "zero tolerance" for "good old boy" behavior. See "'Laohaoren' shi wei 'laohairen'" (The Reality of Being a Good Old Boy Is to Harm People), *Zhongguo jijian*

At both the center and local levels (such as the provinces or counties), there are certain positions that should be filled by allies of the party secretary. That is why Deng Xiaoping said that the party needed to consolidate good "squads" (*banzi*) to bring order out of chaos. At the central level, as we have seen, there are certain critical positions – the heads of the Organization Department, the Propaganda Department, the CDIC, and so forth – that a party leader needs filled by allies in order to be effective. This creates both an effective *banzi* and a political faction.

The same is true at the local levels. A county party secretary, for instance, needs allies in certain positions, such as the heads of the Organization Department, the DIC, and the local police force. A party secretary's relationship with the county head can be problematic, though the decision by the Nineteenth Party Congress (in 2017) to emphasize the leading role of the party makes it clear who is in charge. The county head is in charge of the budget, and he may or may not be forthcoming about how much revenue the county has. There may be "small treasuries" of extra-budgetary funds that the party secretary does not know about. If the county head has already been in position for a period of time before the party secretary takes over, their relationship can be difficult. If the county head is transferred in the course of a party secretary's term, then appointing a new county head can bring in an ally.

The party secretary's personal secretary, usually from that county and assigned to the party secretary by the Organization Department (though the party secretary can approve or decline a secretary), may be a useful asset. Because the secretary's career depends a great deal on evaluation by the party secretary, that relationship tends to be close. Being from the locality, the secretary can sometimes interpret local politics, though there are others at higher levels who can better explain the intricacies of social relations in the area.

It is precisely because of the authority that party secretaries exercise at various levels that there is an effort to balance their power. A county party secretary, for instance, cannot simply choose the people on the party standing committee. First of all, a new party secretary will move into his position surrounded by cadres left over from the previous party committee (at all levels, new party committees are chosen at party congresses, but new party secretaries can be transferred in between

jiancha zazhi, No. 13 (July 1, 2018), available at http://zgjjjc.ccdi.gov.cn/bqml/bqxx/201806/t20180629_174741.html, accessed September 16, 2020.

congresses). Second, at party congresses, or when positions come open, the party secretary can nominate, but not name, people to take up those positions. In considering people for the open positions, the party secretary needs to take into consideration not only the qualifications of a given candidate but also how he or she is connected to others in and around the county. If one knows that one's superior really wants a certain person to be promoted, one is well advised to nominate that person. After one nominates one or more people, the list is submitted to the superior, who approves, or sometimes vetoes, the selection.[12]

The authority of the local party secretary is important economically as well. Particularly during the early years of reform, many policies were delegated downward under the policy of "delegating authority and allowing benefits" (*fangquan rangli*). Under China's planning system, the central government could not allocate funds for local development. But it could grant permission for lower-level governments to have greater authority in certain respects, such as the amount that could be invested without asking the higher authorities for permission. It was such policies that allowed the market-oriented reforms enough room to take off. Although in recent years the development of the market appears to have weakened the role of local party secretaries, for much of the reform period local administration had a great deal to do with the development of the local economy. This is the basis of what Jean Oi calls "local state corporatism," the idea that the local party would run the economy like a corporation with several divisions.[13] To the extent that county party organizations became ingrown and developed their own interests in the economy, there was an inevitable tendency to pursue local interests rather than national interests. Supervision was difficult.

This tendency to have separate interests was strengthened when, in 1984, the party adopted the "one-level-down" system of promotions. Previously, one level had been responsible for evaluating and promoting cadres two levels down, so provincial party secretaries (who are ministerial-level (*bu*) cadres), for instance, had been responsible for cadres at the bureau-director level (*ting*). This meant that the number of cadres they had to keep track of was really quite large. So it made sense to contract the scope of their responsibility so they could really get to know the cadres

---

[12] Interviews with local officials.
[13] Jean Oi, "Fiscal Reform and the Foundations of Local State Corporatism," *World Politics*, Vol. 45, No. 1 (October 1992): 99–126.

whom they were evaluating. But by switching to the one-level-down approach, the party made cadres responsible for evaluating their direct subordinates. Although there are systems in place, particularly the discipline inspection system, to try to prevent corruption and other disciplinary infractions, it goes against human nature for relations not to become personalized, for better or for worse.

The one-level-down system accentuated personal relations. Whether a party secretary was trying to please his boss or trying to build a network of supporters below him, personal relations were of the essence. This is particularly true with personnel decisions. If, for instance, a position opened up because of a promotion or transfer and the party secretary announced that there was an opening, supporters of one candidate or another would mobilize on his or her behalf. This mobilization would deepen whatever political differences existed in the county and the losers would no doubt be resentful. In theory, personnel decisions are supposed to be made by the local party committee as a whole, usually eleven people (at the county level). But concern that mobilization on behalf of different candidates will deepen political cleavages means that personnel decisions are usually made by a small number of people, often just three or four. As a result, personnel decisions are generally made by a rather cohesive inner circle.

Therefore, the sort of mobilization that would exacerbate differences at the local level and create local factions is avoided, but the very effort to avoid contending factions tends to create smaller, but very real, factions among party elites, who tend to promote those they know. The implication of this process is that promotions tend to be biased toward people with the right connections – perhaps people from the same township, perhaps classmates, perhaps even relatives. Choosing people with the "right connections" tended to open the system to corruption. Certainly in the days before Xi Jinping's crackdown on corruption, when corruption was a routine part of the promotion process (at least for certain positions), the giving of bribes was a necessary part of the process. After all, the party secretary needed to accumulate capital to bribe his superior in order to secure a hoped-for promotion.[14]

---

[14] On local government, see Graeme Smith, "Getting Ahead in Rural China: The Elite–Cadre Divide and Its Implications for Rural Governance," *Journal of Contemporary China*, Vol. 24, No. 94 (2015): 594–612; Graeme Smith, "Measurement, Promotions and Patterns of Behavior in Chinese Local Government," *Journal of Peasant Studies*, Vol. 40, No. 6 (2013): 1027–1059;

Perhaps the classic case of such networks of corruption occurred in coal-rich Shanxi province. The combination of corruption, local economic development, and power led to the creation of local factions and organizational dysfunction, at least when viewed from Beijing's perspective. Because Xi Jinping and Wang Qishan cracked down on corruption in Shanxi, we have many accounts of local networks.[15] Also, perhaps because Shanxi's economy is less developed and less marketized than more developed east coast provinces and no doubt because much of the provincial economy revolves around the coal industry and a few large SOEs, the province was particularly susceptible to local factions. Yuncheng in the southern part of the province was one area that generated powerful local factions. Although Yuncheng has long generated such local cliques, it became a particular focal point of the campaign against corruption because it is where Ling Jihua, head of the General Office, hailed from. Ling's father, Linghu Ye, had left his family to join the revolution in 1936, plying his knowledge of traditional Chinese medicine to become a section chief in the Yan'an revolutionary hospital. This put him in close association with many of the Communist elite, including fellow provincial and future vice premier Bo Yibo, father of Bo Xilai, the controversial party secretary of Chongqing whose dramatic fall from power in 2012 heralded the broader campaign against corruption. Bo Yibo seems to have been critical some years later in recommending the young Ling Jihua to the central CYL, thus paving the way for Ling to move from provincial politics to national politics.

As the young Ling Jihua was making his way up the ladder in Beijing, his older brother, Ling Zhengce, was rising, albeit more slowly, in provincial politics. He started out in the Confidential Affairs Office (*jiyao chu*) in 1971, finally becoming a deputy department head (*fu chuzhang*) in the office of the provincial party committee. In 1997, Ling became deputy head (*fu ting zhang*) of the provincial grain office,

Graeme Smith, "The Hollow State: Rural Governance in China," *China Quarterly*, No. 203 (September 2010): 610–618; and Sig Thørersen, "Frontline Soldiers of the CCP: The Selection of China's Township Leaders," *China Quarterly*, No. 194 (2008): 414–423.

[15] The following description is based on my "China's Political Ecology and the Fight against Corruption," *China Leadership Monitor*, No. 46 (Winter 2015), retrieved from www.hoover.org/sites/default/files/research/docs/clm46jf.pdf, accessed September 16, 2020.

a department dominated by people from Yuncheng. Finally, in the year 2000, as his younger brother was making waves in Beijing, Ling Zhengce was promoted to deputy head, then head, of the powerful Development and Reform Commission.

It was while he was head of this commission that Ling Zhengce was in position to approve plans for a major upgrading of the Taiyuan Iron and Steel Plant, run by Yuncheng native Chen Chuanping. It was this upgrading that made Taiyuan Iron and Steel globally competitive and boosted Chen Chuanping's political career. Chen became Taiyuan party secretary and a member of the provincial party standing committee. He also gave a Ferrari to Ling Gu, son of Ling Jihua, which became famous when Ling Gu crashed it into a pillar on the Fourth Ring Road in Beijing, killing himself and one of the two scantily clad women with whom he was riding. It was that incident that led directly to his father's downfall.

Another part of Shanxi that is well known for strong local factions is Lüliang. Nie Chunyu, a member of the provincial party standing committee who was detained for corruption in 2014, had served for eight years as party secretary in Lüliang. When he was transferred out in 2011, Du Shanxue, originally from Yuncheng, replaced him as party secretary. Du Shanxue was later charged with selling offices, an enterprise in which he apparently co-operated with his brother. Ten months after being appointed party secretary, Du was promoted to the provincial party standing committee. From 2003 to 2006, Bai Yun was deputy secretary of Lüliang, and when Nie Chunyu was promoted, Bai Yun took his place as head of the United Front Work Department. She, too, was charged with corruption.

The local networks in Shanxi were tight enough that officials sent in from Beijing either could not penetrate them or did not try. Going along seemed to be the only viable strategy. A case in point is Jin Daoming. Jin was born in Beijing and would spend most of his career in the CDIC. In 2006 he was sent to Shanxi to head the provincial DIC office. At first, it appeared that Jin was determined to crack down on corruption. He sent out fifty-six inspection teams to various units in the coal industry. In August 2008 a provincial leading group to fight corruption in the coal and coking industry was established. The group included not only Jin Daoming, but also Chen Chuanping (whose background is discussed above) and others who would be cashiered in the subsequent campaign against corruption. Altogether, prior to March 2011, Jin investigated some 2,000 cases and recovered 30 billion RMB worth of bribes. This seemingly impressive result was nevertheless later described as "putting up a show" and more than one mine owner was protected by Jin, who was subsequently jailed for corruption.[16]

What the Shanxi case shows, like the broader literature on local government, is that local networks were deeply embedded in the local political economy. They were self-serving networks reaching from the county level all the way up to the provincial party standing committee, and, with respect to Ling Jihua, all the way into the halls of Zhongnanhai in Beijing. In the case of Ling Jihua, he allegedly organized a Xishan Club to bring together officials from Shanxi working in Beijing. Such networks are good for enriching one another and for their networks in Shanxi. If they are good from the perspective of party leaders in Shanxi, it marks extreme dysfunction from Beijing's point of view. Beijing can send out orders, but the degree to which the orders are implemented in the localities is open to question. With such networks so deeply embedded in local society, they are extremely difficult to root out. In the case of Shanxi, over 15,000 cadres were disciplined during the campaign against corruption. This extensive intervention raises the question whether, if Shanxi becomes more responsive to Beijing, will it become less responsive to Shanxi society and lead to more civil disorder?

Conflict with Society

The structure of Leninism naturally inclines cadres to seek out alliances that act as a "mutual benefit society," helping one another seek out promotions and perks that can go with the job on the one hand, but clash with the interests of the peasants or other "vulnerable groups" (*ruoshi qunti*) on the other. The nature of these frictions can change significantly, depending on the demands of higher levels and the opportunities present in local society.

In the 1980s, as is well documented by Kevin O'Brian and Li Lianjiang, conflicts between cadres and peasants focused on taxes. Such conflicts were particularly serious in central China, the "rice belt" of the country, stretching roughly from Hebei in the north through Hunan in the south. In the prosperous East, there was enough

---

[16] This description of the Shanxi case is drawn from ibid.

money that taxation was generally not an issue (conflicts revolved around other issues, such as land), and in the poor West there was no way to extract much extra revenue. So conflict tended to be concentrated in those areas that had some money but not a lot – that is, the rice belt.[17]

By the 1990s, and especially after the tax reform of 1994, conflict focused on land takings. In the course of tax reform, the center negotiated with the provinces, and then the provinces demanded that counties pay them more taxes. By that time, land values were increasing as industry began to look for new places to grow. With the growing demand for land, local officials increased incentives to seize land for minimum compensation, sharply increasing the conflict between peasants and local cadres. It was largely this dynamic that generated the rise in mass incidents from 8,700 in 1993 to 180,000 in 2010.

As these figures suggest, the situation in the countryside was quite serious by the mid- to late 1990s. Industrialization and the demands by local party secretaries in the interior for local cadres to bring in investment for further industrialization (*zhaoshang yinzi*) were causing land prices to increase. At the same time, the central government felt that its relative decline in revenue was making it more difficult to exercise macroeconomic control. Hong Kong scholar Wang Shaoguang and Qinghua University researcher Hu Angang wrote an emotional book decrying the decline of state capacity and even warning that it could, as in Yugoslavia, lead to the breakup of the country.[18] In 1994, Zhu Rongji pushed through a tax reform that greatly increased the percentage of funds going to Beijing. Zhu had struck his deal with the provincial party secretaries (in one-on-one discussions), leaving China's cities and counties to negotiate their tax burdens with their respective provinces. Localities along the prosperous east coast were able to make do, but those in poorer regions were under great pressure. Local cadres were under even greater pressure to extract funds, either by finding investors or by squeezing it out of local industries and residents. The inevitable outcome was conflict.

---

[17] Kevin O'Brien and Lianjiang Li, *Rightful Resistance in Rural China* (New York: Cambridge University Press, 2006).
[18] Wang Shaoguang and Hu Angang, *The Chinese Economy in Crisis: State Capacity and Tax Reform* (Armonk, NY: M. E. Sharpe, 2001).

The case that exploded in Weng'an county, mentioned in the Introduction, was typical, and fortunately is well documented. In Weng'an resentment had been building for some years as local authorities were forcibly moved from one location to another and as local gangs, working with local authorities, kept order in the mines. One evening, a sixteen-year-old girl went out with three well-connected boys and somehow drowned in the course of the night. The family and townspeople suspected rape, though two autopsies judged that to be unfounded. The girl's classmates and friends carried her casket through the town, demanding justice. As they marched on, the crowd grew larger, reaching over 10,000 people. When the marchers reached party headquarters, a quarrel broke out. Angered townspeople soon forced their way into the party building and burned it. They then moved to the police department next door and started to burn it as well.[19]

With similar incidents occurring in other parts of the country, the CCP once again contemplated political reform. Just as the introduction of village elections was intended to defuse tensions in the countryside, this new round of reform, focusing on the selection of township officials, was intended to break up local networks, control the behavior of township cadres, and relieve social tensions.

One way to break up such local networks was to expand the number of people involved in the selection and promotion of local officials. And the way to do this was to set up an election procedure in which many people were involved. But, of course, both local and central officials agreed that elections could not be allowed to get "out of control," which, of course, meant that the very people whose grip should have been loosened actually maintained control.

Both the logic and difficulty of using election procedures, however limited, to reform local government are illustrated in the case of Pingchang county in the northeast corner of Sichuan province. Pingchang, which was administratively under the city of Bazhong, is famous for being the site of many social disturbances, which were caused in part by the fact that it was administratively bloated and therefore in debt. In 2002, the party decided to appoint one Liu Qingxiang to Pingchang county as party secretary. Liu decided that in order to deal with the debt burden, several townships and villages

---

[19] Fewsmith, *The Logic and Limits of Political Reform in China*, Chapter 2.

should be merged, but such a merger meant eliminating jobs. How was it to be decided who should retain their jobs and who should be removed? Encouraged by the atmosphere then prevailing in Sichuan to develop "intra-party democracy," Liu Qingxiang decided to hold "public recommendations and direct elections" (*gongtui zhixuan*) in one-third of the townships in the county. "Public recommendations and direct elections" meant that those running for office were to be self-nominated, supported by party members, or recommended by the party committee – not a very open process but still more open than the simple decision of a party committee to appoint someone. After being nominated, the candidates would be voted on by all party members and sometimes by "representatives of the masses" as well. Such representatives were not chosen at random; rather they included such people as village heads who, although trusted, were not party members. They could provide a degree of representativeness and thus a degree of credibility.

The voting was conducted in three rounds, starting with the contest for township party secretary. There was a logic to starting at the top. It meant that the loser in that round was still eligible to run as deputy party secretary and thus would not be completely out of a job. The loser in the election for deputy party secretary could then run for party committee. The Pingchang elections marked the most extensive experiment with the public-recommendation and direct-election system and were widely regarded as successful.

But two factors undermined Liu Qingxiang and this experiment. First, in the course of these elections some cadres lost their jobs, and these cadres were well equipped to complain. They tended to be well connected and to be skilled at using party rhetoric to allege violations of party procedures. Second, a new party secretary was appointed to Bazhong city. Although this secretary was a strong reformer, he soon clashed with Liu Qingxiang, mostly over who should get credit for the experiment. It was perhaps inevitable that Liu, the lower-ranked official, was placed under investigation for corruption. Although no evidence of corruption was found, Liu was nevertheless soon forced out of his job.[20]

From Beijing's point of view, there were two things wrong with the local elections. First, it was difficult to make the elections do what they

[20] Ibid., pp. 90–97.

should do; that is, to control the behavior of local cadres. For instance, frustrated cadres in Pingchang county fought back against the reform-minded party secretary. In this case, those cadres with many local connections were able to mobilize such connections successfully, thus forcing out Liu Qingxiang. Second, to the extent that township elections did work to promote new blood in local party organizations, they worked against the central organizational practice of Leninist parties, namely *dangguan ganbu* (the party controls the cadres – meaning appointments from the top down). The basic problem with elections, from a Leninist point of view, is that candidates inevitably appeal to their constituents for support, thus weakening vertical control. This is one reason why successful candidates were quickly moved out of one locality to another. It is perhaps discouraging that such successful candidates were happy to follow party orders to move elsewhere. After all, their intention in running for office is to hasten the process of being named to a higher position, not to promote democracy.

The example of Shanxi illustrates how extensive local networks can be. Such local networks inevitably bend the hierarchical, disciplined nature of a Leninist party so that they serve local interests. Given that the local party organizations control a scarce resource – positions – it is only natural that local party organizations found ways to monetize their power. The result is that corruption became woven into the organization. Rules governing recruitment and promotion may have been followed, but there were more people who wanted promotions than there were spaces, so people were willing to pay for positions. The sale of positions provided income for those selling the positions, so they could purchase a higher position for themselves. Because the purchase of positions was a sort of investment, the purchaser needed to find ways to get a return on his or her investment. Moreover, to the extent that the sale of offices became an expected way of doing things, not to participate would have marked someone as suspicious, thus hurting his or her chances of being promoted.

The example of Pingchang further suggests how difficult it is for seemingly radical reform to break up local networks. The township elections adopted in Pingchang county and elsewhere were not intended to introduce democracy, but elections of any sort posed a challenge to hierarchical party control. Furthermore, it really was radical for elections to be introduced at the township level because townships, unlike villages, are part of the administrative system.

Public Opinion and Efforts to Revive the Party

As noted above, the turn to reform broke the spell of Maoist thought and faith in Marxism in general. In this retreat from ideology, students led the way, particularly following the demonstrations of 1986, when the demand for political reform ended in the ouster of Hu Yaobang in January 1987. Students of Chinese public opinion note that "the CCP's ability to attract the masses had weakened and the political enthusiasm of the students had declined."[21] By the late 1980s, but before the Tiananmen events, one survey of the image of the CCP found that nearly 62 percent of the Chinese public thought the image of the CCP was "not good." Part of the same survey asked, "Are you proud to be a party member?" and 43 percent answered "no," including 38.5 percent of cadres.[22] The Tiananmen events exacerbated the lack of faith in the party. Furthermore, the collapse of the Communist Party of the Soviet Union (CPSU) in 1991 revealed what could happen to a Leninist party, indeed the oldest Leninist party in the world, if the public lost faith in it. The CCP seemed to be headed down the same path, as the attitudes of students and others showed how little faith much of the Chinese population, particularly its best and brightest, had in Marxism–Leninism.

The CCP launched a major effort to turn around attitudes. As Deng Xiaoping said in 1989, "We did not tell [students and the people in general] enough about the need for hard struggle, about what China was like in the old days."[23] The CCP would make up for that lapse by launching an "unprecedented" campaign for patriotic education in 1991. It was a campaign that encompassed print, TV, movies, the establishment of new historical sites, and organized visits to such

---

[21] Stanley Rosen, "The Effect of Post-4 June Re-education Campaigns on Chinese Students," *China Quarterly*, No. 134 (June 1993): 325.

[22] Stanley Rosen, "The Chinese Communist Party and Chinese Society: Popular Attitudes toward Party Membership and the Party's Image," *Australian Journal of Chinese Affairs*, No. 24 (July 1990): 51–92, at 80–88.

[23] Deng Xiaoping. "Zai jiejian shoudu xieyan budui junyishang ganbu shi de jianghua" (Address to Officers at the Rank of General and Above in Command of Enforcing Martial Law in Beijing), in *Deng Xiaoping wenxuan, disan juan* (Selected Works of Deng Xiaoping, Vol. 3), p. 306.

sites. In the course of this campaign, nationalism was mobilized in the service of the party. This campaign, which was based on a narrative of China as a victim, identified the "party with the nation," and turned criticism of the party into an "unpatriotic act."[24] Later, the exhibit to which Xi Jinping led his Standing Committee colleagues to at the Museum of Revolutionary History on Tiananmen Square in 2012 was called The Road to Renaissance (*fuxing zhilu*) and it repeated the basic lessons of the Patriotic Education campaign – under the oppression of foreign imperialism China had struggled in the dark for many years, but finally, under the leadership of the CCP, it had been able to recover sovereignty and attain wealth and power.

Still, the party was pounded by news coming from overseas. Starting in 2003, "color revolutions" broke out in Georgia, Ukraine, and Kyrgyzstan. These political upheavals were too similar to what had happened in the former Soviet Union and Eastern Europe, and, indeed, to the protests in China, for comfort. Analysis by Chinese scholars revolved around the US taking advantage of "contradictions" in these countries – contradictions such as the growing disparities in wealth and corruption – to stir up dissatisfaction and protests. Nongovernmental organizations (NGOs), often directly supported by American NGOs, were key to organizing such protests and eventually to carrying out the peaceful overturn of nondemocratic governments. The color revolutions and the nervousness of the party brought the experiments with township elections discussed above to a halt.

The Campaign for Patriotic Education did not turn things around quickly or easily. Surveys of the "post-1980s" generation find that its members were both pragmatic and cynical. Party membership was seen as desirable but primarily for finding a good job. In one survey, only

---

[24] Suisheng Zhao, "State-Led Nationalism: The Patriotic Education Campaign in Post-Tiananmen China," *Communist and Post-communist Studies*, Vol. 31, No. 3 (1998): 289; Zheng Wang, "National Humiliation, History Education, and the Politics of Historical Memory: Patriotic Education Campaign in China," *International Studies Quarterly*, Vol. 52, No. 4 (2008): 783–806; and Elizabeth J. Perry, "Cultural Governance in Contemporary China: 'Re-orienting' Party Propaganda," Harvard-Yenching Institute Working Papers, 2013, available at www.harvard-yenching.org/sites/harvard-yenching.org/files/featurefiles/Elizabeth%20Perry_Cultural%20Governance%20in%20Contemporary%20China_0.pdf, accessed September 16, 2020.

11.5 percent of students said that they wanted to join the party because they believed in "communism."[25]

Over time, however, some combination of economic growth, general social stability, nationalism, and, perhaps, increasingly poor performance by democratic countries, particularly the United States, rebuilt public support. Zhengxu Wang's analysis of the 2000–2001 World Values Survey and East Asia Barometer found that more that 95 percent of Chinese respondents in both surveys had a "great deal" or "quite a lot" of confidence in the national government and the CCP.[26] Similarly, Dickson finds high levels of trust (78.5 percent) in the central government, but a level of only 49.7 percent trust in local governments.[27] This gap between a high level of trust in the central government and a more modest level of trust in local government raises an interesting issue. As Zhengxu Wang points out, most citizens never encounter the central government, so it is, to some extent, an "imaginary state," but they do have encounters with the local state. Thus, the high levels of trust reported in the central state may be illusory and more easily shaken than many expect. Nevertheless, levels of support for the party and government are substantially higher than they were in the late 1980s and throughout the 1990s.[28]

Conclusion

The adoption of reform poses many challenges for Leninism as a system. As the center stepped back from everyday control of society and as the party relaxed its mass mobilization campaigns, it was impossible to maintain the same sort of control and discipline over either society or the party. Indeed, in the case of China, many resentments had been built up over the years so when the pressure was finally released, frustration boiled over. Intellectuals cast the blame on Mao Zedong, and students mocked those trying to carry out political work.

[25] Stanley Rosen, "Contemporary Chinese Youth and the State," *Journal of Asian Studies*, Vol. 68, No. 2 (May 2009): 365.
[26] Cited in Wenfang Tang, *Populist Authoritarianism: Chinese Political Culture and Regime Sustainability* (Oxford: Oxford University Press, 2016), p. 25. See Zhengxu Wang, "Explaining Regime Strength in China," *China: An International Journal*, Vol. 4, No. 2 (September 2006), pp. 217–237.
[27] Bruce J. Dickson, *The Dictator's Dilemma: The Chinese Communist Party's Strategy for Survival* (New York: Oxford University Press, 2016), p. 216.
[28] Wang Zhengxu, "Public Support for Democracy in China," *Journal of Contemporary China*, Vol. 16, No. 11 (2007): 561–579.

More importantly, from an organizational perspective, party discipline atrophied as individuals sought out alliances. The importance of devolving economic power to promote reform made it increasingly difficult for the higher levels to exert control over the local levels. Beijing was even willing to experiment with local elections in an effort to break up local networks.

The threat to the party as an organization was real. The CPSU had collapsed in the Soviet Union and the socialist parties in Eastern Europe had followed it into oblivion. The color revolutions in Central Asia suggested the threat was a continuing one. The alienation of youth was serious, prompting them to look abroad, either for study or inspiration. Two decades of patriotic education was perhaps helpful, but more likely two decades of economic growth and China's emergence as a wealthy and powerful country did more to restore pride and patriotism than did any propaganda. The inability of the United States to avoid the 2008 financial crisis suggested to many Chinese that they had outgrown the need for a "teacher"; China had its own ways of doing things and could manage on its own.

But organizational dysfunction remained, as the factions in Shanxi illustrate, and dysfunction at the top was clearly reflected in the divided government of Jiang Zemin, who should have been retired, and Hu Jintao, who was not powerful enough to force Jiang to step down. The Bo Xilai case, in which his wife, Gu Kailai, was accused (and later convicted) of murdering British businessman Neil Heywood, and he himself later stood convicted of massive corruption, suggested the lawlessness that had infected the elite. Most serious from an organizational point of view, Bo had defied the decision of the Seventeenth Party Congress, which had decided that Xi Jinping would become general secretary and Li Keqiang would be premier. From his mountain lair up the Yangtze river in Chongqing, Bo apparently could not stand it. His efforts to root out secret gangs and his campaign to sing "Red songs" taunted the center, saying in effect that he was more capable and "redder" than Xi Jinping.

As every person who joins the CCP knows, the minority submits to the majority, and lower levels submit to higher levels. Yet here was Bo, raised his whole life in the party and in the household of one of its most senior members, defying the decision of a party congress. The corruption and raw political ambition exposed by the Bo Xilai case, the factionalism and dysfunction revealed in Shanxi, and the conflicts with society apparent in the Weng'an case all suggest a party losing its organizational coherence. "Peaceful evolution" seemed like a real possibility, and experiments in the democratic selection of leaders threatened the sacred principle of the "party controls the cadres."

5 | Xi Jinping's Centralization of Power

As the new century got under way, one frequently heard people in China say, "Deng Xiaoping was not as strong as Mao Zedong, Jiang Zemin was not as strong as Deng Xiaoping, and Hu Jintao was not as strong as Jiang Zemin." It seemed that there had been a four-decade secular decline in central authority. This was not altogether bad. The economy was booming, personal freedoms were expanding, travel was growing, entertainment was flourishing, and educational opportunities were opening up, both domestically and abroad. There were downsides, however, particularly corruption and the abuse of power, but there did not seem to be much chance of turning these back anytime soon, just as there seemed to be little chance of restoring central power.

On November 15, 2011, the body of a British businessman, Neil Heywood, was found dead in a room at the Lucky Holiday Hotel in Chongqing. A night earlier, he had dined with Gu Kailai, the wife of PB member Bo Xilai and had been poisoned with cyanide. Heywood's body was quickly cremated and his wife, Wang Lulu, was told that he had died of a heart attack. Had Wang Lijun, the police chief who had followed Bo Xilai to Chongqing from Tieling in Liaoning, not had a falling out with Bo and fled to Chengdu in a desperate effort to gain political asylum, the murder might never have been discovered. As the investigation into Gu Kailai, and then Bo Xilai, deepened, Bo attended the NPC meeting held in Beijing, on March 5–14, and, after the meeting was adjourned, was taken into custody.[1]

As in most such cases, the Bo Xilai case is not as simple as it seemed. In May 2012, investigators had begun digging into corruption charges against one Gu Fengjie, who had succeeded Wang Lijun as police chief in Tieling. By digging into Gu Fengjie, the investigators hoped to

---

[1] Jamil Anderlini, "Bo Xilai: Power, Death, and Politics," *Financial Times*, July 20, 2012, available at www.ft.com/content/d67b90f0-d140-11e1-8957-00144feab dc0, accessed September 16, 2020.

pressure Wang, and thus gain information on Bo Xilai. Wang Lijun was an ambitious man. He may have encouraged Gu Kailai to kill Heywood so he would have leverage over Bo. He certainly kept forensic evidence from Heywood's body for such purposes. He no doubt hoped to gain Bo's protection when the two met on January 29, 2012. But Bo exploded in anger, slapping Wang in the face, thus setting off Wang's flight to the US consulate in Chengdu on February 6.[2]

Then on March 18, 2012, Ling Gu, son of Ling Jihua, head of the powerful General Office, crashed a Ferarri into a pillar on Beijing's Fourth Ring Road. This was the same Ferarri that Chen Chuanping had given Ling Gu in the web of corruption described in the previous chapter. Ling was killed and the two scantily clothed young women with whom he was riding were seriously injured, one dying shortly thereafter. The Beijing rumor mill, active as ever, alleged that Ling Jihua viewed his son's body at the morgue and denied that it was his son. He then contacted Zhou Yongkang, head of the Political and Legal Commission, and conspired to have the incident covered up.

The fatal crash apparently stayed hidden until August, when it came to Jiang Zemin's attention. On September 1, Ling was suddenly transferred from the General Office to the United Front Work Department Office, an important but still lesser department. In the past, the heads of the party's General Office have routinely been promoted to the PB and, in this case, such a move would have been important in retaining influence for the retiring Hu Jintao. But the crash and demotion of Ling made that impossible. Even worse for Hu was that Ling Jihua was replaced by Li Zhanshu, who would emerge as perhaps Xi Jinping's closest aide.[3]

[2] David Bandurski, "Wang Lijun and the Tieling Corruption Case, *China Media Project*, February 14, 2012, available at http://chinamediaproject.org/2012/02/14/wang-lijun-and-the-tieling-corruption-case, accessed September 16, 2020; "Bo Xilai Admits Slapping Former Police Chief Wang Lijun 'because He Was Two-Faced'," *South China Morning Post*, August 24, 2013, available at www.scmp.com/news/china/article/1299189/murder-violence-and-distrust-bo-xilai-recounts-dramatic-events-police, accessed May 31, 2020.

[3] Edward Wong, "Anti-corruption Campaign in China Snares Former Top Party Official," *New York Times*, May 13, 2016, available at www.nytimes.com/2016/05/14/world/asia/china-ling-jihua.html, accessed September 16, 2020; Clarles Clover, "Chinese Ex-presidential Aide Ling Arrested," *Financial Times*, July 20, 2015, available at www.ft.com/content/a1e33ca6-2f4f-11e5-8873-775ba7c2ea3d, accessed September 16, 2020.

Figure 5.1 Newly appointed General Secretary Xi Jinping introduces the new Politburo Standing Committee in 2012 (Lintao Zhang via Getty Images)

September 1 proved significant for another reason as well – Xi Jinping disappeared. He was scheduled to meet with Secretary of State Hillary Clinton that day, but the appointment was cancelled without explanation. Xi made no public appearances for two weeks, until September 15, giving rise to much speculation. One such guess was that he had been targeted in an assassination attempt, while another guess was that he had hurt his back swimming. Neither guess is particularly persuasive since his disappearance seems so closely tied to Ling Jihua's transfer. Coming in the wake of Bo Xilai's detention, the scandal over Ling Jihua and his son suggests that senior leaders had to renegotiate some of the previously agreed-upon leadership arrangements. At a minimum, it was clear that Ling Jihua would not be promoted to the PB.

A month later, in late October and early November, twenty-two PLA leaders were moved in an effort to stabilize the PLA leadership in the wake of the Bo Xilai scandal. Fan Chonglong and Xu Qiliang were made vice chairmen of the CMC.[4] These transfers reflected the great uncertainty at the top of the system as Xi Jinping prepared to take over.

---

[4] Chien-wei Kou, "Xi in Command," p. 878; *Jiefangjun 22 wei gaoji jiangling lüxin* (22 PLA Senior Generals Assume Their New Offices), *Xinjing bao*, November 22,

Xi seemed fortunate in that all members of the Seventeenth PBSC, selected in October 2012, except himself and Premier Li Keqiang, would have to retire because of age. There were eight members of the outgoing PB eligible for promotion (assuming that the age rule was upheld, which it was), but the question was whether the PBSC would be kept at nine seats, as it had been for the Sixteenth and Seventeenth PBs, or whether it would return to the more normal number of seven members. In the end, it was reduced to seven seats, which meant that Wang Yang, Li Yuanchao, and Liu Yandong were not promoted. Wang Yang, born in 1955, was young enough that he could still serve on the Nineteenth and Twentieth PBSCs, so one could make an argument that he could wait another term (indeed, he was promoted in 2017), and Li Yuanchao faced significant opposition. Li had been editor of the *Zhongguo Qingnianbao* (China Youth Daily) in 1989 and, apparently, had offended Li Peng with his coverage of the student demonstrations. He may also have offended Xi Jinping with some of the appointments he had made while he was head of the Organization Department (2007–2012). Liu Yandong was simply a victim of gender politics; no woman has ever made it to the PBSC, so her exclusion was simply a matter of sexism.

The impact of the politics over the preceding months, however, was significant. Assuming that Hu Jintao hoped to extend his influence over the Eighteenth Central Committee, much as Jiang Zemin had formerly extended his influence, the reduction in the size of the PBSC had eliminated the possibility for Wang Yang and Li Yuanchao to join the elite group, while the Ling Jihua scandal had prevented him from joining the broader PB.

If we look at those who did join the PBSC, we see it was very much divided (Table 5.1).

Xi Jinping was surrounded by Li Keqiang, a Hu Jintao protégé; Zhang Dejiang, Liu Yunshan, and Zhang Gaoli had all come up through Jiang Zemin's network; and Yu Zhengsheng was a princeling in his own right, but because he was more than a decade older than Xi, he was not necessarily an ally. That left Wang Qishan. Wang had certainly worked closely with Jiang Zemin and others in the past, but he was a close friend of Xi Jinping's from the Cultural Revolution days and he had been given the position of head of the CDIC, which would prove critical.

2012, available at http://epaper.bjnews.com.cn/html/2012-11/22/content_391843 .htm?div=1, accessed August 28, 2020.

Table 5.1 *Eighteenth Central Committee Politburo Standing Committee, 2012–2017*

Name	Position	Date of birth
Xi Jinping	General secretary	1953
Li Keqiang	Premier	1955
Zhang Dejiang	Chongqing party secretary	1946
Yu Zhengsheng	Head, CPPCC	1945
Liu Yunshan	Propaganda Department	1947
Wang Qishan	CDIC	1948
Zhang Gaoli	Vice premier	1946

Table 5.2 *Eighteenth Central Committee Politburo Members, 2012–2017*

Name	Position	Date of birth	Probable political alignment
Fan Changlong	Vice chairman, CMC	1947	
Guo Jinlong	Beijing party secretary	1947	Hu Jintao network
Han Zheng	Shanghai party secretary	1954	
Hu Chunhua	Guangdong party secretary	1963	Hu Jintao network
Li Jianguo	NPC, general secretary	1946	Li Ruihuan's secretary
Li Yuanchao	Vice president (2013)	1950	Hu Jintao network
Li Zhanshu	Organization Department	1950	Xi Jinping network
Liu Qibao	Propaganda Department	1953	Hu Jintao network
Liu Yandong (f)	State councilor	1945	
Ma Kai	State councilor	1946	
Meng Jianzhu	Minister, public security	1947	Jiang Zemin network

Table 5.2 (*cont.*)

Name	Position	Date of birth	Probable political alignment
Sun Chunlan (f)	Tianjin party secretary	1950	
Sun Zhengcai	Chongqing party secretary	1963	Jiang Zemin network
Wang Huning	Policy Research Office	1955	
Wang Yang	Vice premier (2013)	1955	Hu Jintao network
Xu Qiliang	Vice chairman, CMC	1950	Jiang Zemin network
Zhang Chunxian	Xinjiang, party secretary	1953	

Looking at the rest of the PB, we see that the Jiang Zemin network continued to have a significant influence. In the military, Xu Qiliang was identified with the Jiang Zemin network and maybe also Fan Changlong (who had once served directly under Xu Caihou). Meng Jianzhu came out of the Shanghai Gang, and Sun Zhengcai was associated with Jiang, though not as closely.

Those associated with Hu Jintao include Guo Jinlong, Hu Chunhua, Li Yuanchao, and Wang Yang. Moreover, the CYL as a group fared remarkably well, perhaps because the decisions were made before the Ling Gu scandal. Of the twenty-nine people with CYL backgrounds who joined the Seventeenth Central Committee, twenty-two were retained on the Eighteenth Central Committee. They were joined by twenty-one others newly elected to the Eighteenth Central Committee. Together, these people made up forty-three members of the new Central Committee, or about 20 percent. But few of these people held important posts. Perhaps the most prominent member of this group, below the PB level, was Xia Baolong, party secretary of Zhejiang and a certified good friend of Xi Jinping. Discerning "factional" alignments is difficult!

Unlike those elected to the Seventeenth Central Committee, most of those with CYL affiliations who joined the Eighteenth Central Committee were too old to be retained on the Nineteenth Central Committee – only six made the cut. Another six were investigated for corruption under Xi's new campaign, so the influence of the CYL at lower levels faded, even apart from the group being denounced in 2015 (see below).

So, as one would expect for a congress in which new leadership was installed, the new general secretary did not have a lot of visible support and a lot of the leadership came from different parts of the party and was more or less closely associated with different former leaders. This does not mean that some leaders would oppose Xi Jinping because they had been associated with one or another previous leader, but it does suggest that Xi would be a cautious leader, trying to feel out the policy preferences of his colleagues.

Obviously, things did not work out that way. Rather than offering the sort of careful, guarded leadership that the PB lineup suggested, Xi moved confidently to take charge. Indeed, as we will see, he moved swiftly against his perceived enemies and to centralize power to an extent not seen since Deng Xiaoping.

The main instrument Xi would use to go after his opponents and establish his authority was the CDIC. Although the CDIC was supposed to be the party's watchdog, it was also not supposed to serve partisan interests. Even though settling some partisan scores is inevitable, the CDIC had never before been used in such a clearly political way to attack the leader's perceived opponents. If extra leverage were required, Xi headed the newly created Leadership Small Group for Comprehensive Change and another newly created small group, the National Security Leadership Small Group. The first of these two groups clearly put a layer between Xi and Premier Li Keqiang, constraining the premier's power in a way that had not been done previously in the reform era.

When one looks back at these early months of Xi's rule, it is clear that he had a plan. There were at least three major themes that he stressed right out of the gate: populist nationalism, opposing corruption, and strengthening the party. On the day that the new PBSC was introduced to the world, Xi appealed to national pride, saying without apparent embarrassment, "Our people are a great people . . ... The Chinese people have opened up a good and beautiful home where all ethnic groups live in harmony and have fostered an excellent culture that never fades."[5] Two weeks later, as mentioned in the previous chapter, Xi led his colleagues to the exhibition on The Road to Renaissance (*fuxing*

---

[5] *Renmin ribao*, November 16, 2012.

zhilu). Wearing a windbreaker and no tie, in contrast to his business-suited predecessors, Xi declared that China had finally found the "correct path" to achieve the "China Dream." Building on the victim narrative that had become a staple of "patriotic education," Xi said: "In modern times, the Chinese nation was subjected to untold miseries and sacrifices rarely seen in the world's history." News commentary made clear that the Chinese people owed the development of China to the CCP. As one authoritative article in *People's Daily* put it, "to realize the China Dream, the political leadership that plays a leading role is extremely important ... the key to running things well in China and realizing the China Dream lies in the party."[6]

The meme of the "China Dream" has been around for a long time. As *People's Daily* helpfully pointed out, Liang Qichao mentioned the "China Dream" in his 1902 essay "The Future of New China," in which he envisions a rich and powerful country, and there are echoes of the China Dream narrative in Sun Yat-sen's calls to "revive China" and in Chiang Kai-shek's *China's Destiny*. About a decade earlier, there had been a Chinese television show called *China Dream* that, perhaps ironically, depicted a young Chinese couple trying to make it in New York City. More recently the idea of a China dream had been given a more cosmopolitan twist in the Olympic slogan "One World, One Dream."

However, in recent years the China Dream has been associated with a nationalistic discourse embodied in such books as *Zhongguo bu gaoxing* (*China Is Unhappy*), *Huobi zhanzheng* (*Currency Wars*), and, of course, Colonel Liu Mingfu's infamous *Zhongguo meng* (*China Dream*). In 2010, Wang Jisi, then dean of Peking University's School of International Relations, had already worried that such discourse, feeding off the global financial crisis and China's increased confidence, might widen the gulf of perceptions between the US and China and lead to conflict.[7]

Although Xi has said that the China Dream is "the dream of every Chinese," it is clearly a collective, not an individual, dream. As one commentary put it, "Compared with the 'American dream' that

---

[6] *Renmin ribao*, April 20, 2013.
[7] Wang Jisi, "ZhongMei guanxi zhongda zhanlüe jiaoliang nanyi bimian" (It Is Difficult to Avoid a Major Strategic Struggle between the US and China), *Guoji xianqu daobao*, August 9, 2010, available at https://news.qq.com/a/20100809/001152.htm, accessed September 16, 2020.

emphasizes personal struggles, the 'China dream' is a dream built on the foundation of patriotism and collectivism."[8] As Xi Jinping said in his closing address to the NPC, "To realize the Chinese dream, we must carry forward the Chinese spirit. This is the national spirit with patriotism as the core."[9]

Launching the Campaign against Corruption

Just as Xi was prepared to hit nationalist and populist themes following the end of the congress, he was also prepared to take on corruption with a force unprecedented in the reform era. The Eighteenth Party Congress was held on November 4–18, 2012. On the day the congress closed, Xi presided over the PB's first collective study session and gave a talk about upholding the party's (not the state's) constitution. With an eye clearly on the campaign against corruption that was about to unfold, he stated bluntly, "There have been serious breaches of discipline in the party in recent years. Some of these cases were very bad, and they have had a terrible, appalling political impact." In other countries, he said, "corruption has played a big role in conflicts that grew over lengthy periods, and it has led to popular discontent, social unrest, and the overthrow of political power." Lest anyone might miss the point, Xi added, "A large number of facts show that corruption could kill the party and ruin the party."[10] It was not yet known publicly that Xi was about to launch a massive campaign against corruption, but it is clear in retrospect that Xi had already decided to move against corruption, and specifically against Zhou Yongkang.

Xi's decision to launch immediately an assault on corruption seemed to catch Wang Qishan, the new head of the CDIC, by surprise. At the study session, Wang reportedly raised some comments to the effect that the CDIC was not prepared for such a large-scale assault. As they were leaving the session, Xi allegedly turned to Wang and said that he should have talked with Wang beforehand, but this was an issue he had thought about for a long time. Xi's words contained a double message. First, they were going to go ahead with the campaign and Wang would

---

[8] Xin Ming, "'Zhongguomeng,' Zhongguo daolu yu Zhongguo tese shehui zhuyi" (The "China Dream," the Chinese Path, and Socialism with Chinese Characteristics), *Xuexi shibao*, March 11, 2013.
[9] *Renmin ribao*, March 18, 2013. [10] *Renmin ribao*, November 17, 2012.

lead it, and, second, despite their long-term personal friendship, Xi was now the boss.

In any event, the campaign got under way quickly. Less than one month later, on December 6, the first "tiger," Li Chuncheng, fell. Although the term "tiger" is often used by the media in a general way to mean an "important" official, it actually has a very specific meaning – it means anyone of the ministerial or vice ministerial rank who thus fell under the purview of the central *nomenklatura*. We often use the Russian term for those cadres appointed by the central party apparatus, but its specific meaning refers to cadres who are under the purview of the central authorities, the centrally managed cadres, *zhongguan ganbu*, of which there are approximately 2,500. Those at lower levels were referred to as "flies," meaning cadres managed by provinces or municipalities.

At the time of his detention, Li Chuncheng was a deputy party secretary of Sichuan province and mayor of Chengdu, a cadre at the level of deputy minister *(fu buji)*. In 1999, when Zhou Yongkang was appointed party secretary of Sichuan, Li moved within only half a year's time, from deputy mayor of Chengdu, to party secretary of Luzhou county in southern Sichuan, and back again to mayor of Chengdu. The decision that sentenced Li Chuncheng to thirteen years in jail declared that during Li's ten years as mayor of Chengdu, he had, "at the instigation of Zhou Yongkang," helped others to acquire illegitimate wealth. As in most such cases, corruption was not a matter of one person taking bribes but rather of a group, what the press started calling "nests," working together to profit one another. This was the same sort of "political ecology" that had developed in Shanxi. In the case of Chengdu, at least twenty-two people were involved, ten of whom were directly involved with Li Chuncheng.[11] The connection between Li and Zhou was thus clear, so a decision to investigate Li would have to have involved a discussion of investigating Zhou.

It seems that Li's problems were well known. He was a powerful person, known for rebuilding the city, which required the destruction

---

[11] "Wang Shu, "Zhe 13 ming luoma guanyuan, gen Zhou Yongkang you duoda guanlian?" (How Much Do These 13 Sacked Officials Have to Do with Zhou Yongkang?), *Xinjing baowang* (New Capital News Web), November 24, 2015, available at www.bjnews.com.cn/news/2015/11/24/385458.html, accessed June 1, 2020.

of much of the city's cultural history. This was during a period when *chaiqian*, the bulldozing of houses, was occurring all over the country, often provoking popular outbursts. In Chengdu, Li was known as "Li Tear-Down-the-City." He also ran media, real-estate and investment firms. A former police commissioner by the name of Shen Yong had been involved in investigations of Li as early as 2002. Li was named an alternate member of the Sixteenth Central Committee in 2002 but he was dropped from the Seventeenth Central Committee, apparently because his problems were already known. Nevertheless, he continued in powerful positions in Sichuan until his arrest in 2012.[12]

One of Li's Chuncheng's close associates was a man named Dai Xiaoming, previously the party secretary of Qingbaijiang district in Chengdu and director of the Chengdu Economic and Information Commission before becoming head of Chengdu Industrial Investment Corporation. Known as Li's "right-hand man," Dai was allegedly involved in many corrupt schemes involving Li. Dai was detained for investigation in August or September, and Xi Jinping may well have become aware of the results of the investigation. If so, he was fully prepared to go after Li as soon as the party congress ended.[13]

Following this fast start, it took the campaign against corruption quite a while to gain momentum. It was not until May of the following year that the campaign claimed its second high-level victim, and that may well have been by accident. Luo Changping was a popular blogger who wrote for *Caijing* magazine. In his serialized blog, he exposed the corruption of Liu Tienan, the deputy head of the National Reform and Development Commission (NDRC). This was one of the few cases of corruption exposed by an unofficial source. Although the media for a time seemed to invite public exposure, it quickly backed off and bottom-up accusations of high-level officials stopped.

[12] Sascha, "Chengdu Ex-mayor Faces Corruption Charges," *Chengdu Living*, December 10, 2012, available at www.chengduliving.com/the-case-of-li-chuncheng, accessed June 11, 2012; Zhang Pinghui, "Li Chuncheng Graft Probe Linked to Chengdu Businessman," *South China Morning Post*, December 6, 2012, available at www.scmp.com/news/china/article/1098437/li-chuncheng-graft-probe-linked-chengdu-businessman, accessed June 11, 2012.
[13] Zhang Pinghui, "Li Chuncheng Graft Probe Linked to Chengdu Businessman."

Figure 5.2 Zhou Yongkang, former head of the Political and Legal Affairs Commission and member of the Politburo Standing Committee, was convicted of corruption in June 2015 (Feng Li via Getty Images)

The Liu Tienan case had nothing to do with Zhou Yongkang, but soon the CDIC was following the trail that led to Zhou Yongkang's door. In June, Guo Yongxiang, a deputy governor of Sichuan, was detained, and in September Jiang Jiemin, chairman of the Natural Resources Commission and former deputy CEO of Petrochina, was detained. Both of these men had close ties to Zhou Yongkang. In July 2014, Xinhua finally announced that Zhou Yongkang had been placed under investigation, although apparently he had been under investigation since late 2013. He was convicted in June 2015.

In early 2014, the CDIC turned its attention to associates of Ling Jihua, and Ling himself was detained in December 2014 and convicted in May 2016. At the same time, Xi also turned his attention to the military. Retired vice chair of the CMC, Xu Caihou, was cashiered on corruption charges in June 2014. Xu seems to have been enormously corrupt – press accounts reported that it took twelve trucks to clear his apartment of ill-gotten gains – but his arrest clearly demonstrated to all, especially the military, that Xi Jinping was in charge. After all, between Xu being named deputy director general of the GPD in September 1999 and his retirement in 2012, Xu had screened some eighty-three officers for promotion to the rank of full general.[14] The purge of Xu Caihou was quickly followed by the purge of Guo Boxiong, the other long-serving and then retired vice chair of the CMC.[15] The purge of Xu and Guo would pave the way for Xi to restructure the PLA (see below).

Altogether during Xi Jinping's first term, twenty-six officials at or above the ministerial level were detained and investigated, along with 129 officials at the vice ministerial level.

What Xi Jinping had managed to do within months of assuming his position was to wrap a long-standing issue – corruption – together with the fate of the party and make it an issue of patriotism and national survival. The collapse of the CPSU and the disintegration of the Soviet Union made this case easier to make. Xi's use of the CDIC and the various leadership small groups he headed allowed him to bypass his colleagues on the PBSC. It turned out not to matter that he did not have overwhelming support on the PB or PBSC.

Saving the Party as a Nationalist Project

Setting out nationalist themes, pumping up populist hopes with the "China Dream," and purging corrupt officials did not define a political program. Xi came much closer to doing this when he went to Shenzhen in December 2012. At first, this trip seemed to pay obeisance to the "architect" of reform and opening, Deng Xiaoping (later on, Xi would begin to denigrate Deng). But he also had a different message for party leaders in Shenzhen. In an internal speech, Xi revealed the depth of his concern that the CCP, like the CPSU, would lose power. He told his listeners that the Communist Party in the Soviet Union had lost power because it had lost its ideals and confidence, because the military did not defend the party, and because, "in the end, no one was a real man,

---

[14] Bo Zhiyue, "The Rise and Fall of Xu Caihou, China's Corrupt General," *The Diplomat,* March 18, 2015, available at http://thediplomat.com/2015/03/the-rise-and-fall-of-xu-caihou-chinas-corrupt-general, accessed June 5, 2020.

[15] Chris Buckley, "Guo Boxiong, Ex-top Military Official in China, Gets Life Sentence for Graft," *New York Times,* July 25, 2016, available at www.nytimes.com/2016/07/26/world/asia/china-guo-boxiong-sentence.html, accessed September 16, 2020.

no one came out to resist."[16] More than anything else, this mission of saving the party would define Xi's administration.

This warning about the precedent of the Soviet Union was not a one-off. A "Ren Zhongping" article in *People's Daily* stated, "Today, the Soviet Union, with its history of 74 years, has been gone for 22 years. For more than two decades, China has never stopped reflecting on how the Communist Party and nation were lost by the Soviet Communists."[17] In September 2013 China's National Defense University put out a film called *Silent Contest (Jiaoliang wusheng)* that cited the alleged US strategy of "peaceful evolution" as the main cause of the collapse of the CPSU.[18] In October–November 2013, Chinese television broadcast a four-part documentary, *Commemorating the Collapse of the CPSU and the Soviet Union (Sulian wangdang wangguo 20 nian ji.)*. Then, in November 2013, Xi's close ally, Li Zhanshu, said that "reform" in the Soviet Union had led to the "burying of the socialist enterprise." "The lesson," he went on, "is extremely deep."[19]

There is no doubt that the party faced real problems, but defining Xi's mission in these terms was also useful politically. Cleaning up corruption required such harsh measures because it was a matter of life and death. Opposition would be seen as undermining the party and socialism. The degree to which this was the case soon became evident.

December 5 is Constitution Day in China, the day the party promulgated China's first post-Cultural Revolution state constitution and vowed to adhere to it (it is the same constitution that, although amended, is still in effect today). When the constitution was

---

[16] Chris Buckley, "Vows of Change in China Belie Private Warning," *New York Times*, February 15, 2013, available at www.nytimes.com/2013/02/15/world/asia/vowing-reform-chinas-leader-xi-jinping-airs-other-message-in-private.html, accessed September 16, 2020; Gao Yu, "Beijing Observation: Xi Jinping the Man," *China Change*, January 26, 2013, available at https://chinachange.org/2013/01/26/beijing-observation-xi-jinping-the-man-by-gao-yu, accessed September 16, 2020.

[17] Ren Zhongping, "Shouhu renmin zhengdang de shengmingxian" (Protect the Lifeline of the Party), *Renmin ribao*, October 14, 2013, available at http://opinion.people.com.cn/n/2013/1014/c1003-23187114.htm, accessed September 16, 2020.

[18] This film can be found on YouTube, at www.youtube.com/watch?v=XhHvhm3Ey_0, accessed October 3, 2020.

[19] Li Zhanshu, "Zunxun 'sige jianchi' de gaige jingyan" (Adhering to the Experience of Reform with the "Four Upholds"), *Renmin ribao*, November 26, 2013, available at http://cpc.people.com.cn/n/2013/1126/c64094-23653391.html, accessed June 4, 2020.

promulgated in 1982, an editorial in *People's Daily* declared, "our party is the party in power, and it occupies the position of leadership in the political life of the state, but before the constitution and laws, our party, like all other parties, groups, and organizations, must conduct its activities within the limits permitted by the constitution and the laws."[20] It seemed at the time that China might really commit itself to a path of institutionalization.

In 2002, on the twentieth anniversary of promulgating the constitution, China seemed to go even further, saying, "no organization or individual can be permitted the special privilege of going outside the constitution and law" and "all party organizations at various levels and all party members must act as models in upholding the constitution, strictly managing affairs in accordance with the constitution, and conscientiously operating within the scope of the constitution and law."[21]

Not to be outdone, Xi Jinping gave a major speech on December 5, 2012, declaring, "Protecting the authority of the constitution means protecting the authority of the common will of the party and the people." He continued:

To manage state affairs according to law, first we must manage the country in accordance with the constitution. The key to holding power in accordance with the law is to first rule in accordance with the constitution. The party leadership formulates the constitution and the law, and the party itself must act within the scope of the constitution and the law to truly achieve the party leadership's establishment of the law, ensuring the enforcement of the law, and taking the lead in abiding by the law.[22]

These seemingly strong words energized the liberal intellectual community. Seventy scholars signed a petition calling for political reform, in particular calling for constitutional government.[23] Picking up on Xi's theme of the China Dream and the seemingly relaxed atmosphere, the liberal Guangzhou-based paper *Southern Weekend* wrote a New

---

[20] Cited in Tang Tsou, "Reflections on the Formation and Foundations of the Communist Party-State," p. 313, in Tang Tsou, *The Cultural Revolution and Post-Mao Reforms: A Historical Perspective* (Chicago: The University of Chicago Press, 1986).

[21] Fewsmith, *China since Tiananmen*, pp. 242–243.

[22] *Renmin ribao*, December 5, 2012.

[23] Zhang Qianfang, "Proposal for Consensus on Reform," *Caijing Online*, December 26, 2012.

Year's editorial, "China's Dream Is the Dream of Constitutional Government." Before it could hit the streets, however, the editorial was rewritten by the head of the Guangdong provincial propaganda department as a paean to the party. The journalists at *Southern Weekend* objected and went out on strike – a movement that only resulted in the removal of the editor. The nationalistic paper *Global Times* then ran an article that stated with unusual bluntness and honesty that "anyone with common sense knows that in China there is no room for a 'free press,' and that the media should not harbor the unrealistic hope of becoming a 'political special zone'."[24]

Tightening Ideology

The reaction to the *Southern Weekend* editorial proved to be just the opening shot in a multiyear effort to tighten controls over media and education. It is not that controls over media were ever loose. In 2004, Hu Jintao had praised North Korea and Cuba for their tight controls over ideology, suggesting that China should emulate them. But, over time, controls would inevitably loosen and debates would resume. The publishing of debates in the media was often a way for reform-minded intellectuals to get their ideas into the public arena and to build support. As the Hu Jintao period wore on, the media atmosphere seemed to become somewhat more relaxed. It was that momentum that *Southern Weekend* had hoped to build on.

However, the Xi administration would sharply reverse this trend. In April 2013, the General Office of the CCP issued so-called "Document No. 9," meaning the ninth centrally issued circular of the year, decrying ideological laxity in seven spheres. The first one, not surprisingly, was "Western constitutional democracy." The document declared that opponents of socialism "use Western constitutional democracy to undermine the Party's leadership, abolish People's Democracy, negate our country's constitution as well as our established system and

---

[24] Ching Cheong, "Xi Faces the Test of His Reform Image," *Straits Times Online*, January 11, 2013; David Bandurski, "Inside the Southern Weekly Incident," *China Media Project*, January 7, 2013, available at http://chinamediaproject.o rg/2013/01/07/inside-the-southern-weekly-incident, accessed September 16, 2020.

principles, and bring about a change of allegiance by bringing Western political systems to China."[25]

The other six ideological trends were "universal values" (such as human rights and democracy), civil society, neoliberalism, freedom of the press, "historical nihilism," and the idea that "reform and opening up" had gone too far and deviated from socialism. The first six trends were identified with liberal intellectuals and the final trend was identified with the neo-Maoist "leftists." This divide, between "liberals" and "leftists" was obviously serious and deep.

The term "historical nihilism" does not strike a visceral response with most Western readers, but it was deeply important to party propagandists. As Xi's visit to The Road to Renaissance exhibit showed, the way history is told is critical to the legitimacy of the CCP. As noted above, this history is a victim narrative. In it, China is brought to its knees by imperialist greed. The Taiping Rebellion (-1850–1864), during which 20 million or more perished, was unable to bring about real revolution. Sun Yat-sen's revolution of 1911 demonstrated that democracy is not right for China. The Nationalist revolution could not free itself from the clutches of imperialism or the greed of landlords and bureaucratic capitalists. Finally, the Communist Party, after undergoing its own trials and tribulations, was able to lead the peasants to victory, restoring unity and sovereignty to the country. After more twists and turns, China had finally emerged as a wealthy and powerful country – the wish of so many patriots over so many years. But the sense of struggle had to be nurtured. If that sense of struggle were to be loosened, China might, once again, become an economic appendage of the West.

There is no mention in this narrative of China's population explosion that pushed the imperial system to its limit;[26] the liberal ideas that inspired many intellectuals, including early members of the CCP; the costs of revolution (Communist or otherwise); or reasons why, having completed the revolution and having gained full sovereignty, democracy was still not appropriate. It certainly does not address the issue of

---

[25] "Document No. 9: A ChinaFile Translation," November 8, 2013, available at www.chinafile.com/document-9-chinafile-translation, accessed June 6, 2020.

[26] Philip Kuhn, *Rebellion and Its Enemies in Late Imperial China: Militarization and Social Structure*, 1796–1984 (Cambridge, MA: Harvard University Press, 1970).

legitimacy; why does victory in war confer legitimacy on leaders seventy years later?[27]

Asking questions of party history threatens the legitimacy of the party perhaps more than abstract ideas such as "universal values" because such inquiries are specific to China and can be documented.

Document No. 9 was hardly the last effort to tighten control over ideology. In August, Xi Jinping addressed a national Meeting on Propaganda and Thought Work and told the attendees that it was necessary to strengthen the "socialist core value system" and that all propaganda and thought workers "must clearly uphold the principles of party spirit."[28] In December 2015, Xi visited the PLA paper, *Liberation Army Daily*, which may have been necessary in the wake of Xu Caihou's detention.[29] Then, in February 2016, Xi visited *People's Daily*, Xinhua, and CCTV to remind them that it is necessary to "put politics in the first place," to "firmly uphold the party's principles, and firmly uphold positive propaganda as primary." When he visited CCTV, he was greeted by a banner that declared, "CCTV is surnamed 'party'; we are absolutely loyal, please inspect."[30] Journalists, believing they had outgrown such servility, were deeply embarrassed.

Dealing with Mao's Shadow

In the telling of modern Chinese history, no figure is more important than Mao Zedong. Deng Xiaoping's approach to Mao was to "museum-ify" him, to borrow a term from the great historian Joseph

---

[27] See Jiwei Ci, *Democracy in China: The Coming Crisis* (Cambridge, MA: Harvard University Press, 2019), for an insightful discussion of legitimacy.

[28] "Xi Jinping zongshuji zai quangguo xuanchuan sixiang gongnzuo huiyi shang de zhongyao jianghua yinqi xuanchuan sixiang wenhua zhanxian he shehui gejie jiji fanxiang" (General Secretary Xi Jinping's Important Speech at the National Propaganda and Thought Work Forum Inspires the Enthusiastic Response of All Circles of Society and the Propaganda, Thought, and Culture Front), *Renmin ribao*, September 9, 2013, available at http://cpc.people.com.cn/n/201 3/0909/c64387-22860470.html, accessed September 29, 2020.

[29] "Xi Jinping shicha Jiefangjun baoshe" (Xi Jinping Inspects the Offices of *Liberation Army Daily*), *Xinhuawang*, December 26, 2015, available at www .xinhuanet.com/politics/2015-12/26/c_1117588434.htm, accessed June 8, 2020.

[30] "President Xi Jinping Makes Research Tour to People's Daily," *People's Daily* online, February 19, 2016, available at http://en.people.cn/n3/2016/0219/c900 00-9018740.html, accessed February 14, 2021.

Levenson. The party's 1981 history resolution ("Resolution on Certain Questions in the History of Our Party since the Founding of the State") praised Mao as "a great Marxist and a great proletarian revolutionary, strategist, and theorist," but it went on to say that Mao had made "gross mistakes during the 'Cultural Revolution.'" It concluded that "[h]is merits are primary and errors secondary." It is worth noting that it did *not* say that Mao was 70 percent good and 30 percent bad.

The history resolution was supposed to put the issue of Mao to rest. Mao should not be repudiated *in toto*, as more liberal members of the party wanted, but his "leftist" errors had to be criticized harshly, both to legitimate the return to power of those purged during the Cultural Revolution and to justify the party's turn from class struggle to economic construction (a shift endorsed by the party's watershed Third Plenary Session of the Eleventh Central Committee in December 1978). Tensions between the "conservative" wing of the party and the "liberal" wing persisted through the 1980s, but the history resolution, despite its ambiguities, held firm.

The march of economic reform perhaps made revisiting Mao inevitable. China had made enormous economic progress between 1978 and 2012 when Xi took over. Indeed, most people, whether Chinese or not, would judge that China had developed precisely because it had turned away from Mao. The gap between the Maoist period of rule and the prosperity after Deng had inaugurated reform and opening was glaring. These two periods became known as the "two thirty years" (*liangge sanshi nian*), and Xi, for the first time, decided to address them as two separate but indivisible periods. On the occasion of the 120th anniversary of Mao's birth, in a major speech to new members of the Central Committee, Xi started off by stating firmly that the spirit of the Eighteenth Party Congress could be summed up in one point: the need to uphold and develop socialism with Chinese characteristics. But in reaffirming the Dengist path, Xi gave it a new twist. He pointed out:[31]

---

[31] "Hao bu dongyao jianchi he fazhan Zhongguo tese shehui zhuyi zai shijian zhong buduan yousuo faxian yousuo chuangzao yousuo qianjin" (Unhesitatingly Uphold and Develop Socialism with Chinese Characteristics; Make Some New Discoveries, Some New Innovations, and Some Advances in the Course of Practice), *Renmin ribao*, January 6, 2013.

In carrying out the construction of socialism by our party, leaders, and people, there have been the two periods, [namely that] before reform and opening and [that] after reform and opening up. These two periods are mutually related but also have major differences, but in essence they are our party's leaders' and people's practical explorations in carrying out the construction of socialism. Socialism with Chinese characteristics was opened up by the new period of reform and opening, but it was opened up on the foundation of the fundamental socialist system that had already been established and the more than 20 years during which construction had been carried out. Although the ideological direction, orientation, and policies of these two historical periods of carrying out socialist construction had major differences, they cannot be cut apart. Even more, they are not in opposition. One cannot use the historical period following reform and opening to negate the historical period prior to reform and opening, and one cannot use the historical period prior to reform and opening to negate the historical period following reform and opening.

In November 2013, the Central Party History Research Office published a full-page article in *People's Daily* that laid out an authoritative view of the "two thirty years." It stated that the Cultural Revolution "brought untold disasters to the party, state, and the people of all nationalities," but it warned sharply against "deliberately negating Comrade Mao Zedong's mistakes in his later years, much less completely negating Comrade Mao Zedong and Mao Zedong Thought." On the contrary, the article argued, the periods before and after reform "are never to be separated from each other, let alone fundamentally opposed to each other."[32]

The importance of "historical nihilism" – the "misunderstanding" of history – was critical, the article stated: "Failure to properly handle this important political issue will create serious political consequences." Raising once again the specter of the former Soviet Union, the article went on, "One important reason for the disintegration of the Soviet Union and the collapse of the CPSU is the complete negation of the history of the Soviet Union and the CPSU, the negation of Lenin and other leading figures, and the practice of historical nihilism, which confused people's minds."[33]

---

[32] Central Party History Research Office, "Zhengque kandai gaige kaifang qianhou liangge lishi shiqi" (Correctly View the Two Historical Periods Prior to and after Reform and Opening Up), *Renmin ribao*, November 8, 2013.
[33] Ibid.

Figure 5.3 Bo Xilai (l), then party secretary of Chongqing, conferring with General Xu Caihou (r), then vice chairman of the Central Military Commission (Feng Li via Getty Images)

Military Reform

As the detention of Xu Caihou, then retired, showed, Xi was determined to take direct control of the PLA, both for his own political purposes and to bring about the reforms that the vested interests and structural impediments in the military had resisted. In November 2014, Xi led over 420 leaders of the PLA to Gutian, the town in Fujian province where, in December 1929, Mao Zedong, after receiving the backing of Zhou Enlai, was able to reimpose his leadership on Zhu De and the Red Fourth Army, which had rejected his leadership the previous June.[34] Forging a party army is not an easy matter. If leadership is too heavily political, the military's professionalism is likely to be compromised; if the military side is too strong, it escapes political control. Even though Xu Caihou was retired and charged with corruption (and Guo Boxiong was about to be similarly

---

[34] James Mulvenon, "Hotel Gutian: We Haven't Had That Spirit Here since 1929," *China Leadership Monitor*, No. 46 (Winter 2015), available at www .hoover.org/research/hotel-gutian-we-havent-had-spirit-here-1929, accessed September 16, 2020.

charged), the military chain of command had largely been promoted by the two of them, and the military had conducted its affairs largely independently of the political leadership. There was even talk of "nationalization" (the idea that the military should be subordinate to the state rather than the party), something that the party leadership beat back repeatedly.

So Xi Jinping felt that the lessons of Gutian needed repeating. He paid special attention to the lessons of Xu Caihou, calling on those present to "deeply reflect on the lessons learned and thoroughly exterminate the influence [of Xu's corrupt acts]." This must have been a deeply unsettling moment since most of the people in the room had been screened and promoted at Xu's behest. Military analyst James Mulvenon judges that the Xu case must have "rock[ed] the very foundations of the military"; after all, "Xu's 'bribes for promotion' scheme [was] reportedly standard practice at every level of the military-promotion system and *every officer attending the Gutian meeting therefore was an unindicted co-conspirator in Xu's larger crime by participating in that system.*"[35]

Not since Deng Xiaoping had someone taken control of the PLA in this manner, and Xi followed up first by charging Guo Boxiong with corruption just a few months later (in April 2015). Then, in late 2015, Xi launched the most extensive reorganization of the PLA since its founding. The essence of the reorganization was that the four general departments – the General Staff Department, the GPD, the General Logistics Department, and the General Armaments Department – were abolished and the seven military regions were replaced by five joint theater commands. There were many reasons for these changes, including the inability of the old structure to implement the joint operations that are necessary for modern warfare, but there is no question that the new structure greatly increased the personal control by Xi Jinping.[36]

[35] Ibid., original emphasis.
[36] David Finklestein, "Breaking the Paradigm: Drivers behind the PLA's Current Period of Reform," pp. 45–83, in *Chairman Xi Remakes the PLA: Assessing the Chinese Military* Reforms, ed. Phillip C. Saunders. Arthur S. Ding, Andrew N. D. Yang, and Joel Wuthnow (Washington, DC: National Defense University Press, 2019).

Curbing the Communist Youth League

In the summer of 2015, Xi gave a speech on the party's mass work, a topic that included the CYL.[37] The CYL has a history that goes back to the 1920s, and it has always been regarded as the junior partner of the CCP, helping the latter to recruit and cultivate party members. During the reform era, the CYL has played a surprisingly strong role in providing the party with major leaders. Hu Yaobang had been head of the CYL prior to the Cultural Revolution and one of his contributions to the reform effort was to tap his network of younger leaders to take up important positions. Although not part of Hu Yaobang's network, Hu Jintao (not related) became a CYL leader in the early 1980s, rising to head the organization in 1984. His protégés at the CYL, including current premier Li Keqiang and PB member Hu Chunhua, followed Hu Jintao up the political ladder. Ling Jihua had also come up through the CYL, working in its Propaganda Department before taking time off to attend college and then to join the central party.

After Xi's speech on mass work, an investigation team was sent to inspect the central offices of the CYL. It returned with a scathing report. The report called the CYL "bureaucratic, administrative, nepotistic, and hedonistic." In April 2016, the CDIC website posted the CYL's response, essentially a self-criticism.[38] But a reorganization of the CYL, laid out in August, cut its budget, put the organization more firmly under the party's control, and stressed its function of reaching out to youth rather than reaching for power.[39] Although Li Keqiang and Hu Chunhua would survive the purge that ensued, a few other once promising leaders would not. The CYL's days as a center of power were over.

---

[37] "Zhonggong zhongyang guanyu jiaqiang ge gaijin dang de quntuan gongzuo de yi jian (quan wen)" (Views of the Party Center on Strengthening and Improving the Work of Mass Organizations (complete text)), *Xinhuashe*, July 8, 2015, available at http://news.china.com.cn/2015-07/09/content_36023933.htm, accessed September 15, 2020.

[38] "Tuanzhongyang fuzeren jiu qongqingtuan gaige da jizhe wen" (A Responsible Person from the CYL Center Answers Reporters' Questions), *Renminwang*, August 3, 2016, available at http://cpc.people.cn/gqt/n1/2016/0803/c363174-286 05839.html, accessed June 22, 2020.

[39] Chris Buckley, "China Reins in Communist Youth League, and Its Alumni's Prospects," *New York Times*, August 3, 2016, available at www.nytimes.com/2016/08/04/world/asia/china-communist-youth-league.html, accessed September 16, 2020.

Wrapping up Xi's First Term

An extremely fast-moving first term began wrapping up with the Fifth Plenum of the Eighteenth Central Committee in October 2015, which was primarily about the Thirteenth Five-Year Plan. This plan period would run through 2020, thus putting the country on the cusp of the hundredth anniversary of the founding of the CCP (in July 2021). To meet this benchmark, the party set the goal of attaining a "moderately prosperous" (*xiaokang*) society, a goal later put in jeopardy by the COVID-19 pandemic.

Although it was unknown at the time, Xi was also upping the stakes in his battle against Bo Xilai and others. When Bo was arrested and convicted, the *People's Daily* repeatedly assured its readers that corruption was the issue. It was all a matter of adhering to the law. In this, everyone is equal; no one is above the law. But in December 2015, the party published a slim volume of statements Xi Jinping had made about strict enforcement of discipline and regulations in the party. Most of the statements had been published before, but on page 28 readers were startled to read:

In recent years [we] have investigated cases of some high-level cadres who have seriously violated discipline and law, especially those of Zhou Yongkang, Bo Xilai, Xu Caihou, Ling Jihua, and Su Rong, who have broken the party's political discipline and political regulations. These must be viewed seriously. These people, the greater their power and the higher their position, the more they don't think of the party's political discipline and political regulations as anything at all. Their actions are unscrupulous and audacious in the extreme. In some of them, their political ambition swells, and for their own interest or for the interest of a small group. They turn their backs on the party organization and engage in political conspiracy; they collaborate with each other to wreck and divide the party. Some leading cadres put themselves above the party, they think of themselves as number one, and they take wherever the party sends them as their own independent kingdom. In using cadres and making decisions, they don't report to the center as they should, and they engage in small-mountaintop-ism, small factions, small groups . . . [40]

All of a sudden, these cases were not only matters of corruption; instead, they reflected deep divisions within the party. Xi Jinping was

[40] Xi Jinping, *Xi Jinping guanyu yanming dang de jilu he guiju lunshu zhebian* (Selected Quotes from Xi Jinping on Making Clear the Party's Discipline and Regulations) (Beijing: Zhongguo fangzheng chubanshu, 2016), p. 28.

saying as openly as possible that institutional processes had not worked within the party. He would work to implement and strengthen party mechanisms – but only under his own domination.

One year later, at the party's Sixth Plenum, the party focused on precisely those issues, passing "Some Principles Regarding the CCP's Intra-party Political Life" and "Regulations of the CCP on Intra-party Supervision." Such regulations, Xi hoped, would regularize activities within the party and prevent the factionalism and conspiratorial activities in which, as Xi charged, Bo Xilai and others had engaged

The big news out of the plenum, however, was that Xi Jinping now officially known as the "core." The term "core" (*hexin*) is not an official title but a description of one's place at the top of the system. When Deng Xiaoping introduced Jiang Zemin as the new leader of the party, he said that Mao had been core of the first generation of leadership, that he (Deng) had been core of the second generation, and, now, he said, Jiang would be the core of the third generation of leadership. Although, as we have seen, Jiang could hardly be considered the core of the party in 1989, Deng designating him as such constituted important political backing. Deng certainly had never called Zhao Ziyang or Hu Yaobang the "core."

When Hu Jintao took over as general secretary in 2002, no one referred to him as the "core." Those watching China wondered whether this absence reflected a normalization and institutionalization of Chinese politics. It did not. It reflected the simple fact that Jiang Zemin continued to hold the designation, informal though it was, until 2016, when Xi declared that he was then the core. Hu Jintao was never considered the core.

Conclusion

Xi Jinping's assumption of office was fundamentally different from that of any of his three predecessors during the reform period. He did not have the ready base that allowed Deng to push Hua Guofeng and others aside and to remake the elite. Indeed, looking at the outcome of the Eighteenth Party Congress, it seemed that Xi, like Hu Jintao, would be hemmed in by elders and a PLA hierarchy that he had not appointed. He was challenged by Bo Xilai before he took office and he faced a potentially recalcitrant PLA leadership, not to mention leaders willing to conspire against him (if his charges against Xu Caihou and Guo Boxiong are accurate).

Determined to escape the influences of the retirees who had dominated Hu Jintao, Xi opened with a full-scale campaign against corruption. It was a smart move. There was probably no one in the Central Committee who was not vulnerable to charges of corruption, and once Xi was able to take down Zhou Yongkang, Ling Jihua, Xu Caihou, and Guo Boxiong, conspiring against Xi would have been very dangerous indeed. In repeatedly invoking the fate of the CPSU, Xi leveraged the threat of "peaceful evolution" that hung over the regime, and he used that threat, which was at least in part real, to remake the elite. Deng had continued as a force while Jiang tried to consolidate power, and Jiang did the same, only worse, to Hu Jintao. Xi made sure that the retirees and their protégés could not do the same to him. But in doing so, he opened a new chapter in intra-party struggle. While we do not know where that will take the party in the future, institutionalization is an unlikely destination.

6 | *The Nineteenth Party Congress and Reinvigorating Leninism*

During his first term, Xi Jinping asserted his power, jailed his enemies, and ended interference by the elders. The last of these ended one form of balance that had been in place since Deng Xiaoping established the CAC in 1982. The CAC had ceased to exist in 1992, but the informal influence of the retirees continued, as the Eighteenth Party Congress clearly shows. The impact of curtailing the influence of retirees such as Jiang Zemin and Hu Jintao was to limit voices at the highest level and to centralize greater power in Xi Jinping. However, Xi had not yet remade the political elite or centralized power through structural changes. These were the tasks of the Nineteenth Party Congress and the period that followed. The Nineteenth Party Congress convened on October 18, 2017, amidst a light rain on a chilly Beijing morning. It would reverse the thrust of Deng Xiaoping's reforms and the trend toward intra-party democracy in favor of a more personalized and centralized system.

If there is anything that distinguishes the Dengist reforms it is the emphasis on breaking up the overconcentration of power and the belief that the party could be separated from the government. In contrast, at the Nineteenth Party Congress, Xi called for "firmly uphold[ing] the party's leadership in all work. Party, government, military, people and intellectuals, whether north, south, east, or west, the party leads in everything."[1] The party, of course, had always led in everything, but this was the first time that this injunction was written into the party

---

[1] Xi Jinping, "Juesheng quanmian jiancheng xiaokang shehui duoqu xin shidai Zhongguo tese shehui zhuyi weida shengli – zai Zhongguo gongchandang shijiuci quanguo daibiao dahui shangde baogao" (Secure a Decisive Victory in Building a Moderately Prosperous Society in All Respects and Strive for the Great Success of Socialism with Chinese Characteristics for a New Era), available at www .xinhuanet.com//politics/19cpcnc/2017-10/27/c_1121867529.htm, accessed September 16, 2020. An English translation is available at www.xinhuanet.com /english/download/Xi_Jinping's_report_at_19th_CPC_National_Congress.pdf, accessed November 3, 2020.

constitution. The separation of party and state had been de-emphasized since the Tiananmen events, but the idea that they could be separated, and perhaps should be, had never been refuted. So reasserting the primacy of the party in this way was jarring. In his report to the Nineteenth Party Congress, Xi went on to emphasize that cadres need to "strengthen their political consciousness, their consciousness of the overall situation, their consciousness of the core (*hexin yishi*), and their consciousness of lining up (*kanqi yishi*)." This call highlighted the "four consciousnesses" (*sige yishi*) that had been formally adopted at the Sixth Plenum of the Eighteenth Party Congress in November 2016. The last two consciousnesses – of the "core" and of "lining up" – put Xi Jinping squarely in the center of the party and political life. The term for "lining up," *kanqi*, is a military term to "dress left" or "dress right" – in other words, to be perfectly aligned with the party line and authority, particularly the leader. It was the loss of party discipline that haunted Xi, and he demanded that party members once again *kanqi*. As he put it, "We must work harder to uphold the authority and centralized, unified leadership of the Central Committee."[2]

The idea of intra-party democracy had been gaining ground even as party leaders undermined it in practice. In Chapter 5, we looked briefly at the experimentation with local elections at the township level starting in 1998. That was one form of intra-party democracy. In the summer of 2007, the Central Committee adopted a very different form of intra-party democracy. The Central Committee met in Beijing for an informal meeting at which the members cast straw ballots recommending people for the twenty-five-person PB. This vote was nonbinding. Perhaps it had no impact on the lineup that was announced that fall at the Seventeenth Party Congress, but it was the first time since the Eighth Party Congress in 1956 that intra-party democracy had been tried out at such a high level. The experiment was repeated five years later, even being extended to recommend people for the seven-person PBSC. Again, we do not know if this straw poll had any impact on the leadership that emerged at the Eighteenth Party Congress, but it suggests that the party leadership understood what had long been obvious – that the legitimacy conferred by victory in a revolutionary war seventy years earlier did not automatically confer legitimacy on the current party leadership. It also suggests that the building of informal networks in an effort to consolidate

[2] Ibid.

leadership cannot build unity in the party. Some form of voting, perhaps even *cha'e* elections (having more candidates than seats), is required.[3]

In 2017, however, this experiment with straw polls was dropped. As the Xinhua News Agency explained:

The Seventeenth and Eighteenth Party Congresses explored using meeting recommendations, but because they gave too much weight to votes, there were some problems. Some comrades in the course of these meeting recommendations simply marked their ballots, leading to voting arbitrarily, missing the sense of the public [good], and even the casting of ballots based on relationships [*guanxi*] and personal feelings [*renqing*]. The center has already investigated and found that Zhou Yongkang, Sun Zhengcai, Ling Jihua, and others had used these recommendations to attract votes and to buy votes and [engage in] extra-organizational activities.[4]

Instead of voting, Xi Jinping personally interviewed fifty-seven current and retired leaders. In addition, other top leaders solicited the views of 258 high-ranking cadres and generals. Moreover, top generals on the CMC spoke with thirty-two senior military leaders about military representation on the PB.[5]

The result, as was clearly intended, was to bring a Xi Jinping faction – I do not think the word is too strong in this case – to power. The party leadership was more centralized and more personalized than at any other time during the reform era. Whereas, previously, party norms had been bent and manipulated, now they were now discarded where needed to pursue the centralization of power, both personal and party.

As expected, Xi Jinping was elected – unanimously – for a second term. Following the retirement norm, five members of the former PBSC, including Wang Qishan, about whom there had been much speculation, retired. The five were replaced by:

---

[3] Wang Xiangwei, "How Xi Jinping Revived Old Methods by Abandoning Intraparty Democracy," *South China Morning Post*, November 5, 2017, available at www.scmp.com/week-asia/opinion/article/2118352/analysis-how-xi-jinping-revived-old-methods-abandoning-intraparty, accessed September 16, 2020.

[4] "Linghang xinshidai de jianqiang lingdao jiti – Dangde xinyijie zhongyang lingdao jigou changsheng jishi" (The Strong Leadership Collective That Will Guide the New Age – An Account of How the New Central Leadership Organs Were produced), Xinhua, October 26, 2017, available at www.xinhuanet.com //politics/19cpcnc/2017-10/26/c_1121860147.htm, accessed June 16, 2020.

[5] Ibid.; Wang Xiangwei, "How Xi Jinping Revived Old Methods by Abandoning Intraparty Democracy."

- Li Zhanshu, Xi's old friend from when both were secretaries in adjoining Hebei counties and former head of the General Office;
- Wang Yang, former party secretary of Chongqing and Guangdong who had joined the PB (but not its Standing Committee) in 2012 and who had spent the previous five years as vice premier in charge of economic relations;
- Wang Huning, former Fudan University professor who was brought to Beijing by Jiang Zemin and who had served as head of the Policy Research Office and speech writer and policy adviser not only for Jiang but also for Hu Jintao and Xi Jinping during his first term;
- Zhao Leji, former party secretary of Shaanxi province who was elected to the PB in 2012 and put in charge of the Organization Department; and
- Han Zheng, party secretary of Shanghai who was elected to the PB in 2012.

Thus, Xi followed the basic norms that have been established in recent years; those who should have retired did retire and those who replaced them were all elevated from the body of the PB, as in past years.

But Xi did not follow the usual practice of elevating people from the PB according to age. On the contrary, the oldest three members

Table 6.1 *Nineteenth Central Committee Politburo Standing Committee, 2017*

Name	Position	Previous position
Xi Jinping	General secretary	General secretary
Li Keqiang*	Premier	Premier
Li Zhanshu*	Chair, NPC	PB; Secretariat; Head, General Office
Wang Yang*	Chair, CPPCC	PB; Vice premier
Wang Huning*	Secretariat	PB; Head, Policy Research Office
Zhao Leji*	Head, CDIC	PB; Secretariat, Head, Organization Department
Han Zheng	Vice premier	PB; Party secretary, Shanghai

Note: Asterisks indicate leaders who are age-eligible to remain on the PBSC in 2022, assuming the age limit of 67 is adhered to.

on the PB, all aged sixty-seven and therefore age-eligible according to the *qishang baxia* rule (sixty-seven goes up, sixty-eight steps down), were all skipped over in order to elevate those named above. Two of those skipped over, Liu Qibao and Zhang Chunxian, were allowed to retain seats on the Central Committee, a highly unusual practice. Previously, only former party chief Hua Guofeng had been allowed to retain his Central Committee seat after stepping down from the PB, and that decision was no doubt based on Hua's unique role as Chairman Mao's successor. The other sixty-seven-year-old who was skipped over was Li Yuanchao, Hu Jintao's close associate who worked as head of the Organization Department under Hu and who had seemed to be a possible selection for the PBSC in 2012. Nevertheless, being forced to retire completely suggests that he did not find favor with Xi or others high in the political hierarchy. The last PB member to be dropped before reaching the retirement age was Li Tieying in 2002, but Li had already served two terms. Five of the seven PBSC members are age-eligible to remain on the Standing Committee in 2022, making the issue of whether or not Xi Jinping will retire perhaps the only outstanding issue to be decided in 2022.

One way of looking at the new PBSC is as a body that draws from the three main political networks in Chinese politics. Li Zhanshu and Zhao Leji are close to Xi. Li Keqiang and Wang Yang are associated with Hu Jintao and the CYL, and Han Zheng is a protégé of Jiang Zemin, though he apparently worked well with Xi Jinping both in Shanghai and on the PB. Wang Huning was brought to Beijing by Jiang Zemin, but he has worked closely with Hu Jintao and Xi Jinping, suggesting he has provided all three with policy advice in an unbiased fashion. Just as important, he has no political base of his own, having never served as a local administrator. In this way, he is nearly unique – the only other policy intellectual to join the PBSC in party history is Chen Boda, Mao's political secretary, who joined in 1969. Pulling together people who have been associated with different networks in China does not mean that the new PBSC is composed of three "factions." On the contrary, it is clear that Xi is dominant, even more so than during his first term. Rather, Xi demonstrated his "inclusivity" in the Chinese tradition of drawing on the "five lakes and four seas" (*wuhu sihai*). "Inclusion" does not mean "checks and balances"; it is more of a consolation prize acknowledging the importance, if not the power, of a group.

The Politburo

Perhaps even more interesting is the makeup of the broader PB; that is, those not on the PBSC. An unusually large number of seats had to be filled. Five members of the outgoing PB were promoted to the PBSC; another six had to retire for reasons of age; three more were dropped (two to the Central Committee); and Sun Zhengcai, the young party secretary of Chongqing who was once thought to be a candidate for successor, was suddenly purged in July 2017, for a total of fifteen open seats. At least ten of the people promoted to fill these seats had worked with Xi in the past and can be counted as close associates.

There are now eight people on the PB who will be eligible for promotion to the PBSC at the Twentieth Party Congress in 2022, six of whom are closely associated with Xi. It thus seems clear, whether Xi decides to step down in 2022 or not, that he will continue to have an outsized influence on Chinese politics for years to come. Given the fact that the Nineteenth Party Congress produced no obvious successor, i.e., someone put in charge of party affairs, it seems increasingly likely that Xi will stay on for a third term (or more).

Table 6.2 *Non-PBSC members of the Nineteenth Central Committee Politburo, 2017 (listed by age)*

Name	Position	Age in 2017	Previous position
Hu Chunhua*	Vice premier	54	Party secretary, Guangdong; PB
Ding Xuexiang*	Head, General Office	55	Deputy head, General Office
Chen Min'er*	Party secretary, Chongqing	57	Party secretary, Guizhou
Li Qiang*	Party secretary, Shanghai	58	Party secretary, Jiangsu
Li Hongzhong*	Party secretary, Tianjin	61	Party secretary, Hubei

Table 6.2 (*cont.*)

Name	Position	Age in 2017	Previous position
Li Xi*	Party secretary, Guangdong	61	Party secretary, Liaoning
Huang Kunming*	Propaganda Department	61	Deputy head, Propaganda Department; party secretary, Hangzhou,
Cai Qi*	Party secretary, Beijing	62	Deputy head, National Security Commission
Chen Quanguo*	Party secretary, Xinjiang	62	Party secretary, Tibet
Guo Shengkun	Politics and Law Commission; Secretariat	63	Minister, Public Security
Chen Xi	Organization Department; Secretariat	64	Deputy head, Organization Department
Yang Xiaodu	Deputy head, CDIC; Secretariat	64	Deputy secretary, CDIC
Liu He	Vice premier; Head, Finance and Economic Leadership Small Group	65	Head, Finance and Economic Leadership Small Group; Vice chairman, NDRC
Xu Qiliang	Vice chairman, CMC	67	Head, air force, Mbr. CMC
Zhang Youxia	Vice chairman, CMC	67	Head, General Armaments Department
Wang Chen	Vice chairman, NPC	67	Deputy head, Propaganda Department
Sun Chunlan	Vice premier	67	Politburo; Head, United Front Work Department

Table 6.2 (*cont.*)

Name	Position	Age in 2017	Previous position
Yang Jiechi	State councilor; Head, External Affairs Leadership Small Group	67	Head, National Security Commission Work Leadership Small Group; Head, Uphold Sea Rights Leadership Small Group

Note: Asterisks indicate age-eligibility for promotion to the PBSC in 2022.

It should be noted that there are four special municipalities whose party secretaries routinely sit on the PB. Beijing is the most important of these cities, and in June 2017, Cai Qi replaced Guo Jinlong as party secretary of Beijing. Guo had served in Tibet, from 2000 to 2004, and was close to Hu Jintao. Cai Qi had served in various positions in Zhejiang when Xi Jinping was party secretary. Sun Zhengcai, once thought of as a potential leader of China, until he was charged with "attempting to seize state power," had governed Chongqing. He was replaced by Chen Min'er, who had headed Zhejiang's Department of Propaganda under Xi Jinping. In Tianjin, Li Hongzhong replaced Huang Xingguo in May 2017. Huang had been acting party secretary since December 2014, an unusually long time to serve in an acting capacity, no doubt indicating that his tenure was likely to be brief, as it proved to be when he was charged with corruption. Li Hongzhong seemed an unusual choice to replace Huang Xingguo. Li had started out as a protégé in Jiang Zemin's network and he had never worked for Xi. But he was the very first provincial party secretary to declare in favor of Xi as "core" in early 2016 when a number of provincial party secretaries clarified their loyalties. Finally, Han Zheng continued on as party secretary of Shanghai until after the party congress. With Han being promoted to the PBSC, Xi appointed his close associate Li Qiang to replace him. Thus, Xi managed to fill at least three of these important positions with his protégés. In addition, Xi replaced Hu Chunhua, party secretary of Guangdong, with another close associate, Li Xi.

Hu Chunhua was promoted to vice premier, but it is a position that may well carry less power.

Some PB choices reflect interesting developments. Cai Qi had never served on the Central Committee, even as an alternate. The same is true of Yang Xiaodu. Yang spent many years in Tibet (1976–2001) before becoming a deputy mayor in Shanghai, then head of Shanghai's United Front Work Department and head of its DIC. In 2014, he moved to the center as CDIC deputy secretary, working under Wang Qishan. Wang and Xi must have been persuaded about his ability and loyalty because he now sits on the PB and the Secretariat, and he heads the State Supervision Commission, a position held concurrently with the deputy chair of the CDIC. But promoting two people to the PB without their first serving on the Central Committee is highly unusual. The last person with such a helicopter promotion was Zhu Rongji, who was promoted from alternate status to PBSC and premier.

In addition, four members of the PB (Huang Kunming, Li Xi, Li Qiang, and Ding Xuexiang) were promoted from alternate status, again highly unusual.

Figure 6.1 Xi Jinping, Hu Jintao, and Jiang Zemin at National Day reception, 2014 (Feng Li via Getty Images)

Table 6.3 *The Nineteenth Secretariat, 2017*

Name	Position
Wang Huning	Chair, Central Civilization Commission (Ideology)
Ding Xuexiang	Head, General Office
Yang Xiaodu	Minister of supervision
Chen Xi	Head, Organization Department
Guo Shengkun	Secretary, Politics and Law Commission
Huang Kunming	Head, Propaganda Department
You Quan	Executive secretary of the Secretariat and head, United Front Work Department

The Secretariat

The Secretariat, as we have noted above, is normally composed of representatives of important party and state bodies, including those in charge of ideology, security, organization, and so forth. Xu Caihou, who retired from the Secretariat in 2007, was the last military representative on the Secretariat.

Few, if any, Secretariats have been as tightly controlled by the general secretary as this one. Ding Xuexiang, Chen Xi, and Huang Kunming have to be counted as particularly close to Xi Jinping. Wang Huning has worked closely with Xi since the Eighteenth Party Congress in 2012. Yang Xiaodu, as mentioned above, worked for many years in Tibet before moving to Shanghai. But he earned the trust of Wang Qishan and Xi Jinping.

The Central Military Commission

Of the eight members of Eighteenth CMC (that is, the members below the chair and two vice chairs), one was promoted to vice chair (Zhang Youxia), one (Wei Fenghe) was retained as a member, four others retired (Chang Wanquan, Zhao Keshi, Wu Shengli, and Ma Xiaotian), and two (Fang Fenghui and Zhang Yang) were investigated for corruption. Zhang Yang committed suicide while in custody. As Table 6.4 shows, the new CMC, revamped to eliminate the four General Staff positions during the military reforms discussed in the previous chapter, provided for only four regular members. Two of these four (Zhang Shengmin and Li Zuocheng) had never served on the Central Committee, normally a prerequisite for promotion to the CMC.

Table 6.4 *The 2012 and 2017 Central Military Commissions*

2012 CMC	Position	2017 CMC	Position
Xi Jinping	Chair	Xi Jinping	Chair
Fan Changlong	Vice chair	Xu Qiliang	Vice chair
Xu Qiliang	Vice chair	Zhang Youxia	Vice chair
Chang Wanquan	Minister of national defense	Wei Fenghe	Commander, rocket forces
Fang Fenghui	Chief of joint staff	Li Zuocheng	Commander, ground forces
Zhang Yang	Political commissar, Guangdong military region	Miao Hua	Chair, GPD
Zhao Keshi	Director, Logistics Department	Zhang Shengmin	Secretary, PLA Discipline Inspection Commission
Zhang Youxia	Director, General Armaments Department		
Wu Shengli	Commander, People's Liberation Army Navy		
Ma Xiaotian	Commander, People's Liberation Army Air Force		
Wei Fenghe	Commander, Second Artillery		

The Central Committee

Xi obviously dominated the leadership of the CCP – the PB, the PBSC, the Secretariat, and the CMC. It is more difficult to trace relationships between the leadership and the members of the Central Committee serving at lower levels. One can start, however, by noting the scope of the change.

Before the congress even opened, Xi's campaign against corruption had taken its toll. A total of seventeen full members of the Central Committee were investigated and removed. Never before during the reform era had there been such a purging of the Central Committee, even following the Tiananmen events. Previously the high-water mark was set by the Eighteenth Party Congress when four people were removed from the Seventeenth Central Committee: Bo Xilai, Liu Zhijun, Yu Youjun, and Kang Rixin. Before that, the norm was only one or two people being removed. Thus, the impact of the campaign against corruption had extensive political repercussions (there were also seventeen alternate members of the Central Committee removed for corruption).

There were 205 people elected as full members of the Eighteenth Central Committee and 161 elected as alternates. Of the 205 full members, only seventy-three retained seats on the Nineteenth Central Committee (36 percent), and only thirty-seven people were promoted from the list of alternate members (18.1 percent). This means that ninety-four were freshly appointed to the new Central Committee (64 percent), giving Xi Jinping unprecedented latitude in shaping the new Central Committee. Normally about one-half of the Central Committee selected at every congress is new (specifically 53 percent, 55 percent, 51 percent, and 56 percent at the Fifteenth, Sixteenth, Seventeenth, and Eighteenth Party Congresses, respectively), so the 64 percent of new entrants to the Central Committee in 2017 is well above the norm.

Perhaps not surprisingly, the largest share of the direct promotions is in the military, where Xi's reforms are rapidly weeding out those promoted under previous leaders. We discussed the changes in the CMC above, but in the broader composition of PLA members of the Central Committee, it is apparent that there was a serious effort to root out the influence of Guo Boxiong and Xu Caihou. Purging PLA officers started in November 2012 and accelerated with the reform of the PLA command structure in 2015. Since Xi's military reforms were announced, over 100 senior military officers have been charged with corruption.[6]

Including members of the CMC, there were forty-two PLA members on the Eighteenth Central Committee (20 percent of the 205 full members). Of the thirty-two full members not on the CMC, all but three were either retired or investigated (Yang Jinshan and Tian Xiusi were investigated). Of the twenty-seven who retired, eleven retired early; that is, before they reached the retirement age of sixty-five. Therefore, of the forty-two military members of the Central Committee, including those on the CMC, only six were retained, a turnover rate of 85 percent.

The Nineteenth Party Congress elected forty-one PLA people as full members of the Central Committee (forty-two, if one includes Xi). Of the thirty-five military people elected to the Nineteenth Central Committee who were not on the CMC, only three were retained from the Eighteenth Central Committee, and only four were promoted from the list of alternates. Thus, twenty-eight members were named directly to full membership. Of the forty-one military members on the Nineteenth Central Committee as full members, thirty-one (76 percent) are serving on the Central Committee in any capacity for the first time. There has never been such a large turnover during the reform period.

The sweeping nature of the changes is obvious in the list of alternate members as well. There are twenty-three people from the PLA who served as alternate members of the Eighteenth Central Committee, nineteen of whom were age-eligible to be promoted to the Central Committee (that is, born in 1953 or later). But two of these people were under investigation, so there were thirteen people who were passed over and dropped from the alternate list. In other words, of the twenty-three PLA people who were alternate members of the Eighteenth Central Committee, only four (Gao Jin, Yi Xiaoguang, Yang Xuejun, and Wang Ning) were promoted to full membership on the Nineteenth Central Committee. All the others (83 percent) were dropped.

[6] Jun Mai, "Xi Jinping's Anti-corruption Drive Brings Down More Generals than 20th Century Warfare," *South China Morning Post*, November 17, 2012. Available at www.scmp.com/news/china/policies-politics/article/2120430/xi-jinpings-anti-corruption-drive-brings-down-more, accessed September 16, 2020.

Whether one looks at the composition of the PBSC, the broader PB, the Secretariat, the CMC, the holders of critical positions, or the broader Central Committee, it is apparent that Xi Jinping won an overwhelming victory. Perhaps the only anomaly was Minister of State Security Guo Shengkun. State security is obviously a critical position, but Guo had come up through the nonferrous metal and aluminum industries before becoming deputy secretary of Guangxi in 2004. After rising to party secretary, he was able to jump to minister of public security in 2012, despite not having any background in police work. At the time Guo made the switch to a political track, Zeng Qinghong and He Guoqiang were heads of the Organization Department (He taking over in 2002). Guo Shengkun is reportedly indirectly related to Zeng (both are from Jiangxi) – Guo's wife's grandmother was Zeng Qinghong's mother's younger sister.[7] In July 2020, Chen Yixin, secretary general of the Political and Legal Affairs Commission, announced that there would be a major purge of the security forces. It was necessary, he said, to "scrape the poison off the bones" of the political and legal system.[8]

Xi's New Order

During his first term, Xi earned a reputation for cracking down on corruption, tightening ideological strictures, and centralizing power in the party, both in Beijing and in himself. As time went by, however, it became evident that Xi had in mind a model of governance quite different from that of either Deng Xiaoping or Jiang Zemin. One can view Xi's efforts as a way to reverse the trends toward institutional decay surveyed in Chapter 4. From Xi's point of view, those trends opened the door to "peaceful evolution" – and the collapse of the CCP. For Xi, the growth of factions meant the weakening of discipline; intellectual debate meant the loss of ideological authority; corruption

---

[7] "Heima Guo Shengkun: Qule ge hao taitai, Zheng Qinghong shi biaojiu" (Dark Horse Guo Shengkun: He Married a Good Wife and Zeng Qinghong Is His Uncle), available at www.boxun.com/news/gb/china/2013/03/20130320 1141.shtml, accessed June 16, 2020.

[8] William Zheng, "China's Top Law Enforcement Body Unveils Campaign to Purge 'Corrupt Elements'," *South China Morning Post*, July 10, 2020, available at www.scmp.com/news/china/politics/article/3092559/chinas-top-law-enforce ment-body-unveils-campaign-purge-corrupt, accessed September 16, 2020.

meant the weakening of party purpose; the growth of group interests within the CCP meant a challenge to centralization; the development of expertise in the state (as opposed to the party) meant a dilution of ideological purity; and the emergence of civil society, particularly the rights-protection movement, meant defiance of party authority. As noted above, one of Xi's "four consciousnesses" is *kanqi*, to line up. That is precisely what Xi wants the party – indeed, all of Chinese society – to do.

Xi's overwhelming victory at the Nineteenth Party Congress, similar to his view of party governance, changed substantially the informal balances that had characterized political life in the CCP throughout the reform period. During the Dengist period there had been a number of balances between conservatives and reformers that, unfortunately, broke down in the late 1980s. The Jiang Zemin period was characterized by a number of balances that shifted gradually in Jiang's favor over time, as party elders left the scene and as Jiang was able to gain greater control over the military and critical positions. Indeed, Jiang was so successful, as I have argued, that Hu Jintao was never able to be fully in control – he was never the "core." But there was, in any case, room for different views within the party. Xi's campaign against corruption eliminated open opposition (Bo Xilai, Zhou Yongkang, Ling Jihua, and many others), ended intervention by the elders, and greatly diminished the role of the CYL. The use of leadership small groups concentrated power in Xi's hands, diminished the power of the State Council, and allowed Xi to override other organizations. As the Nineteenth Party Congress put it, the party led in everything, and everyone should heighten his or her consciousness of the core (*hexi yishi*) and line up properly (*kanqi*). It seemed to many observers, both inside and outside China, that Xi was attempting to reverse the trends toward diversity that had been so evident in Chinese society, forcing everything back into a straitjacket.

Although efforts to expand surveillance of the Chinese population pre-date Xi's rise to power, one gets a better sense of Xi's efforts to tighten control by looking first at what he has been doing in the party. As noted above, the move to "one-level-down" management of cadres in 1984 created incentives for lower-level cadres to curry favor with their superiors. This system fostered corruption and those networks that usually accompany corruption. It is the

DIC at various levels that is supposed to check this tendency. The DIC is supposed to be under dual management, meaning horizontally by the local party secretary and vertically by the DIC at the next level up. However, the party secretary at the same level controls resources needed or desired by the head of the DIC, so he or she reports primarily to the party secretary at the same level and only secondarily to the DIC at the next level up. The result is that top-down supervision is weakened and party dysfunction – the inability of higher levers to control lower levels – corrodes the system.

Xi has moved strongly to tighten vertical control and thus weaken the relative autonomy of local party secretaries. This effort can be seen in the "merger" of the Ministry of Supervision (MOS), a state organization, and the CDIC. These two organs have long overlapped in their functions, but there has been an effort to maintain some separation. The CDIC investigated party people and the MOS investigated nonparty civil servants. In November 2016, the General Office promulgated the "Plan for Experimenting with Reform of the State Supervisory Structure in Beijing, Shanxi, and Zhejiang."[9] The choice of these three localities hardly seems coincidental. Beijing, of course, is the national capital. Xi's protégé Cai Qi is the party secretary, so progress can be observed particularly closely. Zhejiang, of course, is where Xi had served for five years as party secretary, so he is very familiar with that province. Finally, Shanxi had been a particular target of Xi's efforts to clean out the local factions that had supported Ling Jihua. Constructing a new system of supervision there would break down whatever was left of the old "political ecology" and provide a model for implementation elsewhere. In January 2017, it was announced that Yang Xiaodu, who would become a member of the PB and Secretariat at the Nineteenth Party Congress in November of that year, would be office director of the newly established Central Leadership Small Group for Deepening the

---

[9] See "Zhongban yinfa 'Guanyu zai Beijing, Shanxi sheng, Zhejiang sheng kaizhan guojia jiancha tizhi gaige shidian fang'an'" (The General Office Promulgates "Experimental Program for Opening the Reform of the Supervision System in Beijing, Shanxi Province, and Zhejiang Province"), available at http://cpc .people.com.cn/n1/2016/1108/c64387-28842803.html, accessed June 23, 2020.

Reform of the State Supervision Structure (*Zhongyang shenhua jiancha tizhi gaige shidian gongzuo lingdao xiaozu*).

The experiment in all three localities moved very quickly. By April 2019, the prosecuting functions of the supervisory commissions at various levels had been transferred to the DICs at the corresponding levels. Although the task was to create a National Supervisory Commission with subordinate units branching downward, in actuality the DICs at various levels were being strengthened. Employees of the old People's Procuratorate and of the DIC at the corresponding level were working in the same building. Officials of the new supervisory commissions were members both of the DIC *and* of the supervisory commissions.[10] In other words, they were both state and party officials, meaning that the new organizations had the authority to investigate both party and nonparty people.[11]

Although one stated purpose of the reform was to reduce redundant investigations by the DICs and the procuratorate, the more important reason was to strengthen the supervision of lower-level offices and to make the investigative offices more independent of the local party secretary. Under the new rules, although local DICs still need the party secretary's approval to initiate certain investigations, they can initiate other investigations on their own. In either case, they must pass the same materials on to their superior DIC – and the higher-level DIC not only leads the casework, it can also overturn the decision of a local party secretary if the secretary declines prosecution.[12]

This tightened management of investigative organs has resulted in the prosecution of an unprecedented number of cadres. According to figures released by China, many leading cadres, called "tigers," have been caught. "Tigers" are generally defined as cadres of vice ministerial rank and above. In other words, they are the centrally managed cadres (*zhongguan ganbu*). Although there is no official figure for the number of centrally managed cadres, it is believed that there

[10] Jinting Deng, "The National Supervision Commission: A New Anti-corruption Model in China," *International Journal of Law, Crime and Justice*, Vol. 52 (2018): p. 70.

[11] "Guojia jiancha tizhi gaige shidian qude shixiao" (The Experiments with the Reform of the National Supervision Structure Have Achieved Real Results), *Renminwang*, November 6, 2017, available at http://dangjian.people.com.cn/n1/2017/1106/c117 092-29628258.html, accessed October 7, 2019.

[12] Jinting Deng, "The National Supervision Commission," pp. 65–66.

are about 2,500. In 2017, Yang Xiaodu stated that since the Eighteenth Party Congress in 2012, 440 centrally managed cadres had been investigated. Of these, 43 were full or alternate members of the Central Committee, and 9 were members of the CDIC. Moreover, over 8,900 cadres at the bureau-director (*ting*) level had been investigated and 63,000 cadres at the division (*chu*) level had been investigated. Some 278,000 basic-level cadres had been disciplined, and 3,453 cadres had been brought back from overseas.[13] In 2019, the CDIC opened investigations on 68 centrally controlled cadres, sending 15 to the judicial system for prosecution. Throughout the country, supervisory commissions cited 526,000 cadres for violations of party discipline (*dangji chufen*) and cited 135,000 nonparty cadres for violations of public affairs (*zhengwu chufen*).[14] These figures suggest a closeness of central supervision over lower-level cadres far exceeding that during the Jiang Zemin or the Hu Jintao eras.

At the same time, Xi has paid great attention to intra-party rules. In June 2012, the General Office began the first effort in the history of the PRC to comb through the 23,000 documents issued by the Center since the establishment of the People's Republic. They found 1,178 documents regarding the organizational work, activities, and behavior of party members. It discarded 322 of them, announced that 369 were no longer applicable, and found that 487 were still in effect. In cases where such rules were inconsistent, they have been revised so they are compatible and appropriate for governing the party.[15] The fact that this

---

[13] "Yang Xiaodu: Shibada yilai li'an shencha shengjunji yishang dangyuan ganbu ji qita zhongguan ganbu 440 ren" (Yang Xiaodu: Since the Eighteenth Party Congress, 440 Cadres at or above the Provincial, Army and Other Centrally Managed Cadres Have Been Investigated), available at http://cpc.people.com.cn /19th/n1/2017/1019/c414536-29596644.html, accessed November 5, 2020.

[14] Zhao Leji, "Zhongshi lüxing dangzhang he xianfa fuyu de zhize nuli shixian xinshidai jijian jiancha gongzuo gaozhi fazhan" (Loyally Carry Out the Responsibilities Conferred by the Party Charter and Constitution; Strive to Realize High-Quality Discipline Inspection and Supervisory Work in the New Era), January 11, 2019, available at http://dangjian.people.com.cn/n1/2019/ 0221/c117092-30851340.html, accessed November 5, 2020.

[15] "Zhongyang dangnei fagui he guifanxing wenjian jizhong qingli gongzuo quanbu wancheng" (The Work of Comprehensively Sorting through Central Intra-party Regulations and Standardizing Documents Has Been Completed), Xinhua, November 17, 2014, available at http://politics.people.com.cn/n/2014/ 1117/c1001-26041917.html, accessed September 16, 2020.

body of rules had not been gone through and revised from time to time suggests how important local cadres were in governing the party. It was local cadres who interpreted and enforced (or not) the party rules. Again, Xi's emphasis has been on strengthening the system at the expense of individual cadres.

As Minxin Pei points out, in revising these rules and promulgating new ones, Xi has not been shy about strengthening centralized control. For instance, "the CCP's Politburo's Regulations on Strengthening and Maintaining the Party Center's Centralized and Unified Leadership of the Party Center" and the "Code on Seeking Instructions and Reporting Matters" have "formalized the personalization of power through the establishment of loyalty to Xi as one of the most important political principles guiding actions by members of the party-state."[16]

Loyalty to Xi was made even more explicit on September 29, 2020, when the PB adopted the "Work Regulations of the Central Committee." These regulations appear to act as a supplement to the Party Charter, in effect amending that document without going through the process of gaining approval of a Party Congress. The Party Charter, of course, is written in impersonal terms because it governs the organization and responsibilities of the whole party over time (although it is revised at every party congress). In contrast, the new regulations are remarkably personal. They start by repeating the formula from the Party Charter, saying that the party takes "Marxism–Leninism, Mao Zedong Thought, Deng Xiaoping Theory, the Important Thought of the 'Three Represents,' the Scientific Development Perspective, and Xi Jinping's Thought on Socialism with Chinese Characteristics for the New Age" as its guidance. However, it then goes on to state that the Central Committee must "take the lead, among other things, in strengthening the 'four consciousnesses' and carrying out the 'two upholds'." It will be recalled that the "four consciousnesses" refers to "political consciousness," "consciousness of the overall situation," "consciousness of the core," and "consciousness of lining up (*kanqi*)." Xi is, of course, the core, and "lining up" means maintaining solidarity with him. The "two

---

[16] Minxin Pei, "Rewriting the Rules of the Chinese Party-State: Xi's Progress in Reinvigorating the CCP," *China Leadership Monitor*, No. 59 (June 1, 2019), available at www.prcleader.org/peiclm60, accessed September 28, 2020.

upholds" refers to upholding general secretary Xi Jinping as the core of the center and upholding the authority and centralized unity of the leadership. In other words, the work of the whole party must revolve around Xi Jinping.[17] If it is possible to codify personalistic leadership, this document does it.

These efforts to tighten control over party and state cadres have been accompanied by continued efforts to strengthen surveillance over the Chinese population. In 1998 the Ministry of Public Security, in response to the rapid expansion of the Internet, and perhaps the formation of the China Democratic Party during the same year, established a program known as the "Golden Shield Project" (*jindun gongcheng*). Part of this project was to create a "Great Firewall" to block undesirable content from being viewed in China. But the Golden Shield Project goes far beyond this function, collecting information on all Chinese citizens, essentially replacing the old *dang'an* (dossier) files that had been maintained manually. By 2003, the Ministry of Public Security had already collected data on 96 percent of the Chinese population.[18]

In 2015, the State Council approved an "Outline for Accelerating the Development of Big Data."[19] This outline ushered in the "police cloud" (*jingwuyun*), an effort to build on the information collected by the Golden Shield Project by automating everything and making everything accessible throughout the country. The aim of Golden Shield Project and the Police Cloud is to "link up all information on all Chinese citizens." "At a basic level it would allow authorities to know everything about a particular person within seconds," British analyst Charles Parton explains. "But it aimed to go beyond that, predicting who might cause trouble to the regime, anticipating the

---

[17] "Zhongguo gongchandang zhongyang weiyuanhui gongzuo tiaoli" (Work Regulations of the Central Committee), available at http://politics .people.com.cn/n1/2020/1013/c1001-31889182.html, accessed November 5, 2020.

[18] "Jindun gongcheng shujuku baokuo 12 yi duo Zhongguoren de xinxi" (The Data Bank of the Golden Shield Project Includes Information on More than 1.2 Billion Chinese), *Boxun*, April 9, 2006, available at https://web.archive.org/we b/20160305214310/http://www.boxun.com/news/gb/china/2006/04/2006040 91432.shtml, accessed September 16, 2020.

[19] Liu Wei and Li Jisheng, "'Jingwuyun' kaichuang zhihui gong'an xinshidai" ("'Police Cloud' Opens a New Era for Smart Policing"), *Jilin ribao*, August 7, 2018, available at http://jlrbszb.cnjiwang.com/pc/paper/c/201808/07/con tent_59869.html, accessed November 5, 2020.

organizing of any action deemed inimical to the party, and curtailing the freedom and actions of any suspect citizen, for example, by taking away the ability to fill up a car with petrol."[20]

Inside Out

This is not the place to review China's foreign policy, but one has to be struck by the degree to which China's approach to the outside world has changed over the past decade and wonder how these changes are related to Chinese domestic changes. Although international-relations specialists are inclined to see nations as having enduring interests and thus relative continuity in their foreign policy, China's foreign policy seems very tightly bound to its domestic politics. When Deng Xiaoping announced that China faced a period of "peace and development" during which it could prosper by opening the country to foreign investment and cultural interactions (including particularly education), it was not because he did not perceive threats to China's interests. Rather, he thought that these threats were manageable. As he put it in one of his more colorful aphorisms, "Open the windows, breathe the fresh air, and at the same time fight the flies and insects";[21] that is, keep out the "spiritual pollution" that was bound to come in. There was much that China needed and wanted to learn from the outside world, so Deng's foreign policy was radically different from Mao's.

Even after the Tiananmen events, when "peaceful evolution" seemed much more threatening, China pursued closer economic integration with the global community through its application to join the World Trade Organization (WTO). Part of its application involved the scrubbing of domestic laws to make them compliant with the international trade regime. At the time, a commonly used phrase was "join tracks with international norms" (*yu guoji guize jiegui*). My argument is not that China complied completely with international norms, but simply that it saw its interests as largely compatible with maintaining friendly relations with the outside

---

[20] Charles Parton, "China's Bigger Brother," *World Today*, Vol. 74, No. 4 (August 2018): 24–27.
[21] Quoted in George J. Church, "Old Wounds: Deng Xiaoping," *Time*, Vol. 127, No. 1 (January 6, 1986): 24.

world. China did not see its interests being threatened by joining the world.

One no longer hears the phrase "join tracks with international norms." Efforts to redefine China's interests began as the Soviet Union tottered on the brink of collapse following the failed coup attempt against Gorbachev in August 1991. A group of New Left intellectuals gathered and hammered out a program of "neoconservatism" that defined China's interests as separate from the "socialist utopia" embraced by members of the Old Left who had dominated Chinese politics during the period since the Tiananmen events and the "capitalist utopia" that they believed dominated the thinking of liberal intellectuals and the international order.[22] As the New Left intellectuals explored alternatives to Western liberalism, they began to reimagine Chinese history. They started to question the way the May Fourth Movement – the 1919 iconic movement that was both nationalistic and liberal in its initial inspiration – defined "modernity" in largely Western terms. These intellectuals increasingly came to argue that Mao Zedong's socialist thought was a type of "modernist thought that was opposed to capitalist modernity."[23] Such thinking delegitimized the pursuit of Western-style modernity and valorized the Chinese revolution and the search for a different route to modernity. These intellectual explorations were largely the purview of a small group of young intellectuals who hailed from the fields of literary criticism, the social sciences, and intellectual history. The intellectual battles with liberals enlivened the pages of China's journals and blogs (this was before WeChat had been introduced).

In 2004, Joshua Cooper Ramo, then a senior editor at *Time* magazine, wrote a short book called *The Beijing Consensus*, pointing out that China was following a course of development quite different from that of the so-called "Washington consensus."[24] The years 2008–2009

---

[22] China Youth Daily, Ideology and Theory Department, "Realistic Responses and Strategic Options for China after the Soviet Union Upheaval," *Chinese Law and Government*, Vol. 29, No. 2 (March–April 1996): 13–31.

[23] Wang Hui, "Dangdai Zhongguo de sixiang zhuangkuang yu xiandaixing wenti" (The Circumstances of Contemporary Chinese Thought and the Problem of Modernity), *Wenyi zhengming* No. 6 (November 1998): 7–26.

[24] Joshua Cooper Ramo, *The Beijing Consensus* (London: The Foreign Policy Centre, 2004).

were an especially bad time for China, both domestically and internationally. Charter '08 had stirred "civil society," mass incidents were growing in numbers, riots broke out in Xinjiang, and the international financial crisis had hit China, particularly its export sector, extremely hard. It was a perfect storm of domestic and international troubles at a time of leadership change and a decaying party system.[25] By 2008–2009, China was ready to respond more aggressively to challenges. The global financial crisis threw into question the American neoliberal economic model in particular and global leadership in general. As Vice Premier Wang Qishan told US secretary of the Treasury Hank Paulson, "You were my teacher . . . But I look at your system, Hank. We aren't sure we should be learning from you anymore."[26]

The financial crisis in 2008 and the sixtieth anniversary of the People's Republic in the following year spurred the use of a different term – the "China model" (*Zhongguo moshi*). The China model was intended to highlight the importance of the state and SOEs in China's development. It came to prominence at a time when many SOEs were being disbanded in favor of private enterprises (China never used the term "privatization"). Peking University scholar Pan Wei helped popularize the term by coediting a thick book called *The China Model*. In a long essay, Pan harshly criticizes China's liberals, saying that liberals believe China should "tear down the Palace Museum and build a White House"; in other words, they favor complete Westernization.[27]

Perhaps what is most striking about Pan's essay is his argument that the sixty years of the PRC reflected a basic continuity. Anticipating Xi Jinping's 2013 speech on the two thirty-year periods, Pan argued, "The successes of the first 30 years [of the PRC] cannot be neglected," for they laid the bases for the later successes.[28] Pan points to state control

---

[25] Wu Guoguang, "China in 2009: Muddling through Crises," *Asian Survey*, Vol. 50, No. 1 (February 2010): 25–39.

[26] Quoted in Richard McGregor, *Asia's Reckoning: China, Japan, and the Fate of U.S. Power in the Pacific Century* (New York: Viking, 2017), p. 240.

[27] Pan Wei, *Dangdai Zhonghua tizhi: Zhongguo moshi de jingji, zhengzhi, shehui jiexi* (The Structure of Contemporary China: An Analysis of the Economy, Polity, and Society of the China Model) (Hong Kong: Sanlian chubanshe, 2010).

[28] Pan Wei, "Zhongguo moshi: Zhonghua tizhi de jingji, zhengzhi, shehui jiexi" (The China Model: An Analysis of the Economy, Politics, and Society of the Chinese Structure), available at www.chinaelections.org/printnews.asp?newsi d=177983, accessed September 16, 2020.

over land and finance established during the Maoist period, believing that if that had not occurred, reform would have led quickly to large concentrations of land and resulting inequalities.

This growing critique of liberalism established the foundations for a new nationalism, one that was not so open to "joining tracks with international norms." This critique was largely aimed at domestic trends, but it was suddenly joined by virulent nationalism when the US, in the course of the war against Serbia, bombed the Chinese embassy in Belgrade in May 1999. Accidental though it was, this incident led many Chinese to believe that the US was determined to "contain" China. The idea of containment was never part of US policy, but it was one of those public myths that fed into the growing nationalist sentiment in China. The US, many said, was trying to "hold China down."

Those who had responsibilities in the area of national security and national defense had always been suspicious of the US, and the Belgrade bombing only confirmed such feelings. Following the Tiananmen events, Deng Xiaoping had resisted pressure from the left, advising his colleagues to take a low profile. "Avoid the limelight, nurture one's abilities, there are some things we can do" (*taoguang yanghui, yousuo zuowei*), he counseled. It was a diplomatic approach that recognized China's weakness and realized that taking a high profile would damage China's ability to develop. With the bombing of the Chinese embassy, however, increasing numbers of people, especially those in the security establishment, wanted to take a more adversarial position against the US. They believed that China had developed the capabilities to push back and to assert itself. At first, the Hu Jintao administration resisted this pressure, believing that China was still relatively weak and had to focus on economic growth. But military modernization continued apace. By 2007, China had begun to outfit the *Liaoning*, the carrier hull it had purchased from Ukraine in 1998, and China's 2008 decision to join naval patrols in the Sea of Aden to combat piracy marked a major step forward in China's naval modernization.[29] In 2009, Hu adjusted, however slightly, China's foreign-policy mantra. Hu declared that China should "Uphold *taoguang yanghui*," but there were things "it could do *actively*" (*jianchi taoguang yanghui, jiji yousuo zuowei*). This new formulation (*tifa*),

---

[29] Michael A. McDevitt, *China as a Twenty First Century Naval Power: Theory, Practice, and Implications* (Annapolis, MD: Naval Institute Press, 2020).

reflecting a shift in official thinking, asserted, at least tentatively, taking a higher profile.

This background makes it clear that changes in China's foreign policy pre-dated Xi Jinping, but Xi certainly embraced this new nationalism and promoted it. As we have noted above, Xi's message has been both populist and nationalist. After all, he started his tenure by appealing to Chinese pride: "Our people are a great people," and he has returned repeatedly to nationalist themes during his years in office. "We are closer to the goal of the great rejuvenation of the Chinese nation than at any time in history," he told military leaders on the ninetieth anniversary of the PLA. In June 2018, he greeted Defense Secretary James Mattis in Beijing, saying emphatically, "We cannot lose one inch of territory passed down by our ancestors."[30] This warning seemed to be particularly relevant to Taiwan as Xi had warned that Taiwan "must and will be" reunited with China.[31] Such threats have been accompanied increased intimidation of the island.[32]

Xi's warning also applied to the South China Sea. In 2013, the Philippines took its dispute over the South China Sea to the Permanent Court of Arbitration (PCA), which specializes in ruling on disputes arising from the Law of the Sea. China refused to participate, saying that the case interfered with Chinese sovereignty. Instead of participating, China embarked on a program of land reclamation, creating some 3,000 acres of land on seven reefs, three of which boasted 10,000-foot runways, deep-water harbors, and reinforced hangars.[33] The PCA's subsequent (2016) ruling that China's claim of "historic rights" in the area and China's "nine-dash line" were invalid was simply ignored.

---

[30] Thomas Gibbons-Neff and Steven Lee Myers, "China Won't Yield 'Even One Inch' of South China Sea, Xi Tells Mattis," *New York Times*, June 27, 2018, available at www.nytimes.com/2018/06/27/world/asia/mattis-xi-china-sea.html, accessed September 16, 2020.

[31] Chris Buckley and Chris Horton, "Xi Jinping Warns Taiwan That Unification Is the Goal and Force Is an Option," *New York Times,* January 1, 2019, available at www.nytimes.com/2019/01/01/world/asia/xi-jinping-taiwan-china.html, accessed September 16, 2020.

[32] "With the World Distracted, China Intimidates Taiwan," *The Economist*, April 8, 2020, available at www.economist.com/asia/2020/04/08/with-the-world-distracted-china-intimidates-taiwan, accessed September 16, 2020.

[33] Thomas Shuggart, "China's Artificial Islands Are Bigger (and a Bigger Deal) than You Think," *War on the Rocks*, September 21, 2016, available at https://waron therocks.com/2016/09/chinas-artificial-islands-are-bigger-and-a-bigger-deal-than-you-think, accessed September 16, 2020.

Figure 6.2 Xi Jinping giving speech on the fortieth anniversary of the "Message to Compatriots," January 2, 2019 (Mark Schiefelbein/AFP via Getty Images)

China's increased intimidation of Taiwan, its militarization of the South China Sea, its hardline stance in its dispute with Japan over the Senkaku/Diaoyutai islands, its building of a first overseas base in Djibouti, and Xi's admonition that the PLA train to "fight and win" wars,[34] all reflect the use of nationalism at home that is used to ward off the "peaceful evolution" that seemed a real threat a decade earlier and to justify the harsh measures Xi has used to punish his enemies, centralize authority in the party, and solidify his own power. Xi has found that maintaining the party in power has required turning away from Deng's efforts to join the world.

Conclusion

In terms of reshaping China's political elite and political system, the two terms (so far) of Xi Jinping have been extremely consequential. With his campaign against corruption, Xi was able to oust his political

---

[34] "China Focus: 'Be Ready to Win Wars,' China's Xi Orders Reshaped PLA," *Xinhuanet*, August 1, 2017, available at www.xinhuanet.com//english/2017-0 8/01/c_136491455.htm, accessed July 10, 2020.

rivals and centralize power in a way not done since Deng Xiaoping. But Xi is not replicating Deng's period. On the contrary, Xi's approach has been quite different. Deng came to power extremely confident not only because of his extensive experience, both domestic and international, but also because he knew he had the support of the military. Xi came to power at a time of great contention in the party, when many forces were against him. His campaign against corruption made his taking of power almost coup-like – ousting rivals like Zhou Yongkang, Ling Jihua, Xu Caihou, and Guo Boxiong (Bo Xilai had been ousted by Hu Jintao). There is less talk about the way in which Xi ousted virtually the entire top leadership of the PLA, remaking its structure in a way that would increase both its operational capability and his personal control.

If Deng saw the major fault in the CCP as the overconcentration of power, Xi has seen the major problem as the decentralization of power. This decentralization of power has come about largely because of the inherent pathologies of a Leninist party during a period of reform. Mass incidents reflect higher levels putting pressure on lower levels, but without the ability to control them. The development of the rights-protection movement raises directly the issue of whether the CCP will be constrained by law. Finally, the "color revolutions" in Central Asia demonstrated the very real possibility of peaceful evolution. Jiang Zemin began tightening party control during his "talk politics" campaign, and Hu Jintao presided over a turn toward a more assertive posture following the global financial crisis. However, Xi Jinping has gone far beyond his predecessors, and the contrast between his policies and those of Deng Xiaoping is striking.

Deng wanted to reduce the role of the party in many nonessential parts of the polity, including the SOEs and the government. He saw the party as more of a policy-making body that would set the overall direction of reform, but then allow the enterprises and the state to implement that policy. In contrast, Xi has declared that the party leads in everything. Even though the effort to put party committees in private enterprises pre-dates Xi, Xi has strengthened that policy and extended it to NGOs.

Perhaps most important for the long-term future of the CCP has been the way in which it thinks about succession. Deng saw the regular turnover of leadership as essential (even if he could not refrain from interfering from time to time). In contrast, Xi appears to want to control succession, if and when he decides to step down. Whether that will be regarded as reinvigorating the party or as factionalism remains to be seen. In any event, Xi has demonstrated, even more than his predecessors, the weakness of China's institutions.

Conclusion

Looking in detail at how the four leaders of China during the reform period came to power, how they consolidated power (or not), and their (weak) ability to pass on power, they all reflect not institutionalization but the Leninist framework in which they have worked. One factor that, in various ways, seems important across these four decades is the military. The fact that both Deng Xiaoping and Jiang Zemin held on to the chairmanship of the CMC after giving up their party positions is highly telling. More recently, Xi Jinping has reorganized the military with an eye both to improving military operations and to strengthening personal control.

Looking at these four leaders in this way suggests how different each of their administrations has been. Deng Xiaoping took to power naturally. His self-confidence, which caused some of his colleagues to hesitate to grant him full power, his support from the military, his experience in foreign affairs, and his boldness in adopting (or, in the case of rural reform, accepting) radical reform stand out. Of all four leaders, he was clearly the one who thought the most about the flaws in the Maoist system, tried to correct them, and hoped to institutionalize party procedures. He worried most about the overconcentration of power and hoped to institutionalize a system in which a leader did not pick his own successor ("feudalism"!). The irony, of course, is that ultimately power was concentrated in Deng, and he demanded obedience. In 1989, when Deng had left his party position but still retained his military position, he still expected Zhao Ziyang, the general secretary of the party, to obey ("You simply cannot sing a tune contrary to Deng's"). When he went on his Southern Tour in 1992, at a time when he was fully retired, he still expected that the party would comply with his demands – and it did. Deng may have hoped to institutionalize party procedures, but ultimately his personalization of power undermined the development of party institutions.

After the trauma of the Tiananmen events, one might have expected the party to call a plenary session of the Central Committee to discuss the selection of a new leader and build a new consensus. Instead three senior leaders, none of whom held a formal position in the party, conferred and decided to name Jiang Zemin as general secretary. At first, Jiang's position was weak, and speculation that he might not retain it was not without reason. He did have the support of Chen Yun and Li Xiannian, and he gained Deng's full support, as manifested by the ouster of the Yang brothers following the Fourteenth Party Congress. Jiang simply had to build support in the military if he was to be an effective leader and the purge of the Yang brothers permitted him to do so. As we have seen, Jiang was also able to appoint people to critical positions to fortify his position.

It was this trajectory from a weak political figure to one strong enough to continue to influence personnel decisions through the Hu Jintao period and even to the selection of Xi Jinping (which turned out to be a mistake from Jiang's point of view) that allows one to judge the weakness of institutions and what it takes to rule China.

One of the indicators of the weaknesses of institutions is how often they are manipulated. Many policies were routed through the Secretariat in the 1980s before the Secretariat was restored to its rightful position under the PB at the Thirteenth Party Congress. Jiang expanded and then contracted the PBSC to limit Hu Jintao's ability to bring in allies. Under Jiang, the Political and Legal Commission (run by Zhou Yongkang) became very powerful, but under Xi the power of that organization has been much reduced and that of the CDIC has increased beyond anything seen before in party history.

As argued in the Introduction, there is no reason to discard the usage of "Leninist" to describe the CCP (the party itself does not hesitate to use the term). It is useful not only because it helps us to understand the long-term stability of the Chinese political system (centralization, ideology, penetration of society), but also because it renders the difficulties the party has faced more understandable. As China gave up the intense politicization of society and mass mobilization that typified the Maoist period and entered the reform period (the inclusionary phase, according to Jowitt's terminology) the party, qua organization, began to weaken in predictable ways. Cadres were more secure in their positions and found alliances with other cadres, often those above and below them, that were useful for controlling power and accumulating wealth. Vertical discipline was weakened accordingly, and the party was increasingly dominated by *laohaoren* ('good old boys'), and higher levels found it more difficult to control lower levels. There was an asymmetry of knowledge, so local levels could often outmaneuver higher levels. Corruption became a part of the system.

The interests of local government frequently came into conflict with those of local citizens, especially those in the broad "rice belt" that dominates the middle of the country. Though the central party had no interest in allowing local society to express itself through elections, it wanted to control the predatory instincts of local governments. It could ameliorate conditions by adopting new regulations, but there was no question that its control over local party organizations was weakening, especially in places such as Shanxi.

Moreover, as the economy grew, so did the diversity of society. Social groups, from environmental groups to entrepreneurial interests to native-place associations to religious organizations, emerged to produce a much more diverse society, placing new demands on the party. Furthermore, as the diversity of such groups increased, the control of ideology weakened. Many groups had ties overseas and/or became aware of new ideas. Intellectuals frequently dismissed Marxism–Leninism as they explored foreign ideas, frequently in collaboration with colleagues abroad. Lawyers, especially those with an interest in human rights, began to challenge the party to constrain itself within the contours of the law, as the party had vowed it would do. The regime's fear of "peaceful evolution" was well founded, especially after the breakup of the Soviet Union and the "color revolutions" in Georgia, Ukraine, and Kyrgyzstan.

Thus not only does "Leninism" describe the way the party works at the highest level; it is also useful for understanding the way in which decay sets in.

The dysfunctionalities the party developed – exemplified by the cases of Bo Xilai, Ling Jihua, Zhou Yongkang, and others – provide a perspective for understanding Xi Jinping. No doubt, biography matters. Xi is not only the son of a first-generation revolutionary but also the one who saw his father purged by Mao and who was himself a victim of the Cultural Revolution. He has a clear vision of how the party is supposed to work and, unfortunately, he has a deep understanding of how power works. He also watched from his perch on the PBSC as Hu Jintao tried to parry the forces around him. He has made it his mission to put the Lenin back in the Leninist party, demanding a degree of loyalty perhaps even exceeding that demanded by Deng.

Xi's campaign against corruption was used first and foremost to purge his political enemies. If, indeed, as Xi seems to suggest, Bo Xilai tried to collude with Zhou Yongkang and Xu Caihou, to produce a very different outcome at the Eighteenth Party Congress, then the party was deeply divided. The relative strength of Hu Jintao and the CYL at the Eighteenth Party Congress suggests another dimension of division. The Xi administration could have emerged as a very weak administration. Instead, Xi boldly used the CDIC to strike at his enemies, including the followers of Jiang Zemin and Hu Jintao. Xi may well have been granted permission to strike at corruption, but it is doubtful that Jiang and the other elders would have granted him the plenipotentiary powers he has assumed. Xi's actions may well have ended interference from retired elders (no "immortals" in the Xi administration), but they have left a personalized leadership far less constrained by balances within the party. As we have seen, balances have often complemented the Leninist system in ways that allow greater voice within the party, though balances ultimately have proven unstable. Xi's success in placing his own people in critical positions and, insofar as we can tell, throughout the party bureaucracy suggests a party that contains fewer interest groups. Although that may increase compliance in the short run, the shutting out of different groups is likely to create more conflicts over the long term.

Xi's campaign against corruption is also being used to enforce discipline throughout the bureaucracy (not only the party bureaucracy). Reduced income and increased oversight are obviously something not appreciated by cadres, judging by the number who have resigned.[1] The effort to increase centralization is apparent, but it runs against the decentralization that has been at the core of reform and marketization. The effort to strengthen party control over enterprises, including private enterprises, runs against what Deng tried to do three decades ago and appears to account for the weakness of the economy at present.[2]

---

[1] Li Lianjiang, "The Cadre Resignation Tide in the Wake of the 18th Party Congress," *China: An International Journal*, Vol. 17, No. 3 (August 2019): 188–199.

[2] Nicolas Lardy, *The State Strikes Back: The End of Economic Reform in China?* (Washington, DC: The Peterson Institution of International Economics, 2019).

A survey of elite politics across the four leaders of the reform period reveals a surprising amount of variation in how they organized, or tried to organize, their power. Time was a factor. Each leader faced different problems, both domestically and internationally, and each had different resources with which to attempt to accumulate power. Each also faced obstacles in the sense of other people who had different degrees of power. Some relied more on balances, others relied more on factional supporters. Some tried to build, or say they were trying to build, institutions, but, in the final analysis, Leninist structures and their own quests for power doomed such efforts. In the end, Leninism proved stronger than institutionalization.

Bibliography

"2006 nian lianghui Wen Jiabao zongli da zhongwai jizhe wen" (Premier Wen Jiabao Answers the Questions of Chinese and Foreign Reporters during the 2006 Two Sessions). *Renmin ribao*, March 14, 2006. Available at www .gov.cn/2007lh/content_520478.htm, accessed September 28, 2020.

Alford, William. "Double-Edged Swords Cut Both Ways: Law and Legitimacy in the People's Republic of China." *Daedalus*, Vol. 122, No. 2 (Spring 1993). Available at https://go.gale.com/ps/i.do?p=AONE&id= GALE%7CA13802438&v=2.1&it=r&sid=zotero&userGroupName=ml in_b_massblc&isGeoAuthType=true, accessed September 16, 2020.

Anderlini, Jamil. "Bo Xilai: Power, Death, and Politics." *Financial Times*, July 20, 2012. Available at www.ft.com/content/d67b90f0-d140-11e1-8 957-00144feabdc0, accessed September 16, 2020.

Bandurski, David. "Inside the Southern Weekly Incident." *China Media Project*, January 7, 2013. Available at http://chinamediaproject.org/2013/ 01/07/inside-the-southern-weekly-incident, accessed September 16, 2020.

Bandurski, David. "Wang Lijun and the Tieling Corruption Case." *China Media Project*, February 14, 2012. Available at http://chiname diaproject.org/2012/02/14/wang-lijun-and-the-tieling-corruption-case, accessed September 16, 2020.

Baum, Richard. *Burying Mao: Chinese Politics in the Age of Deng Xiaoping*. Princeton, NJ: Princeton University Press, 1994.

"Bo Xilai Admits Slapping Former Police Chief Wang Lijun 'Because He Was Two-Faced.'" *South China Morning Post*, August 24, 2013. Available at www.scmp.com/news/china/article/1299189/murder-violence-and-distrust -bo-xilai-recounts-dramatic-events-police, accessed May 31, 2020.

Bo Zhiyue. "The Institutionalization of Elite Management in China." Pp. 70–100, in Barry Naughton and Dali Yang, eds. *Holding China Together: Diversity and National Integration in the Post-Deng Era*. New York: Cambridge University Press, 2004.

Bo Zhiyue. "The Rise and Fall of Xu Caihou, China's Corrupt General." *The Diplomat*, March 18, 2015. Available at http://thediplomat.com/2015/03/ the-rise-and-fall-of-xu-caihou-chinas-corrupt-general, accessed June 5, 2020.

Buckley, Chris. "China Reins in Communist Youth League, and Its Alumni's Prospects." *New York Times*, August 3, 2016. Available at www.nytimes .com/2016/08/04/world/asia/china-communist-youth-league.html, accessed September 16, 2020.

Buckley, Chris. "Guo Boxiong, Ex-top Military Official in China, Gets Life Sentence for Graft." *New York Times*, July 25, 2016. Available at www .nytimes.com/2016/07/26/world/asia/china-guo-boxiong-sentence.html, accessed September 16, 2020.

Buckley, Chris. "Vows of Change in China Belie Private Warning." *New York Times*, February 15, 2013. Available at www.nytimes.com/20 13/02/15/world/asia/vowing-reform-chinas-leader-xi-jinping-airs-other-message-in-private.html, accessed September 16, 2020.

Buckley, Chris and Chris Horton. "Xi Jinping Warns Taiwan That Unification Is the Goal and Force Is an Option." *New York Times*, January 1, 2019. Available at www.nytimes.com/2019/01/01/world/asia/ xi-jinping-taiwan-china.html, accessed September 16, 2020.

Central Party History Research Office. "Zhengque kandai gaige kaifang qianhou liangge lishi shiqi" (Correctly View the Two Historical Periods Prior to and after Reform and Opening Up). *Renmin ribao*, November 8, 2013.

Cheong, Ching. "China's New Leadership May Rule under Jiang's Shadow." *Straits Times*, August 22, 2002.

Cheong, Ching. "Xi Faces the Test of His Reform Image." *Straits Times Online*, January 11, 2013.

"China Focus: 'Be Ready to Win Wars,' China's Xi Orders Reshaped PLA." Xinhuanet, August 1, 2017. Available at www.xinhuanet.com//english/2 017-08/01/c_136491455.htm, accessed July 10, 2020.

China Youth Daily, Ideology and Theory Department. "Realistic Responses and Strategic Options for China after the Soviet Union Upheaval." *Chinese Law and Government*, Vol. 29, No. 2 (March–April 1996): 13–31.

Church, George J. "Old Wounds: Deng Xiaoping." *Time*, Vol. 127, No. 1 (January 6, 1986): 24.

Ci, Jiwei. *Democracy in China: The Coming Crisis*. Cambridge, MA: Harvard University Press, 2019.

Clover, Clarles. "Chinese Ex-presidential Aide Ling Arrested." *Financial Times*, July 20, 2015. Available at www.ft.com/content/a1e33ca6-2f4f-1 1e5-8873-775ba7c2ea3d, accessed September 16, 2020.

Deng, Jinting. "The National Supervision Commission: A New Anti-corruption Model in China." *International Journal of Law, Crime and Justice*, Vol. 52 (2018): 58–73.

Deng Liqun. *Deng Liqun zishu: Shi'erge chunqiu* (Deng Liqun's Memoir: Twelve Springs and Autumns). n.p., n.d.

Deng Liqun. *FangRi guilai de sisuo* (Thoughts on Returning from a Visit to Japan). Beijing: Zhongguo shehui kexue chubanshe, 1979.

Deng, Xiaoping. "Adhere to the Party Line and Improve Methods of Work." Pp. 259–269, in *Selected Works of Deng Xiaoping (1975–1992)*. Beijing: Foreign Languages Press, 1983.

Deng Xiaoping. "Answers to the Italian Journalist Oriana Fallaci." Pp. 326–334, in *Selected Works of Deng Xiaoping (1975–1992)*. Beijing: Foreign Languages Press, 1983.

Deng Xiaoping. "Dang zai zuzhi zhanxian he sixiang zhanxianshang de poqie renwu" (The Party's Urgent Tasks on the Organizational and Ideological Fronts). P. 37, in *Deng Xiaoping wenxuan, disan juan* (Selected Works of Deng Xiaoping, Vol. 3). Beijing: Renmin chubanshe.

Deng Xiaoping. *Deng Xiaoping wenxuan, disan juan* (Selected Works of Deng Xiaoping, Vol. 3). Beijing: Renmin chubanshe, 1993.

Deng Xiaoping. "On the Reform of the System of Party and State Leadership." Pp. 326–334, in *Selected Works of Deng Xiaoping (1975–1982)*. Beijing: Foreign Languages Press, 1983.

Deng, Xiaoping. *Selected Works of Deng Xiaoping (1975–1982)*. Beijing: Foreign Languages Press, 1983.

Deng Xiaoping. "Senior Cadres Should Take the Lead in Maintaining and Enriching the Party's Fine Tradition." Pp. 208–223, in *Selected Works of Deng Xiaoping (1975–1982)*. Beijing: Foreign Languages Press, 1983.

Deng Xiaoping. "Speech at All-Army Conference on Political Work." Pp. 128–140, in *Selected Works of Deng Xiaoping (1975–1982)*. Beijing: Foreign Languages Press, 1983.

Deng Xiaoping. "Uphold the Four Cardinal Principles," March 30, 1978. Pp. 166–191, in *Selected Works of Deng Xiaoping (1975–1982)*. Beijing: Foreign Languages Press, 1983.

Deng Xiaoping. "Zai jiejian shoudu xieyan budui jun yishang ganbu de jianghua" (Address to Officers at the Rank of General and above in Command of Enforcing Martial Law in Beijing). Pp. 302–308, in *Deng Xiaoping wenxuan, disan juan* (Selected Works of Deng Xiaoping, Vol. 3). Beijing: Renmin chubanshe, 1993.

Deng Xiaoping. "Zai Wuchang, Shenzhen, Zhuhai, Shanghai, dengdi de tanhua yaodian" (Important Points of [Deng's] Talks in Wuchang, Shenzhen, Zhuhai, and Shanghai). Pp. 370–383, in *Deng Xiaoping wenxuan, disan juan* (Selected Works of Deng Xiaoping, Vol. 3). Beijing: Renmin chubanshe, 1993.

Deng Xiaoping. "Zucheng yige shixing gaige de you xiwang de lingdao jiti (Organize a Leading Collective That Will Carry Out Reform and Be Hopeful). Pp. 296–301, in *Deng Xiaoping wenxuan, disan juan*

(Selected Works of Deng Xiaoping, Vol. 3). Beijing: Renmin chubanshe, 1983.

"Document No. 9: A ChinaFile Translation," November 8, 2013. Available at www.chinafile.com/document-9-chinafile-translation, accessed June 6, 2020.

Dickson, Bruce J. *The Dictator's Dilemma: The Chinese Communist Party's Strategy for Survival.* New York: Oxford University Press, 2016.

Dickson, Bruce J. *Red Capitalists in China: The Party, Private Entrepreneurs, and Prospects for Political Change*, Cambridge: Cambridge University Press, 2003.

Erickson, Andrew S. "China's Massive Military Parade Shows Beijing Is Military Superpower." *National Interest*, October 1, 2019. Available at www.theguardian.com/world/2019/oct/01/china-celebrates-70-years mili taryparade-xi-jinping-hong-kong, accessed September 15, 2020.

Fewsmith, Joseph. *China since Tiananmen: From Deng Xiaoping to Hu Jintao*, 2nd ed. Cambridge: Cambridge University Press, 2008.

Fewsmith, Joseph. "China's Political Ecology and the Fight against Corruption." *China Leadership Monitor*, No. 46 (Winter 2015). Available at www.hoover.org/sites/default/files/research/docs/clm46jf .pdf, accessed September 16, 2020.

Fewsmith, Joseph. *Dilemmas of Reform in China: Political Conflict and Economic Debate.* Armonk, NY: M. E. Sharpe, 1994.

Fewsmith, Joseph. *The Logic and Limits of Political Reform in China.* New York: Cambridge University Press, 2013.

Fewsmith, Joseph. "Promoting the Scientific Development Concept." *China Leadership Monitor*, No. 11 (Summer 2004). Available at www .hoover.org/research/promoting-scientific-development-concept, accessed September 15, 2020.

Fewsmith, Joseph. "What Zhao Ziyang Tells Us about Elite Politics in the 1980s." *China Leadership Monitor*, No. 30 (Fall 2009). Available at www .hoover.org/research/what-zhao-ziyang-tells-us-about-elite-politics-1980 s, accessed September 16, 2020

Finklestein, David. "Breaking the Paradigm: Drivers behind the PLA's Current Period of Reform." Pp. 45–83, in Phillip C. Saunders, Arthur S. Ding, Andrew N. D. Yang, and Joel Wuthnow, eds., *Chairman Xi Remakes the PLA: Assessing Chinese Military Reforms.* Washington, DC: National Defense University Press, 2019.

Gandhi, Jennifer and Adam Przeworski. "Authoritarian Institutions and the Survival of Autocrats." *Comparative Political Studies*, Vol. 40, No. 11 (November 2007): 1279–1301.

Gao Xin and Pin He. *Zhu Rongji zhuan* (Biography of Zhu Rongji). Taipei: Xinxinwen, 1993.

Gao, Yu. "Beijing Observation: Xi Jinping the Man." *China Change*, January 26, 2013. Available at https://chinachange.org/2013/01/26/bei jing-observation-xi-jinping-the-man-by-gao-yu, accessed September 16, 2020.

Geddes, Barbara, Joseph Wright, and Erica Frantz. *How Dictatorships Work*. Cambridge: Cambridge University Press, 2018.

Gewirtz, Julian. *Unlikely Partners: Chinese Reformers, Western Economists, and the Making of Global China*. Cambridge, MA: Harvard University Press, 2017.

Gibbons-Neff, Thomas and Steven Lee Myers. "China Won't Yield 'Even One Inch' of South China Sea, Xi Tells Mattis." *New York Times*, June 27, 2018. Available at www.nytimes.com/2018/06/27/world/asia/mattis-xi-china-sea.html, accessed September 16, 2020.

Goldman, Merle. *Sowing the Seeds of Democracy in China: Political Reform in the Deng Xiaoping Era*. Cambridge, MA: Harvard University Press, 1994.

Gong Xintian. "Yibu weibei xianfa he beili shehui zhuyi jiben yuanze de 'wuquanfa' (cao'an) (The Property Law (Draft) Violates the Constitution and Violates the Basic Principles of Socialism). Available at www.boxun.com /news/gb/pubvp/2005/08/200508201243.shtml, accessed September 16, 2020.

"Gongan dashuju yingyong yanjiu" (Research on Public Security's Use of Big Data). *Jingcha jishu*, May 2016, p.1.

Graham-Harrison, Emma and Verna Yu. "China Celebrates 70th Anniversary as Xi Warns 'No Force Can Shake Great Nation.'" *The Guardian*, October 1, 2019. Available at www.theguardian.com/world/2 019/oct/01/china-celebrates-70-years-military-parade-xi-jinping-hong-ko ng, accessed September 20, 2020.

"Guanyu jiaqiang dang de jianshe jige zhongda wenti de jueding" (Decision on Some Major Issues on Strengthening Party Building). *Renmin ribao*, September 28, 1994.

Guo Luoji. "Zhengzhi wenti shi keyi taolunde" (Political Issues Can Be Discussed). *Renmin ribao*, November 14, 1979.

Guo Xuezhi. *The Politics of the Core Leader in China: Culture, Institution, Legitimacy, and Power*. Cambridge: Cambridge University Press, 2019.

"Guojia jiancha tizhi gaige shidian qude shixiao" (The Experiments with the Reform of the National Supervision Structure Have Achieved Real Results). Available at http://dangjian.people.com.cn/n1/2017/1106/c117 092-29628258.html, accessed October 7, 2019.

"Hao bu dongyao jianchi he fazhan Zhongguo tese shehuizhuyi zai shijianzhong buduan yousuo faxian yousuo chuangzao yousuo qianjin" (Unhesitatingly Uphold and Develop Socialism with Chinese

Characteristics; Make Some New Discoveries, Some New Innovations, and Some Advances in the Course of Practice). *Renmin ribao*, January 6, 2013.

He Ping and Siyang Liu. "Jianfu qi jiwang kailai de zhuangyan shiming: dang de xinyijie zhongyang weiyuanhui dansheng ji" (Shouldering the Serious Mission of Inheriting from the Past and Opening the Future: An Account of the Birth of the Party's New Central Committee). Xinhua, November 14, 2002. Available at http://zqb.cyol.content/2002-11/15/content_564726.htm, accessed September 16, 2020.

"Heima Guo Shengkun: Qule ge hao taitai, Zheng Qinghong shi biaojiu" (Dark horse Guo Shengkun: He Married a Good Wife and Zeng Qinghong Is His Uncle). Available at www.boxun.com/news/gb/china/2013/03/201303201141.shtml, accessed June 16, 2020.

Heurlin, Christopher. *Responsive Authoritarianism in China: Land, Protests, and Policy Making*. New York: Cambridge University Press, 2015.

"Hu Jintao, Wu Bangguo, Wen Jiabao, Jia Qinglin, Wu Guanzheng, Li Changchun, Luo Gan fenbie canjia shenyi he taolun" (Hu Jintao, Wu Bangguo, Wen Jiabao, Jia Qinglin, Wu Guanzheng, Li Changchun, Luo Gan Participate in Examination and Discussion). *Renmin ribao*, March 8, 2007. Available at www.china-embassy.or.jp/chn/zgxw/t239160.htm, accessed September 15, 2020.

"Jiang Zemin zai Qiao Shi tuixiu de qianhou" (Jiang Zemin before and after Qiao Shi's Retirement). Aboluo News Network, July 11, 2019. www.aboluowang.com/2019/0711/1313895.html, accessed September 16, 2020.

Jiefangjun 22 wei gaoji jiangling lüxin (22 PLA Senior Generals Assume Their New Offices). *Xinjing bao*, November 22, 2012. Available at http://epaper.bjnews.com.cn/html/2012-11/22/content_391843.htm?div=1, accessed August 28, 2020.

"Jindun gongcheng shujuku baokuo 12 yi duo Zhongguoren de xinxi" (The Databank of the Golden Shield Project Includes Information on More than 1.2 billion Chinese). *Boxun*, April 9, 2006. Available at https://web.archive.org/web/20160305214310/http://www.boxun.com/news/gb/china/2006/04/200604091432.shtml, accessed September 16, 2020.

Jowitt, Ken. "Inclusion and Mobilization in European Leninist Systems." *World Politics*, Vol. 28, No. 1 (October 1975): 69–96.

Jowitt, Ken. "The Leninist Phenomenon." Pp. 1–49, in Ken Jowitt, *New World Disorder: The Leninist Extinction*. Berkeley: University of California Press, 1992.

Jowitt, Ken. *New World Disorder: The Leninist Extinction*. Berkeley, CA: University of California Press, 1992.

Jun Mai. "Xi Jinping's Anti-corruption Drive Brings down More Generals than 20th Century Warfare." *South China Morning Post*, November 17, 2012.

Kiselycznyk, Michael and Phillip C. Saunders. "Civil–Military Relations in China: Assessing the PLA's Role in Elite Politics." *INSS China Strategic Perspectives*, No. 2 (August 2010).

Kou, Chien-wen. "Xi Jinping in Command: Solving the Principal-Agent Problem in the CCP–PLA Relations?" *China Quarterly*, No. 232 (December 2017): 866–885.

Kou, Chien-wen and Tsai, Wen-hsuan. "'Sprinting with Small Steps' towards Promotion: Solutions for the Age Dilemma in the CCP Cadre Appointment System." *China Journal*, No. 71 (January 2014): 153–171.

Kuhn, Philip. *Rebellion and Its Enemies in Late Imperial China: Militarization and Social Structure, 1796–1884*. Cambridge, MA: Harvard University Press, 1970.

Lam, Willy Wo-lap. *The Era of Jiang Zemin*. Singapore and New York: Prentice Hall, 1999.

"'Laohaoren' shi wei 'laohairen'" (The Reality of Being a Good Old Boy Is to Harm People). *Zhongguo jijian jiancha zazhi*, No. 13 (July 1, 2018). Available at http://zgjjjc.ccdi.gov.cn/bqml/bqxx/201806/t20180629_174741.html, accessed September 16, 2020.

Lardy, Nicholas. *The State Strikes Back: The End of Economic Reform in China?* Washington, DC: The Peterson Institution for International Economics, 2019.

Lee, Hong Yung. *From Revolutionary Cadres to Party Technocrats in Socialist China*. Berkeley: University of California Press, 1991.

Li, Cheng. *Chinese Politics in the Xi Jinping Era: Reassessing Collective Leadership*. Washington, DC: The Brookings Institution Press, 2016.

Li, Cheng. "The 'New Deal': Politics and Policy of the Hu Administration." *Journal of Asian and Sudies*, Vol. 38, Nos. 4–5 (2003): 329–346.

Li, Cheng. "Was the Shanghai Gang Shanghaied? The Fall of Chen Liangyu and the Survival of Jiang Zemin's Faction." *China Leadership Monitor*, No. 20 (Winter 2007). Available at www.hoover.org/research/was-shanghai-gang-shanghaied-fall-chen-liangyu-and-survival-jiang-zemins-faction, accessed September 16, 2020.

Li, Cheng and Scott W. Harold. "China's New Military Elite." *China Security*, Vol. 3, No. 4 (Autumn 2007): 62–89.

Li, Cheng and Lynn White. "The Sixteenth Central Committee of the Chinese Communist Party: Hu Gets What?" *Asian Survey*, Vol. 43, No. 4 (August 2003): 553–597.

Li, Hongbin and Li-an Zhou. "Political Turnover and Economic Performance: The Incentive Role of Personnel Control in China." *Journal of Public Economics*, Vol. 80 (2005): 1743–1762.

Li Junru. "Zhengque lijie he jianchi dangde jiejixing" (Correctly Understand and Uphold the Party's Class Nature). *Lilun dongtai*, July 20, 2001, p.3.

Li Liang and Tonghui Liu. "2004–2006 'disanci gaige lunzheng' shimo" (The Whole Story of the 2004–2006 "Third Argument against Reforms"). *Nanfang zhoumo*, March 16, 2006. Available at http://news.sina.com.cn/c/2006-03-16/10379365018.shtml, accessed September 16, 2020.

Li, Lianjiang. "The Cadre Resignation Tide in the Wake of the 18th Party Congress." *China: An International Journal*, Vol. 17, No. 3 (August 2019): 188–199.

Li, Lianjiang and Kevin J. O'Brien. "The Struggle over Village Elections." Pp. 129–144, in Merle Goldman and Roderick MacFarquhar, eds. *The Paradox of China's Post-Mao Reforms*. Cambridge, MA: Harvard University Press, 1999.

Li Zhanshu. "Zunxun 'sige jianchi' de gaige jingyan" (Adhering to the Experience of Reform with the "Four Upholds"). *Renmin ribao*, November 26, 2013. Available at http://cpc.people.com.cn/n/2013/1126/c64094-23653391.html, accessed June 4, 2020.

Lin, Gang. "Leadership Transition, Intra-party Democracy, and Institution Building in China." *Asian Survey*, Vol. 44, No. 2 (March – April 2004): 255–275.

"Linghang xinshidai de jianqiang lingdao jiti: Dangde xinyijie zhongyang lingdao jigou changsheng jishi" (The Strong Leadership Collective That Will Guide the New Age: An Account of How the New Central Leadership Organs Were Produced). Xinhua, October 26, 2017. Available at www.xinhuanet.com//politics/19cpcnc/2017-10/26/c_1121860147.htm, accessed June 16, 2020.

Link, E. Perry, ed. *Stubborn Weeds: Popular and Controversial Chinese Literature after the Cultural Revolution*. Bloomington: Indiana University Press, 1983.

Liu Binyan. *A Higher Kind of Loyalty: A Memoir by China's Foremost Journalist*. New York: Pantheon, 1990.

Liu Wei and Li Jisheng. "'Jingwuyun' kaichuang zhihui gong'an xinshidai" ("Police Cloud" Opens a New Era for Smart Policing), *Jilin ribao*, August 7, 2018. Available at http://jlrbszb.cnjiwang.com/pc/paper/c/201808/07/content_59869.html, accessed November 5, 2020.

McDevitt, Michael A. *China as a Twenty First Century Naval Power: Theory, Practice, and Implications*. Annapolis, MD: Naval Institute Press, 2020.

McGregor, Richard. *Asia's Reckoning: China, Japan, and the Fate of U.S. Power in the Pacific Century*. New York: Viking, 2017.

Mahoney, James and Kathleen Thelen, eds. *Explaining Institutional Change: Ambiguity, Change, and Power*. Cambridge: Cambridge University Press, 2010.

Manion, Melanie. *Information for Autocrats: Representation in Chinese Local Congresses*. New York: Cambridge University Press, 2015.

Miller, Alice L. "Institutionalization and the Changing Dynamics of Chinese Leadership Politics." Pp. 61–70, in Cheng Li, ed. *China's Changing Political Landscape: Prospects for Democracy*. Washington, DC: Brookings Institution Press, 2008.

Montinola, Gabriella, Yingyi Qian, and Barry Weingast. "Federalism, Chinese Style: The Political Basis for Economic Success in China." *World Politics*, Vol. 48, No. 1 (October 1995): 50–81.

Mulvenon, James. "Hotel Gutian: We Haven't Had That Spirit Here since 1929." *China Leadership Monitor*, No. 46 (Winter 2015). Available at www.hoover.org/research/hotel-gutian-we-havent-had-spirit-here-1929, accessed September 16, 2020.

Mulvenon, James. "Reduced Budget, the 'Two Centers,' and Other Mysteries of the 2003 National People's Congress." *China Leadership Monitor*, No. 7 (Summer 2003). Available at www.hoover.org/research/reduced-budgets-two-centers-and-other-mysteries-2003-national-peoples-congress, accessed September 16, 2020.

Mulvenon, James. "Straining against the Yoke? Civil–Military Relations in China after the Seventeenth Party Congress." Pp. 267–279, in Cheng Li, ed. *Chinese Politics in the Xi Jinping Era: Reassessing Collective Leadership*. Washington, DC: Brookings Institution Press, 2016.

Nathan, Andrew J. "Authoritarian Resilience." *Journal of Democracy*, Vol. 14, No. 1 (January 2003): 6–17.

Nathan, Andrew J. and Perry Link, eds., *The Tiananmen Papers: The Chinese Leadership's Decision to Use Force against Their Own People – in Their Own Words*. New York: Public Affairs, 2001.

North, Douglass C. *Institutions, Institutional Change and Economic Performance*. Cambridge: Cambridge University Press, 1990.

O'Brien, Kevin and Lianjiang Li. *Rightful Resistance in Rural China*. New York: Cambridge University Press, 2006.

Oi, Jean. "Fiscal Reform and the Foundations of Local State Corporatism." *World Politics*, Vol. 45, No. 1 (October 1992): 99–126.

Pan Wei. *Dangdai Zhonghua tizhi: Zhongguo moshi de jingji, zhengzhi, shehui jiexi* (The Structure of Contemporary China: An Analysis of the Economy, Politics, and Society of the China Model). Hong Kong: Sanlian chubanshe, 2010.

Pan Wei. "Zhongguo moshi: Zhonghua tizhi de jingji, zhengzhi, shehui jiexi" (The China Model: An Analysis of the Economy, Politics, and Society of the Chinese Structure). *Guanchazhe*, April 24, 2012. Available at www .guancha.cn/PanWei/2012_04_24_70705.shtml, accessed September 16, 2020.

Pang, Baoqing, Shu Keng, and Lingna Zhong. "Sprinting with Small Steps: China's Cadre Management and Authoritarian Resilience." *China Journal*, No. 80 (2018): 68–93.

Parton, Charles. "China's Bigger Brother." *World Today*, Vol. 74, No. 4 (August 2018): 24–27.

Pei, Minxin. *China's Crony Capitalism: The Dynamics of Regime Decay*. Cambridge, MA: Harvard University Press, 2016.

Pei, Minxin. "Rewriting the Rules of the Chinese Party-State: Xi's Progress in Reinvigorating the CCP." *China Leadership Monitor*, No. 59 (June 1, 2019). Available at www.prcleader.org/peiclm60, accessed September 28, 2020.

Perry, Elizabeth J. "Cultural Governance in Contemporary China: 'Reorienting' Party Propaganda." Harvard-Yenching Institute Working Papers, 2013. Available at www.harvard-yenching.org/sites/harvard-yen ching.org/files/featurefiles/Elizabeth%20Perry_Cultural%20Governance %20in%20Contemporary%20China_0.pdf, accessed September 16, 2020.

Pierson, Paul. *Politics in Time: History, Institutions, and Social Analysis*. Princeton, NJ: Princeton University Press, 2004.

"President Xi Jinping Makes Research Tour to *People's Daily*." *People's Daily* online, February 19, 2016, available at http://en.people.cn/n3/2016/0219/c90000-9018740.html, accessed February 14, 2021.

Qin, Amy, Steven Lee Myers, and Elaine Yu. "China Tightens Wuhan Lockdown in 'Wartime' Battle with Coronavirus." *New York Times*, February 7, 2020. Available at www.nytimes.com/2020/02/06/world/asia/cor onavirus-china-wuhan-quarantine.html, accessed September 15, 2020.

Ramo, Joshua Cooper. *The Beijing Consensus*. London: The Foreign Policy Centre, 2004.

Ren Zhongping. "Shouhu renmin zhengdang de shengmingxian" (Protect the Lifeline of the Party). *Renmin ribao*, October 14, 2013. Available at http://opinion.people.com.cn/n/2013/1014/c1003-231871 14.html, accessed September 16, 2020.

Rong Jingben et al. *Cong yalixing tizhi xiang minzhu hezuo tizhi de zhuanbian: Xiang liangji zhengzhi tizhi gaige* (Changing from a High-Pressure System to a System of Democratic Co-operation: Political System Reform at the County and Township Levels). Beijing: Zhongyang bianyi chubanshe, 1998.

Rosen, Stanley. "The Chinese Communist Party and Chinese Society: Popular Attitudes toward Party Membership and the Party's Image." *Australian Journal of Chinese Affairs*, No. 24 (July 1990): 51–92.

Rosen, Stanley. "Contemporary Chinese Youth and the State." *Journal of Asian Studies*, Vol. 68, No. 2 (May 2009): 359–369.

Rosen, Stanley. "The Effect of Post-4 June Re-education Campaigns on Chinese Students." *China Quarterly*, No. 134 (June 1993): 310–334.

Saich, Tony. "China in 2006: Focus on Social Development." *Asian Survey*, Vol. 47, No. 1 (January–February 2007): 32–47.

Sanzhong quanhui yilai zhongyao wenxian xuanbian (Selected Important Documents since the Third Plenum). Guangzhou: Renmin chubanshe, 1982.

Sascha. "Chengdu Ex-mayor Faces Corruption Charges." *Chendu Living*, December 10, 2012. Available at www.chengduliving.com/the-case-of-li-chuncheng, accessed June 11, 2012.

Shen Baoxiang. *Zhenli biaozhun wenti taolun shimo* (The Whole Discussion of the Issue of the Criterion of Truth). Beijing: Zhongguo dangshi chubanshe, 2008.

Shuggart, Thomas. "China's Artificial Islands Are Bigger (and a Bigger Deal) than You Think." *War on the Rocks*, September 21, 2016. Available at https://warontherocks.com/2016/09/chinas-artificial-islands-are-bigger-and-a-bigger-deal-than-you-think, accessed September 16, 2020.

Silberman, Bernard S. *Cages of Reason: The Rise of the Rational State in France, Japan, the United States, and Great Britain*. Chicago: The University of Chicago Press, 1993.

Smith, Graeme. "Getting Ahead in Rural China: The Elite–Cadre Divide and Its Implications for Rural Governance." *Journal of Contemporary China*, Vol. 24, No. 94 (2015): 594–612.

Smith, Graeme. "The Hollow State: Rural Governance in China." *China Quarterly*, No. 203 (September 2010): 610–618.

Smith, Graeme. "Measurement, Promotions and Patterns of Behavior in Chinese Local Government." *Journal of Peasant Studies*, Vol. 40, No. 6 (2013): 1027–1059.

Streek, Wolfgang and Kathleen Thelen, eds. *Beyond Continuity: Institutional Change in Advanced Political Economies*. Oxford: Oxford University Press, 2005.

Streek, Wolfgang and Kathleen Thelen. "Introduction: Institutional Change in Advanced Political Economies." Pp. 1–37 in Wolfgang Streek and Kathleen Thelen, eds. *Beyond Continuity: Institutional Change in Advanced Political Economies*. Oxford: Oxford University Press, 2005.

Sun Liping. "Shehui zhixu shi dangxia de yanjun tiaozhan" (Social Order Is a Serious Challenge at Present). *Jingji guanchabao*, February 25, 2011.

Svolik, Milan W. *The Politics of Authoritarian Rule*. New York: Cambridge University Press, 2012.

Tang, Wenfang. *Populist Authoritarianism: Chinese Political Culture and Regime Sustainability*. Oxford: Oxford University Press, 2016.

Teiwes, Frederick C. and Warren Sun. *The End of the Maoist Era: Chinese Politics during the Twilight of the Cultural Revolution, 1972–1976*. Armonk, NY: M. E. Sharpe, 2007.

Thøgersen, Stig. "Frontline Soldiers of the CCP: The Selection of China's Township Leaders." *China Quarterly*, No. 194 (2008): 414–423.

Tsou, Tang. *The Cultural Revolution and Post-Mao Reforms: A Historical Perspective*. Chicago: The University of Chicago Press, 1986.

Tsou, Tang. "Political Change and Reform: The Middle Course." Pp. 219–258 in Tang Tsou, *The Cultural Revolution and Post-Mao Reforms: A Historical Perspective*. Chicago: The University of Chicago Press, 1986.

Tsou, Tang. "Reflections on the Formation and Foundations of the Communist Party-State." Pp. 259–334, in Tang Tsou, *The Cultural Revolution and Post-Mao Reforms: A Historical Perspective*. Chicago: The University of Chicago Press, 1986.

Tsou, Tang. "The Tiananmen Tragedy: The State–Society Relationship, Choices, and Mechanisms in Historical Perspective." Pp. 265–327 in Brantly Womack, ed. *Contemporary Chinese Politics in Historical Perspective*. Cambridge: Cambridge University Press, 1991.

"Tuanzhongyang fuzeren jiu qongqingtuan gaige da jizhe wen" (A Responsible Person from the CYL Center Answers Reporters' Questions). *Renminwang*, August 3, 2016. Available at http://cpc.people.cn/gqt/n1/20 16/0803/c363174-28605839.html, accessed June 22, 2020.

Vogel, Ezra F. *Deng Xiaoping and the Transformation of China*. Cambridge, MA: Belknap Press of Harvard University Press, 2011.

Walder, Andrew G. *China under Mao: A Revolution Derailed*. Cambridge, MA: Harvard University Press, 2015.

Wang Hui. "Dangdai Zhongguo de sixiang zhuangkuang yu xiandaixing wenti" (The Circumstances of Contemporary Chinese Thought and the Problem of Modernity). *Wenyi zhengming*, No. 6 (November 1998): 7–26.

Wang Jisi. "ZhongMei guanxi zhongda zhanlüe jiaoliang nanyi bimian" (It Is Difficult to Avoid a Major Strategic Struggle between the US and China). *Guoji xianqu daobao*, August 9, 2010. Available at https://news.qq.com /a/20100809/001152.htm, accessed September 16, 2020.

Wang, Shaoguang and Hu Angang. *The Chinese Economy in Crisis: State Capacity and Tax Reform*. Armonk, NY: M. E. Sharpe, 2001.

Wang Shu. "Zhe 13 ming luoma guanyuan, gen Zhou Yongkang you duoda guanlian?" (How Much Do These 13 Sacked Officials Have to Do with Zhou Yongkang?). *Xinjingbao wang* (New Capital News Web), November 24, 2015. Available at www.bjnews.com.cn/news/2015/11/24/385458.html, accessed June 1, 2020.

Wang, Xiangwei. "How Xi Jinping Revived Old Methods by Abandoning Intra-party Democracy." *South China Morning Post*, November 5, 2017. Available at www.scmp.com/week-asia/opinion/article/2118352/analysis-how-xi-jinping-revived-old-methods-abandoning-intraparty, accessed September 16, 2020.

Wang, Zheng. "National Humiliation, History Education, and the Politics of Historical Memory: Patriotic Education Campaign in China." *International Studies Quarterly*, No. 52, No. 4 (2008): 783–806.

Wang, Zhengxu. "Explaining Regime Strength in China." *China: An International Journal*, Vol. 4, No. 2 (September 2006): 217–237.

Wang, Zhengxu. "Public Support for Democracy in China." *Journal of Contemporary China*, Vol. 16, No. 11 (2007): 561–579.

Wei, Jingsheng. "The Fifth Modernization." Available at www.weijingsheng.org/doc/en/THE%20FIFTH%20MODERNIZATION.html, accessed September 28, 2020.

Wei Yung-cheng. "Reveal the Mystery of Huangfu Ping." *Ta kung pao*, October 7, 1992. Trans. FBIS-CHI-92-201, October 16, 1992, p. 19.

"Wen Jiabao zongli da zhongwai jizhe wen" (Premier Wen Jiabao Answers the Questions of Chinese and Foreign Reporters). *Renmin ribao*, March 14, 2006, retrieved from www.gov.cn/2007lh/content_520478.htm, accessed February 5, 2021.

Whiting, Susan H. "Authoritarian 'Rule of Law' and Regime Legitimacy." *Comparative Political Studies*, Vol. 50, No. 14 (December 2017): 1907–1940.

"Why Must We Unremittingly Oppose Bourgeois Liberalization?" *Renmin ribao*, April 24, 1991, p. 5. Trans. FBIS-CHI-91-081, April 26, 1991, pp. 18–21.

"With the World Distracted, China Intimidates Taiwan." *The Economist*, April 8, 2020. Available at www.economist.com/asia/2020/04/08/with-the-world-distracted-china-intimidates-taiwan, accessed September 16, 2020.

Womack, Brantly, ed. *Contemporary Chinese Politics in Historical Perspective*. Cambridge: Cambridge University Press, 1991.

Wong, Edward. "Anti-corruption Campaign in China Snares Former Top Party Official." *New York Times*, May 13, 2016. Available at www.nytimes.com/2016/05/14/world/asia/china-ling-jihua.html, accessed September 16, 2020.

Wu, Guoguang. "China in 2009: Muddling through Crises." *Asian Survey*, Vol. 50, No.1 (February 2010): 25–39.

Wu, Guoguang. "Command Communication: The Politics of Editorial Formulation in the *People's Daily*." *China Quarterly*, No. 137 (1994): 194–211.

Wu Jinglian. "Xiang furen kaiqiang jiang hui daozhi hen yanzhong de shehui houguo" (Opening Fire on the Wealthy Will Bring about Dire Social Consequences), March 12, 2009. Available at www.taoke.com/article/82 78.htm, accessed September 16, 2020.

"Xi Jinping: Juesheng quanmian jiancheng xiaokang shehui, duoqu xinshidai Zhongguo tese shehuizhuyi weida shengli" (Xi Jinping: Decisively Win an Overall Moderately Prosperous Society, Strive for a Great Victory in Creating Socialism with Chinese Characteristics in the New Age). Xinhua, October 27, 2017. Available at www.xinhuanet.com//politics/19cpcnc/20 17-10/27/c_1121867529.htm, accessed September 28, 2020.

"Xi Jinping shicha Jiefangjun baoshe" (Xi Jinping Inspects the Offices of *Liberation Daily*). Xinhuawang, December 25, 2015. Available at www .xinhuanet.com/politics/2015-12/26/c_1117588434.htm, accessed June 8, 2020.

Xi Jinping zongshuji zai quanguo xuanchuan sixiang gongzuo huiyishang de zhongyao jianghua yinqi xuanchuan sixiang wenhua zhanxian he shehui gejie jiji fanxiang" (General Secretary Xi Jinping's Important Speech at the National Propaganda and Thought Work Forum Inspires the Enthusiastic Response of All Circles of Society and the Propaganda, Thought, and Culture Front). *Renmin ribao*, September 9, 2013. Available at http://cpc.people.com.cn/n/2 013/0909/c64387-22860470.html, accessed September 29, 2020.

Xin Ming. "'*Zhongguomeng,*' *Zhongguo daolu yu Zhongguo tese shehui zhuyi*" (The "China Dream," the Chinese Path, and Socialism with Chinese Characteristics). *Xuexi shibao*, March 11, 2013.

Xu Xianglin. "Hou Mao shidai de jingying zhuanhuan he yifuxing jishu guanliao de xingqi" (The Turnover of Elites and the Rise of Dependent Technocrats in the Post-Mao Period). *Zhanlüe yu guanli*, No. 49 (December 2001): 65–76.

Xue Muqiao. *Dangqian woguo jingji ruogan wenti* (Some Problems in China's Contemporary Economy). Beijing: Renmin chubanshe, 1980.

Yang Xuedong. "Yalixing tizhi: Yige gainian de jianmingshi" (High-Pressure System: A History Clarifying a Concept). *Shehui kexue*, No. 11 (2012): 4–12.

Ye Bing. "Xu Caihou shangjiang luoma (1): yi she quandou ji bozhuo mimou" (The Fall of General Xu Caihou (1): The Probable Involvement in Power Struggles and the Bo and Zhou Plot). *Voice of America*,

August 11, 2015. Available at www.voachinese.com/content/top-general-investigated-20140701/1948242.html, accessed November 9, 2020.

You, Ji. "Jiang Zemin: In Quest of Post-Deng Supremacy." Pp. 1–28, in Maurice Brosseau and Suzanne Pepper, eds., *China Review 1996*. Hong Kong: Chinese University Press, 1996.

You, Ji. "Jiang Zemin's Command of the Military." *China Journal*, No. 45 (January 2001): 131–138.

Yu Guangyuan. *Deng Xiaoping Shakes the World: An Eyewitness Account of China's Party Work Conference and Third Plenum (November–December 1978)*, ed. Ezra F. Vogel and Steven I. Levine. Norwalk, CT: EastBridge, 2004.

Zhang Qianfang. "Proposal for Consensus on Reform." *Caijing Online*, December 26, 2012.

Zhao Leji. "Zhongshi luxing dangzhang he xianfa fuyu de zhize nuli shixian xinshidai jijian jiancha gongzuo gaozhi fazhan" (Loyally Carry out the Responsibilities Conferred by the Party Charter and Constitution; Strive to Realize High-Quality Discipline Inspection and Supervisory Work in the New Era), January 11, 2019. Available at http://dangjian.people.com.cn/n1/2019/0221/c117092-30851340.html, accessed November 9, 2020.

Zhao, Suisheng. "The China Model: Can It Replace the Western Model of Modernization?" *Journal of Contemporary China*, Vol. 19, No. 65 (2010): 419–436.

Zhao, Suisheng. "State-Led Nationalism: The Patriotic Education Campaign in Post-Tiananmen China." *Communist and Post-communist Studies*, Vol. 31, No. 3 (1998): 287–302.

Zhao Ziyang. "Advance along the Road of Socialism with Chinese Characteristics." *Beijing Review*, Vol. 30, No. 45 (November 9–15, 1987): 419–436.

Zhao Ziyang. *Gaige licheng* (The Course of Reform). Hong Kong: Xin shiji chubanshe, 2009.

Zheng, William. "China's Top Law Enforcement Body Unveils Campaign to Purge 'Corrupt Elements'." *South China Morning Post*, July 10, 2020. Available at www.scmp.com/news/china/politics/article/3092559/chinas-top-law-enforcement-body-unveils-campaign-purge-corrupt, accessed September 16, 2020.

"Zhongban yinfa 'Guanyu zai Beijing, Shanxi sheng, Zhejiang sheng kaizhan guojia jiancha tizhi gaige shidian fangan'" (The General Office Promulgates an "Experimental Program for Opening the Reform of the Supervision System in Beijing, Shanxi Province, and Zhejiang Province"). *Renminwang*, November 8, 2016. Available at http://cpc.people.com.cn/n1/2016/1108/c64387-28842803.html, accessed June 23, 2020.

"Zhonggong zhongyang bangongting fayin 'Dangzheng lingdao ganbu kaohe gongzuo tiaoli'" (The Central CCP Office Promulgates "Regulations on the Evaluation Work of Leading Party and State Cadres"). Available at www.xinhuanet.com/politics/2019-04/21/c_1124 395835.htm, accessed February 5, 2021.

"Zhonggong zhongyang guanyu jiaqiang ge gaijin dangde quntuan gongzuo de yijian (quan wen) (Views of the Party Center on Strengthening and Improving the Work of Mass Organizations (Complete Text)), July 9, 2015. Available at http://news.china.com.cn/2015-07/09/con tent_36023933.htm, accessed September 15, 2020.

"Zhonggong zhongyang zhengzhiju huiyi tongbao" (Communiqué of the Meeting of the Political Bureau of the CCP Central Committee). Pp. 596–600, in *Sanzhong quanhui yilai zhongyao wenxian xuanbian* (Selected Important Documents since the Third Plenum). Guangzhou: Renmin chubanshe, 1982, Vol. 1.

Zhonggong zhongyang zuzhibu ketizu, ed. *Zhongguo diaocha baogao: Xin xingshixia renmin neibu maodun yanjiu, 2000–2001* (China Investigation Report: Research on Contradictions among the People under the New Situation, 2000–2001). Beijing: Zhongyang bianyi chubanshe.

"Zhongguo gongchandang dishiliujie zhongyang weiyuanhui disanci quanti huiyi gongbao" (Communiqué of the Third Plenary Session of the Sixteenth Central Committee of the Chinese Communist Party). Xinhua News Agency, October 14, 2003.

"Zhongyang dangnei fagui he guifanxing wenjian jizhong qingli gongzuo quanbu wancheng" (The Work of Comprehensively Sorting through Central Intra-party Regulations and Standardizing Documents Has Been Completed). Xinhua, November 17, 2014. Available at http://politics.people.com.cn/n/20 14/1117/c1001-26041917.html, accessed September 16, 2020.

Zhou, Ruijin. "Record of How the Series of 'Huangfu Ping' Essays Came About," May 7, 2008. Available at www3.nd.edu/~pmoody/Text%20 Pages%20-%20Peter%20Moody%20Webpage/Huangfu%20Ping.pdf, accessed September 15, 2010.

Zhuang Pinghui. "Li Chuncheng Graft Probe Linked to Chengdu Businessman." *South China Morning Post*, December 6, 2012. Available at www.scmp.com/news/china/article/1098437/li-chuncheng-graft-probe -linked-chengdu-businessman, accessed June 11, 2012.

Zuihou de mimi: Zhonggong shisanjie sizhong quanhui [liu si] jielun wenjian (The Last Secret: The Final Documents from the Fourth Plenary Session of the Thirteenth Central Committee [June Fourth]). Hong Kong: Xin Shiji ji chuanmei youxuan gongsi, 1919.

Index

CPSIA information can be obtained
at www.ICGtesting.com
Printed in the USA
LVHW081343021222
734417LV00003B/296